UNLIKELY HEROES

UNLIKELY HEROES: ORDINARY PEOPLE WITH EXTRAORDINARY FAITH

A Biblical and Personal Reflection on Hebrews 11

Daniel R. Lockwood, PhD
President
Multnomah University

MULTNOMAH

UNIVERSITY

Published in cooperation with Multnomah University, 8435 NE Glisan St., Portland,
OR 97220. All rights reserved.

21 20 19 18 17 16 15 14 13 12   1 2 3 4 5

Library of Congress Control Number: 2012912762
ISBN-13: 978-0615657578
ISBN-10: 0615657575

All Scripture quotations, unless otherwise indicated, are taken from *The Holy Bible,
English Standard Version*. Copyright © 2000; 2001 by Crossway Bibles, a division of
Good News Publishers. Used by permission. All rights reserved.

Cover: Rembrandt, *Sacrifice of Isaac* (1635); public domain.

Printed in the United States of America

To Jani, my beloved helpmate, my insightful critic, and my dearest friend. You are my unlikely hero!

CONTENTS

BY RANDY ALCORN

In 1970, when I was sixteen and a brand new Christian, a couple in our church invited me to attend an evening class at Mult- nomah School of the Bible. It was the Gospel of John, taught by John G. Mitchell, one of Multnomah's founders in 1936. The following year I attended Dr. Mitchell's class on the book of Hebrews. Later, someone explained that I could go to college at Multnomah and study the Bible. It seemed too good to be true.

I completed my bachelor's work at Multnomah in 1976. While a pastor, I finished the brand new Multnomah master's program in 1979. My theology teacher, Dr. Joseph Wong, wrote a note on one of my papers. "You should consider being a writer," he said. I took it to heart. In 1985 I wrote my first book, pub- lished by Multnomah Press, then the college's publishing arm. In the 1980s I taught Bible study methods part-time at Multnomah, then in the 90s I returned to teach biblical ethics.

I knew Dr. Willard Aldrich, Multnomah's second president, who coined the phrase that defined the school: "If it's Bible you want, then you want Multnomah." I also knew Dr. Joe Aldrich, who, like his father, loved God's Word and faithfully stewarded the school's convictions and vision.

As Multnomah's fourth president, Dan Lockwood inherited a precious legacy of Christ-centeredness and faith in the Scriptures as God's inerrant Word. My first long conversation with Dan occurred in 2006 when I was the visiting lecturer for a chapel series. There was a delicate situation we had to deal with that week, and I found Dan to be thoughtful, biblical, gracious, and wise.

When Dr. Lockwood asked me to read this book, *Unlikely Heroes*, and write the foreword, my appreciation for Multnomah and for him prompted me to say yes. I said I would look at it and write the foreword if I could. Of course, when you say you are open to writing a foreword, you have to pray that the book is not a disappointment. To say the least, it isn't!

Dan Lockwood has written an engaging book about some of the characters pointed to in Hebrews 11. I love that he doesn't waste time doing what has become trendy—trying to be more accurate or clever than the Bible. He simply believes it, then explains it with thoughtful insights and creative application.

I like Dan's tongue-in-cheek style. He takes the Bible seriously, but doesn't take himself too seriously. He *enjoys* God's Word, as His people have throughout the centuries. Dan handles Scripture with care and respect. He treats it as God's unfolding drama of redemption, full of rich meaning waiting to be mined and treasured and lived by. In short, *Unlikely Heroes* is a Multnomah-kind-of-book. Given the school's rich history, I consider that high praise.

In the early and mid-seventies I often heard Dr. Mitchell ask us students a scolding question with a twinkle in his eye: "Don't you people ever read your Bibles?" Dr. Lockwood not only reads his Bible, he explains it with profound discernment and contagious enthusiasm. He believes these Bible characters were real people who walked this planet, people we'll meet in the presence of Christ. They're alive to him, and he makes them come alive to readers. Dan's passion and keenness for Bible study is evident on every page.

In a day when some Christian colleges and professors seem increasingly less concerned about holding true to God's Word, it is refreshing to read a university president who doesn't attempt to invent new truth, but explores and communicates truth God revealed thousands of years ago. Dan writes like a man who knows it is God's words, not ours, that won't return to Him empty, without accomplishing the purpose for which He sent them (Isaiah 55:11).

Dr. Lockwood's confidence, not in the flavor-of-the-month viewpoint but in God's revealed eternal wisdom, infuses this book with lasting value. I'm very happy to recommend *Unlikely Heroes*.

—RANDY ALCORN

New York Times bestselling author of
Heaven and *Safely Home*

UNLIKELY HEROES

Ever dream of being a hero? Ever picture yourself honored in a hall of fame? Professional baseball players work throughout their entire careers hoping for recognition in Cooperstown's Hall of Fame. CEOs strive for top listing in Fortune 500's list of wealthiest people. Celebrities visualize their names in lights on a Broadway marquee, their granite stars inlaid in some Hollywood sidewalk, or their handprints in the concrete squares outside Grauman's Chinese Theatre. Imagine having a name that thousands of people look at—and walk on—every day!

The "Swoosh"

I'll never forget when eight of us toured the Nike, Inc., headquarters in Beaverton, Oregon. The company that Phil Knight built resides on a beautiful campus dedicated to the running shoe and the "swoosh." Each of the main buildings honors a particular athlete. Every lobby displays the equipment, paraphernalia, pictures, and often a life-size statue of the honoree with a vivid retelling of their athletic achievements. Outside, lining the brick-inlaid walkways that crisscross the grounds, pillar after pillar supports the bronze busts of noteworthy athletes, past and present.

I caught myself thinking, *What if my head was displayed atop one of those pedestals?*

Admit it, we all like heroes. Like magnets, remarkable people with enviable achievements draw us in. The media spotlight movie stars, pro athletes, corporate moguls, politicians, and the ostentatiously rich, creating heroes and legends that dazzle and fascinate—and sell merchandise. And when they inevitably falter or flicker, we, like fickle spectators, abandon yesterday's shining stars and turn our eyes toward new lights rising in the social firmament.

Human after All

Being a hero is an elusive—and always temporary—prize. My childhood friend Timmy was a certifiable hero. At least, that's what I believed as a fifth grader at West Hills Christian School.

Our meeting was not coincidental. The Lockwood and Rogers families had been acquaintances for years. My older brothers attended elementary and high school with the Rogers kids since before I could remember. But this was the year that Timmy would stay with us. My mom and Timmy's mom arranged for him to wait after school at our house until his older brother arrived to take him home. Timmy at once became my personal, one-of-a-kind idol.

There were lots of reasons for this. For one thing, he was an eighth grader. For a fifth grader like me, few achievements ranked higher than this. As the new kid in an eighth grade class of only three, Timmy occupied a position of real power. His being my friend imputed a certain cachet down the elementary-school hierarchy to me.

Also, there were the girls. Within days, it seemed, every girl in our three-room elementary school fell in love with Timmy. Not just the seventh and eighth grade girls, mind you. Even my fifth grade female classmates were hooked. I wasn't discouraged by this, because I had known most of them since first grade and wasn't much attracted to them. After all, familiarity breeds, well, familiarity. But the thrill of seeing a real pro at work fascinated me. Timmy was friendly and witty, and earned a schoolgirl's highest compliment: "cute."

Above all, he had the hair. In the days before the Beach Boys and the Beatles, kids my age tried to imitate the pompadour of Elvis. Timmy lacked the dark color or greasy sheen of the King, but he could still make his long hair curve around and sit on his head in a way that made me green with envy.

Timmy had other attributes too. He could play cool songs like "Ghost Riders in the Sky" on the guitar; draw cartoons like Al Hirschfeld; build huge, engine-powered model airplanes that actually flew; shoot squirrels with his own .22 rifle; and whip any boy twice his size. Yes, Timmy was a hero, and he belonged to me.

Our close friendship lasted four years, and we drifted apart when I began high school. Our last conversation occurred on a Saturday evening. I was backstage at Portland's old Civic Auditorium, which Youth for Christ used for their Saturday-night teen rallies. The singing ensemble in which I sang, *The Continentals*, had finished rehearsal and was milling around, waiting for the program to begin. I had just begun a shy conversation with "Squeak," a girl in the group whom I considered really pretty, when Tim (no longer Timmy) appeared. I was glad to see him, but something was different. Missing were his powerful good looks, the commanding presence, the *élan* I remembered. While his easy smile was still there, he lacked the social attraction he once had. In fact, he had a bad case of acne.

Greeting me, he confidently slipped his arm around Squeak. She smiled but without the intensity I had seen on other fresh faces many times before. Then it hit me. *She's not interested in Tim. She'd rather talk with me!*

In a moment, my long-cultivated hero-worship dissolved. It was not because Tim had betrayed my trust or dashed my admiration. No, it was just that we both were growing up. Tim proved to be what I knew myself to be all along—human.

The Unlikely Heroes of Hebrews 11

The Bible has heroes too. We find hundreds of them—men and women from all walks of life. In this book we shall consider the select list of Old Testament personalities found in Hebrews 11. Some people have named this familiar passage "faith's hall of fame" or "faith's list of heroes." Nineteen times the writer uses "by faith" to introduce notable people and deeds: sixteen people are mentioned by name; five groups are included (Moses' parents, the people, the army, the prophets, and us); and a long list of unnamed "victors" concludes the account. In the following chapters, we will inspect these heroes of faith closely for clues on how to travel wisely and courageously as Christian pilgrims walking to the celestial city.

This book's approach may differ from that of others you've read. My interest in this list follows from the observation that these are *unlikely heroes*. Many are seriously flawed. Others face incredible challenges for which they seem ill-prepared. Still others are simply ordinary. Yet the Bible includes them as people of extraordinary faith. In each chapter we'll consider how it is possible for a broken, ill-equipped, faltering, or average person to merit God's highest commendation: "by faith." We'll seek to connect the dots across the centuries by asking, Can ordinary you and me really become people of extraordinary faith? What lessons from this cast of characters emerge to guide us on our journey?

The focus and format of this book is biographical. We will consider each unlikely hero one by one. You'll notice that Hebrews 11 does not begin with a biographical entry. Rather, it opens with a brief, if enigmatic, definition of faith: "Now faith is the assurance of things hoped for, the conviction of things not seen" (Heb. 11:1). We'll postpone our discussion of that important statement until the conclusion of the book, after we've scrutinized each character.

So, welcome to an adventure. Strap on your dusty sandals, shoulder your trail-worn knapsack, pick up your reliable walking stick, and get ready to walk in the footsteps of some remarkably unremarkable individuals. Prepare to meet people whom God himself calls faithful. People like us!

PART 1

THE ANCIENTS

CHAPTER 1

INTRODUCTION: UNLIKELY STANDOUTS

A Hero in Running Shoes

On a hot Friday in August, during Oregon's annual Hood To Coast Relay, I witnessed the actions of an unlikely hero.

The Hood To Coast Relay is a remarkable event. Started in 1981 with just a handful of teams, the event now has a national reputation, drawing thousands of runners from across the country. The race is 197 miles long, starting at venerable Timberline Lodge 6,500 feet up the southern slope of Mount Hood, and concluding in Seaside's loose sand on the Oregon coast. Each team of twelve people requires two vans. Each runner covers three of the thirty-six legs, running an average total of sixteen miles. The elite teams can complete the course in just over sixteen hours. Most take between twenty-five and thirty.

The number of people involved in the event is mind-boggling. The relay is limited to one thousand teams of twelve persons each, adding up to twelve thousand sweaty runners. Throw in two van drivers and three volunteers required for each team, and you have over seventeen thousand crazy participants on racing weekend. The relay handoffs, particularly when the vans exchange, are unforgettable. The handoff areas are like small villages teeming with tents and people.

Our hero in this setting is an unremarkable candidate for heroic status. He is in his early sixties, and his graying hair and aging face hardly evoke the legendary Adonis. Five foot five in sneakers, his stature—a smidge shorter than mine—inspires little awe. His shoes could not have cost much, and his running shorts seem more like the walking variety than the sleek, air-knit style of other athletes. I even recall him wearing a sweat-band around his head.

In a race filled with huge egos, he was hardly noticeable. He was also possibly the slowest member on our team. And with me as a member, that speaks volumes! I speak of this unlikely hero with affection because he is my older brother, Darrell. But what an ordinary runner like Darrell did that day was truly extraordinary.

It happened on the seventh leg of the race, around six o'clock in the evening. We had just dropped off my nephew Bob at the handoff and headed toward the next exchange. As we rounded the corner, we saw what participants fear the most—a downed runner. As we passed the man lying flat on his back, surrounded by a small knot of other racers, Darrell said in a low voice, "Stop the van. I've got to get out." It was the quiet but authoritative command of a man with decades of medical experience. The van stopped, and Darrell and I leaped into the street. As we approached, we saw a woman runner—an RN, it turned out—

working over the lifeless body. Instantly, Darrell took over. I don't recall that he identified himself as a medical doctor, but somehow everyone seemed to know. As Darrell began CPR, the nurse explained that the man had only just collapsed, that he was not responding, and that an ambulance had been called.

For ten minutes that seemed like ten hours, Darrell labored over the runner. Several times the man would come around, and Darrell would shout, "Stay with me!" slapping his face to keep him responding. Then the man would lapse again into unconsciousness. As Darrell worked, he learned from the man's brother who was standing nearby that "Shamir" was a healthy fifty-year-old in the peak of fitness. He'd never had heart trouble, nor was there heart disease in his family. It was unbelievable that Shamir was now lying here on the cusp of death.

Eventually the ambulance arrived, and the EMTs took over, thanking Darrell and the nurse for their quick-thinking intervention. "He just wasn't coming back," Darrell whispered to me as we turned toward the van. "I can't tell whether he'll make it or not."

Since he was on staff at the nearby hospital where Shamir was taken, Darrell kept updated by cell phone. By the time we picked up Bob at the eighth exchange, Shamir was in the ICU. By the ninth, the news was good: Shamir would recover.

I witnessed an unlikely hero in action that day. I learned from Darrell that heroism does not depend on age, height, appearance, speed, or stylish conformity. It is about making choices and acting in the face of risk. It's about knowing the talents you have and putting them to use for what you know to be right regardless of the consequences. With this in mind, we approach Hebrews 11's list of unlikely heroes.

The Most Surprising Entry

It would be natural, after scanning the register of names, to turn away discouraged. *After all,* you might think, *how could I ever qualify for such a roster? I'm seriously flawed. My past is spotted. I've made poor life choices.* Perhaps you believe you're beyond forgiveness.

But the writer of Hebrews does not open with a famous, larger-than-life Bible character. The text begins with the most surprising and unlikely heroes of all: "By faith we understand that the universe was created by the word of God, so that what is seen was not made out of things that are visible" (Heb. 11:3). By faith *we* understand. The first space for the name of a faithful man or woman of God is reserved for you and me! It's as if this divine roster of faithful saints begins with a blank. If we qualify—and each of us can—we are invited to inscribe our own names at the top of the list.

Maybe we should wear laminated nametags at our next social icebreaker that look like this:

By Faith

Phil

(write your name here)

**understands that God created the world
by simply speaking the word.**

What a tribute to God's surprising grace! Christian faith, we discover right from the start, is not an elitist faith. It is God's invitation to ordinary people to dare to do the impossible: to enter into a relationship with the living Creator. With faith as your stylus, you can engrave your name here.

So, how do we qualify? By *understanding* that the worlds were prepared by the word of God. The genesis of genuine faith is theological. It involves one of the great themes of Hebrews 11: the willingness to believe in something—or someone—you cannot see. Specifically, it is to understand that our Creator is the God who makes and speaks.

Where's Adam?

A quick reading of the chapter shows that it is organized chronologically. It is not surprising, therefore, that creation is front and center. This is where the interaction between God and the human race begins. But what is surprising is that Adam, the first patriarch and the progenitor of the human race, is so conspicuously absent. Surely Adam deserves a spot!

There are lots of possible explanations for his absence. Those from a liberal perspective question that the Edenic couple really existed at all. Adam is not listed, they reply, because there was no Adam. After all, the word *adam* (literally "earth") simply denotes generic mankind. But for those of us who believe the Bible is the accurate Word of God that simply won't do. The references in the first five chapters of Genesis undeniably refer to an individual who walked with God, who named animals, who had a wife, who ate the forbidden fruit, who was ejected from the garden, and who fathered children. Furthermore, the five New Testament references to Adam make clear that he was a real person.

Another explanation for Adam's absence in Hebrews 11 is theological, namely, that Adam is not a man of faith. Of the five New Testament references, three are negative: Adam is the one through whom sin enters the world (Rom. 5:1–19); Adam is the source of death while Christ brings life (1 Cor. 15:22); Adam was a living soul, while Christ is the life-giving spirit (1 Cor. 15:45). The other two references underscore Adam's historical reality but say nothing about his faith: Adam, the "son of God," tops Christ's genealogy (Luke 3:38); and Adam, created before Eve, was not beguiled by the tempter (1 Tim. 2:13–14). The lack of a New Testament reference to Adam's faith, some say, explains his exclusion from the list of the faithful. With no biblical clue that Adam ever repented from his fallen state, he does not belong.

My opinion is more generous; I'm hesitant to conclude that Adam did not or could not seek God again. I prefer to accept Hebrews' list of heroes as a selective register that includes some, but not all, faithful men and women. Perhaps the author, writing under divine guidance, is prompted to leave the initial spot for people much more relevant—you and me.

But of all the things we should believe, why this? Why are we to understand that the universe is created by the word of God? The answer is simple. Faith is not primarily about believing facts; it is about trusting in a person, trusting in God. Nor is faith belief in a god. It is believing in the one and only true God, acknowledging this God as creator, and understanding his work of creation as coming through his spoken word.

Faith in the God Who Makes and Speaks

Hebrews 11:3 describes God, the object of our faith, with two startling assertions: (1) God makes by speaking, and (2) God makes from nothing.

God Makes by Speaking

First, God created the universe and all it contains simply by speaking. "We understand that the universe was created by the *word of God*," our text reads, confirming the Genesis 1 account. A passage with beautiful symmetry, the Genesis 1 description of the six days of creation begins with the affirmation "And God said." This phrase, repeated eight times (including twice on days three and six), emphatically underscores God's creative power. Day seven also emphasizes God's speaking when it says, "God blessed the seventh day and made it holy" (Gen. 2:3). This remarkable pattern is charted below.

The God Who Creates by Speaking

Day	Formula	God's Creative Word
1	And God said	Let there be light.
2	And God said	Let there be an expanse between the waters.
3	And God said And God said	Let the waters be gathered; Let the land produce vegetation.
4	And God said	Let there be lights in the sky.
5	And God said	Let the waters teem.
6	And God said And God said	Let the land produce living creatures; Let us make man in our image.
7	And God blessed the seventh day and sanctified it.	

Genesis 1's emphasis on God speaking does not, in and of itself, answer the questions of how or when God created the heavens and the earth. He could have, for example, commanded intermediary or secondary processes to begin.

In fact, in the second, complementary account of Adam and Eve's creation (Gen. 2:4–25), God does use means other than speaking. There, the actual act of creating mankind is described in earthy detail. God molded Adam from the dust of the ground and fashioned Eve from Adam's rib. Can you picture the eternal God kneeling in the gooey mud, shaping Adam's head, torso, and limbs from the sticky clay? I once sculpted a miniature human figure from artist's clay. It took a lot of time, patience, and care to produce even a passable sculpture. Though God could have done this in an instant, this remarkable story suggests otherwise. It evokes God's patience, his attention to detail. I can imagine the clay material dropping from his hands as God adds a pellet here, a clump there, to perfect the contour of Adam's face. Perhaps the Lord tilts His head and squints His eyes, just like a human sculptor, to get the proportions just right.

And the creation of Eve? While I hardly think God would stand in scrubs and mask shouting "Scalpel!" to an attending Gabriel, I find the story has the straightforward telling of a literal, historical event. One of my father's medical school professors remembered his Sunday school lessons well when he asked the first-year medical school class on their first exam, "Who was the world's first anesthesiologist?" Imagine their surprise when he smilingly informed them, "God—when he put Adam to sleep and removed his rib for Eve's creation."

This emphasis on God's speaking does not deny his possible uses of other methods, natural or supernatural. Far more important is *why* God's speaking is so central to both the author of Genesis and the writer of Hebrews. The answer, I believe, lies in God's purposes for Israel.

When Moses wrote the Book of the Law (the Pentateuch) of which Genesis is a part, God's people were about to enter the Promised Land of Canaan. Since the Canaanites worshipped their own Baals and embraced their own creation story, how would Israel know the difference between the Canaanite gods and Yahweh, the true God of Israel? According to Akkadian mythology (Babylonian legends borrowed by the Canaanites), creation came about from a struggle between Marduk, their supreme god, and Tiamat, a great sea monster. After a bloody, extended battle, the victorious Marduk formed the earth and heavens out of Tiamat's battered carcass. Now there's a bedtime story to lull your kids to sleep!

So, who is Israel's God? Is he a deity who creates through struggle, strife, and battle? No, he is the God who stands at the edge of nothing and speaks the entire cosmos into existence. And where are the sea monsters? These "tiamats" are part of God's fifth-day creation; the very word is found in the biblical narrative (Gen. 1:21). They are the leviathans that God formed to frolic in the oceans (Ps. 104:26).

I hope you catch the not-so-subtle sarcasm in the creation story. The so-called powerful gods of the Canaanites are about to be schooled. Who would you like on your side—the schoolyard bullies who beat up kids on the playground, or the schoolmaster who silences the unruly mob of kids with a single word, sending the bullies slinking into a corner? The Canaanite gods are not simply weak; they are "nothings," because there is only one God, Yahweh. One Hebrew word for idol, *elil*, literally means "a nothing."

God Makes from Nothing

Not only does God create by speaking, he also creates out of nothing (*ex nihilo*). Creation from nothing is not explicit in Genesis 1. The activity of the six creative days builds upon an earth that is "without form and void" (the Hebrew *tohu vebohu* is also translated "unformed and unfilled"), cloaked in darkness, covered in water, and brooded over by the Spirit (Gen. 1:2). Because water is mentioned before day one, Genesis 1 is inconclusive on the question of when matter was first created. Water was around before God said, "Let there be light!"

This is where Hebrews 11 helps. "What is seen was not made out of things that are visible," we read. This explicitly describes the *ex-nihilo* origin of matter. God both creates matter and fashions it, a doctrine absolutely essential for understanding the nature of God. To conclude otherwise—to suggest that matter is coeternal with God—elevates matter to divine status. This pantheistic distortion is opposite of biblical theism. The doctrine of creation *ex nihilo* in one deft stroke lays bare the tottering materialistic foundation of naturalism and exalts the sovereign power of the living creator God.

How Big Is Your God?

The life of faith begins with trust in the God who makes and speaks. Do you believe that? If so, you can inscribe your name on the list of God's faithful heroes—right at the top. It all begins with affirming that God is the Creator whose unparalleled power is demonstrated by creating the cosmos through speaking the word and fashioning materials he created from nothing.

J. B. Phillips wrote a wonderful little book called *Your God Is Too Small*. In it he gives seventeen caricatures or distorted perceptions of God and asks the significant question, "How big is your God?" Is he big enough to stand at the edge of the darkness and speak, "Let there be light"? Is he powerful enough to create all there is from nothing? Is he strong enough to stand opposed to all false deities, sending them scurrying away with a simple word? If so, he is big enough to carry you through the valley of the shadow of death and to warm you with the light of his love. He is strong enough to build out of your empty life a temple for his indwelling Spirit.

That's where faith begins: trusting in a God who makes and speaks.

CHAPTER 2

ABEL:

THE UNLIKELY MARTYR

Of Babies and Birth Order

When I graduated from eighth grade, I decided to take on a new identity. I planned to enter high school as "Dan," abandoning forever the name "Danny" I had used for fourteen years. This was not as intriguing as acquiring a secret identity, mind you. I was just making a subtle shift, insignificant to most people but of great importance to me. That simple name change announced my longing to grow up.

Most people accepted this metamorphosis, and my intention behind it, without a fuss. But one group never got the message. Oh, they call me Dan, all right. Yet whenever we get together, I get the feeling I am still "Danny" to them. You may have guessed that I am speaking of my siblings.

I am the youngest of four children, and all of us still live in the Portland, Oregon, area. Fifteen years separate my oldest sister

Marliss and me. Larry, the eldest son, is eight years older than me. Darrell is five. No matter how much we age or how life circumstances affect us, our birth order—and the roles assigned to it—never changes.

Many studies link birth order to personality. One study suggests eight common traits of the youngest child: risk-taker, idealist, good sense of humor, hard-working, immature, attention-seeking, secretive, and sensitive. While this may only be nonsense, I have to admit that I manifest some of these characteristics. But what really caught my attention was the study's follow-up observation. The youngest child is considered the baby of the family, the study concludes, and lives up to this role.

The baby of the family—how true that is! To my brothers and sister I am still Danny. Whenever we get together, I slip to the bottom of the hierarchy. No matter what I achieve in life, no matter what accolades I may receive, I'm still the baby. You could say I am the Rodney Dangerfield of the Lockwood family: "I don't get no respect." And if birth-order studies are reliable, I never will!

Abel, the Unlikely Little Brother

Abel, the unlikely hero of our chapter, is the baby of the "Adam" family. I suspect he got the youngest child treatment.

His story appears with little historical context except that he is the second son of disgraced parents and the younger brother of the firstborn, Cain. Some have even suggested he is the younger twin brother of Cain, because both brothers appear on the biblical stage together when they bring their offerings. However, the way the narrative introduces Abel (Gen. 4:2) suggests that the conceptions and births of Cain and Abel are events separated in time.

We know nothing of Abel's childhood, his spiritual upbringing, his hobbies, his dreams, or his idiosyncrasies. While we know his occupation, we are not told his age nor given any hints of his accomplishments or potential that would commend him as a spiritual model. We have insufficient information to compare Abel with the determined Moses, the robust David, or the courageous Elijah. Abel is almost a footnote, appearing in Scripture unexpectedly and disappearing almost as quickly. A portrait of Abel would be shaded in vanilla tones except for his one simple and epic decision to obey the command of God.

Although Abel is clearly the hero of the story, Cain grabs the center of attention. That would be just like the older brother! To put it in theatrical terms, Cain chews the scenery. He dominates every scene he's in, which is all but one. When he's on stage, it's hard to take your eyes off him. The story in Genesis 4 mentions Cain by name sixteen times to Abel's eight; he is present in almost every verse.

Abel comes across as a supporting character. He's an understudy, a member of the chorus. He gets his lines right, but the pathos of his character doesn't seem to carry beyond the floodlights. It's as if the playwright underwrote his role, considering a full-orbed development unimportant. He is ordinary, pedestrian, lackluster, and—humanly speaking—uninspiring. He is, in a word, the baby of the family.

To discover the scriptural lessons, we must look deeper into this incident. Let's consider the story of Cain and Abel as a brief drama in four acts. And what a dramatic story it is.

Act I: The Two Offerings

In Act I (Gen. 4:1–5) the two sons of Adam and Eve prepare to offer a sacrifice to God. Cain is a farmer; Abel, a shepherd. They each bring an offering to the Lord that reflects their vocation. Cain brings a portion of his crops; Abel, a part of his flock. Yet the results are starkly different: God accepts Abel's sacrifice, but he rejects Cain's.

This story raises many questions. For example, how did the two brothers even know to bring a sacrifice? The biblical text is silent except to say they brought them "in the course of time" (Gen. 4:3). Perhaps Adam encouraged his sons to do so, following the pattern God began when he clothed the first human couple with animal skins prior to their expulsion from Eden. More likely, God instructs Cain and Abel through direct revelation—a vision or a dream. Because of God's later conversations with Cain, we know that direct communication with God occurs in those days.

One thing is clear. The cornerstone of Abel's faith is a sacrifice approved by God. "By faith Abel offered to God a more acceptable sacrifice than Cain" (Heb. 11:4). But this leads to more perplexing questions: What made Abel's sacrifice superior to Cain's? And why was Cain's rejected? Consider the following explanations.

Some suggest that God accepted Abel's sacrifice because it meets God's requirement of the shedding of blood. Cain's vegetable offering does not. True, Old Testament sacrifices usually require the death of an animal. In Eden God makes garments of slain animal skins for the first couple, although there is no specific mention of a sacrifice. We also read of blood sacrifices after the flood (Gen. 8:20), in the sealing of the Abrahamic covenant

(Gen. 15:9–11), and in the Law of Moses. Leviticus 1–7 presents six major categories of sacrifices, and those offered for sin (the sin and guilt offerings) always require the shedding of blood.

However, others do not. The divinely approved grain offering is a bloodless offering of worship (Lev. 2:1–16), and grain and cakes are used in several of the peace offerings (e.g., Lev. 7:11–14). If Abel's sacrifice were an atonement for sin, it would require blood. But the Genesis record does not suggest this, and Hebrews 11:4 uses the word *gifts* to describe the offering, a word more in keeping with the purpose of the bloodless grain and peace offerings. Therefore, I remain uncertain that Abel's offering is accepted by God simply because it involves animal blood.

Still others suggest that Abel offers the best specimen from his flock, whereas Cain brings the surplus—perhaps the overripe surplus—from his crops. Maybe Cain brings zucchini—after all, the stuff grows like crazy!

"What am I going to do with all this squash?" he may have asked himself. "No neighbors are around to take it. Oh, I know," he concludes, his eyes brightening, "I'll give it to God!"

Any parallel between Cain's zucchini offering and Christians who donate a beat-up jalopy to their church in lieu of a tithe, expecting a tax-deductible receipt, of course, is purely coincidental. Biblically there is no denying that God requires the best for himself, an unblemished offering (Mal. 1:11). But again, the text is silent on whether Cain's sacrifice is substandard.

Whether you embrace the blood theory or the surplus theory (with its zucchini corollary), one thing is clear: Cain lacks a sincere, spiritual motivation to please God; Abel offers his sacrifice by faith. We might say the heart of the issue is that *their hearts* are the issue.

Act II: The Warning

Act II of the story (Gen. 4:6–7) highlights God's response to Cain's resentful heart. The Lord approaches him, pointing out that Cain's face reflects his unjustifiable fury.

"Why are you angry?" God asks him. "If you do well, won't you be accepted?" And then comes the warning. "Watch out," the Lord continues. "If you persist in bitterness, then sin, like a crouching animal (or serpent), will fulfill its desire to dominate you. Choose wisely, Cain. Gain the upper hand!"

In this unusual encounter, we glimpse the extraordinary grace of God. Cain, through his own selfishness, offers a sacrifice unworthy of God. He is not a righteous man. But God approaches him, extending the hope of a second chance. Cain's first, rebellious choice is not irrevocable. God implies that Cain has another chance to do the right thing, another opportunity to receive God's approval, just as there is for us. But there is a spiritual battle going on within Cain. He must choose wisely.

Act III: The Murder

In Act III (Gen. 4:8–15) the story takes a devastating turn. Cain does not heed God's sober but gracious warning about the danger of sin. In a chilling fulfillment of God's words, Cain invites Abel to join him in the field, away from watching eyes. There he murders him in cold blood. This deliberate and intentional slaughter suggests that Cain may have formulated his plan even while speaking face to face with God.

"Wait a minute," you might say. "That's not the way it's supposed to end. Abel is the man of faith, the righteous one. He is the hero of this story. He is simply minding his own business, doing what is right. He should be blessed, not bludgeoned. Doesn't the guy in the white hat vanquish the villain, get the girl, and live happily ever after?"

The Bible's answer is: not always. For Abel, his obedient sacrifice becomes "sacrificial obedience." His choice is costly, exacting the ultimate price of his very life. That is the first lesson of Abel's lasting legacy: faith is the willingness to obey God regardless of the consequences.

Think long and hard about this principle because it contradicts our natural instincts. Many people seek religion for how it may benefit them. "Religion helps us to face life better; it makes us fulfilled people," some claim. "God is a kindly old grandfather, the Man Up There, or a jolly Santa Claus who gives wonderful gifts to his kids. Pray to him when you are in a jam."

We evangelical Christians fall for this too. In sharing our faith, we are tempted to say things like, "Come to Jesus; he's all you need. He'll fulfill all your dreams." Some go even further, propounding the popular theology of health, wealth, and prosperity. This distortion maintains that God does not want any of his children to be poor or sick or unsuccessful. "Why pray for a Volkswagen when you can pray for a Cadillac?" I've heard some say. "God wants the best for you, if you'll only ask for it." And what if you fail to experience material prosperity, human success, or a long, healthy life? Well, the problem is you: not enough prayer, not enough faith.

Like any distortion, there is a grain of truth to this. God does want our best and will fulfill all our dreams. But Scripture makes it clear that he does this in his way (often using the tool of adversity) and in his timing (sometimes only in eternity). Jesus makes no promises for a life of ease. To the contrary, he says, "In the world you will have tribulation. Take heart; I have overcome the world" (John 16:33). Abel, along with many others in the register of faith, illustrates the principle that the life of faith may indeed have lethal consequences.

Act IV: The Two Legacies

The Legacy of Cain

After Abel's murder, Cain remains at center stage. Genesis narrates the painful legacy of Cain living on in a world without Abel. Cain's legacy is the consequence of a hardened heart and a heartless act.

The account begins when God initiates a second dialog with Cain (Gen. 4:9–16). "Where is your brother?" the Lord asks. Cain's response to God reverberates down history's corridors as one of the most hateful and willful lies a brother could utter. "I don't know," the murderer retorts. "Am I supposed to babysit my baby brother all the time?"

God does not tolerate dishonesty or cover-ups. "Cain, you murdered your brother," God replies. "Trying to deny it is pointless. Abel's blood cries out to me from the very field where you spilled it." And then, with words that must have chilled even Cain to the bone, God adds a curse. "The ground you so love to till, and the crops whose harvest so delights you, will fail you. Your green thumb will turn black, and every plant you tend will die. You will become nomadic, a wanderer on the earth and a fugitive among men."

Cain's second response to the Lord is equally telling. He shows no remorse, no repentance, no guilt, no shame. Instead, Cain, concerned about his own welfare, complains that God's punishment is unfair. "I'll have no home, no income, and no respect," he protests. "People will have a ready excuse to kill me!"

Again, God responds with compassion. "No one shall kill you," he promises. "I'll put a mark on you for your protection." God extends Cain another second chance. Even in placing Cain under the curse, God does not close the door on him. It is Cain, not God, who departs. It is Cain who chooses to become an exile from the presence of the Lord and settle east of Eden, in Nod (which means "wandering").

The remainder of Genesis 4 concludes Cain's genealogy and earthly legacy. He marries; has children; builds a city named after his eldest son, Enoch; and launches a lineage skilled in civilization-building. One descendant replaces Abel as the father of ranching, another is skilled at musicology, another excels in metallurgy.* God's prediction that sin will master Cain is fulfilled in Lamech, the sixth descendant from Cain. Lamech's brief poem is a terrifying ode to murder, rebellion, violence, and vengeance, setting the stage for the flood.

The Legacy of Abel

Abel is a righteous martyr. While the theme of martyrdom is understated in Genesis, the New Testament portrays Abel as the father of those who pay for their obedience to God with their

---

* Theologically, it is important for Israel to recognize that Cain is the father of civilization and buys his legacy with the price of his brother's blood. I do not agree with those who believe that Cainite origins imply that all civilization and city-building are evil. But I do concur that a successful civilization guarantees neither righteousness of its citizens nor divine approval of its values.

lives (Matt. 23:35; Luke 11:51). In Hebrews Abel's better sacrifice is the means "through which he was commended as righteous" (Heb. 11:4). It is not better because he offers a bigger sacrifice, one that is costlier, bloodier, or more perfect. It is because he offers it "by faith." Seeing that faith, God accepts Abel's offering and pronounces him "righteous," just as he does for you and me when we respond to God in genuine and sincere faith

To punctuate this, Hebrews 11:4 adds that "God [commended Abel] by accepting his gifts." Imagine that! Like a witness in a crowded courtroom, God himself takes the stand and vows that Abel is righteous. In fact, God declares each of us who places his or her trust in Jesus Christ to be righteous like Abel.

Abel leaves a second legacy—an eternal one. "Though he died, he still speaks," Hebrews 11:4 tells us. Abel's spilled blood speaks to God immediately, but Abel's testimony continues to the present day. In the pages of Scripture, this unlikely hero testifies about the importance of faith in the living God. Anytime we read the Genesis account, the testimony rings again.

My mother, who taught a children's Bible club for many years, went even further. "Though Abel was the first to die and see God," she often said, "his reward is not yet complete. Every time someone reads his story, Abel testifies to faith in God. He won't receive his full reward until his story is read for the last time."

Is Your Faith in God Strong Enough?

What does this unlikely hero teach us? Abel is a reliable witness, whose life and death give personal, expert testimony to his faith and righteousness. And God corroborates this testimony. Abel shows us—from beyond the grave—that living by faith involves obeying God regardless of the consequences. Faith may not lead to prosperity, adulation, or peace. Like Abel, we may pay dearly in this life for righteous choices. But when the result of those choices is the eternal approval of an eternal God, it seems a very insignificant price to pay.

In the previous chapter we saw that our presence on the roster of the "hall of faith" compels us to ask, "Is our view of God *large* enough?" Now, Abel's courageous witness challenges us, "Is our faith in God *strong* enough?"

An Applicational Summary

Witness	Principle	Challenge
You and me	Living by faith begins with trust in the God who makes and speaks.	Is our view of God *large* enough?
Abel	Living by faith requires obedience regardless of the consequences.	Is our faith in God *strong* enough?

Unlikely heroes like Abel are still around us. We can learn from and emulate their faith. May our faith in God be strong enough.

CHAPTER 3

ENOCH:

THE UNLIKELY PILGRIM

Otherworld Encounters

Dr. John "Jack" Mitchell, the founder of Multnomah, loved to tell the deathbed story of Bernard B. Sutcliffe, Multnomah's cofounder and first president. Jack was at the side of Dr. Sutcliffe as he lay dying in a hospital bed. The end was near. As Jack watched and prayed, it seemed that his close friend exhaled his last breath. Assuming Bernard's spirit had passed into the presence of the Lord, Jack rose and gently touched his friends elbow. To Jack's surprise, Bernard roused and looked straight into Jack's face. With a look of resignation and with disappointment in his voice, he said, "Oh, Jack, it's only you."

Some deathbed stories are quite spectacular. Two such stories hover in my family tree. My grandmother, Grammie, witnessed the death of her older sister, Evalina Little. Known as Aunt E, Evalina was the wife of an itinerant preacher, David Little, a widower who married her later in life. In her early fifties Aunt E became an invalid. When her death seemed imminent, she summoned Grammie to her hospital bed in Spokane, Washington.

"Aunt E appeared drained of life," Grammie recalled. "Then, as I watched her face, it became transformed. She radiated a divine glory!"

Aunt E roused enough to utter six words. "Oh, Ruth," she gasped, "the Shinings! The Shinings!" With that she expired.

The other story in my family is even more mysterious. John Williams, my mother's beloved uncle, was an itinerant Methodist preacher who rode the circuits in Idaho. After years of hardship on the trail, Uncle John lay at death's door. Doctors did what they could while family members prayed. Eventually, they thought they witnessed his passing. But Uncle John awoke.

"Why did you bring me back? Oh, why did you bring me back?" was all he would say. And for the rest of his years he refused to speak of his otherworldly experience.

Aunt E and Uncle John, like others before them, had close encounters of the divine kind.

Enoch, the Unlikely Pilgrim

Enoch, our second unlikely biblical hero, has a close, supernatural encounter with God too. But, like Abel, there seems to be little about him to commend him to undertake the most supernatural pilgrimage a human can have: a walk with God into heaven.

Enoch appears in Genesis 5 as little more than a cipher, an annotation in an otherwise ordinary genealogy. On the one hand, we know little about Enoch's spiritual successes. There is no record of a stunning victory over a devastating spiritual crisis, just as there is no mention of remarkable acts of spiritual courage or faithfulness. Is he a faint-hearted man who conquers his fear with bravado? Is he a reluctant leader who impacts his generation in an era of decline? Or is he a man of gentle compassion, reaching out with mercy and justice in a self-centered culture? We simply do not know.

On the other hand, we learn of no personal angst, no bitter failure, no depressing brokenness. Does Enoch have psychological issues with his parents or siblings? Is he the youngest brother? Does he fight depression? Is he tempted with lust or troubled with doubt? We don't even know if he was heckled at school. In fact, we cannot describe Enoch in any more colorful hue than common beige, because so little is revealed about him. Yet, while he appears in the pages of Scripture as a genealogical statistic, he will always be known for one important thing: he took a surprising stroll with the living God.

Enoch serves as witness to the evidence of genuine faith. Just as Abel earns God's divine testimony as a righteous man, Enoch's walk remains an everlasting epitaph of one pleasing to God (Heb. 11:5). Like a stack of exhibits on a courtroom table, the evidence that unlikely heroes can reveal extraordinary faith keeps piling up.

Enoch's Profile: A Biblical Sketch

His Boring Genealogy

Enoch's brief citation in Genesis 5 hardly satisfies our biblical curiosity. The chapter could easily contend for one of the Bible's dullest. It is a genealogy with ten patriarchal entries, tracing Adam's ancestral line to Noah's three sons, Shem, Ham, and Japheth. It seems lackluster because, after the wonder and excitement of Genesis 1–4, the narrative grinds to halt.

But within this chapter we discover unexpected insights. For example, each of the ten patriarchs is described within the predictable genealogical formula shown below.

Genealogy Formula in Genesis 5

A lived **x** years and fathered **B**.

After **A** fathered **B**, he lived **y** years
and fathered other sons and daughters.

So all the days of **A** was **x** + **y**.

And he died.

This less-than-stirring chapter, however, has tremendous biblical significance. Historically, it links Adam and Seth with Noah, showing how the line of righteous people is preserved up to the great flood. It anticipates the Genesis 11 genealogy that extends this unbroken line down to Abraham, the patriarchal father of Israel and the spiritual father of all people of faith.

But it is the phrase "and he died" that carries the heaviest theological weight. Repeated eight times, these three words pound like a funeral dirge throughout the chapter. Because God tells Adam he would die on the day he eats of the forbidden fruit, Genesis 5 stands as the stark and accurate fulfillment of God's prediction. It also affirms three immutable truths that still apply today:

- Everyone sins.
- The wages of sin is death.
- Everyone dies.

His Abrupt Rapture

When Enoch's name appears in the genealogy, we find a break from the formula. After he became the father of Methuselah, Enoch "walked with God" three hundred years (Gen. 5:22), something not said of the others. And then the text takes a truly surprising turn: "Enoch walked with God, and he was not, for God took him" (Gen. 5:24).

Perhaps if all we had was the Genesis account, we might miss the miracle. After all, "God took him" is a euphemism for death we still use today. But the abrupt contrast between Enoch's obituary and the genealogical formula strongly suggests something unique and wonderful happens here.

Our hunch is confirmed when we read, "Enoch was taken up so that he should not see death" (Heb. 11:5). He did not die. Apparently he arises one dawn, kisses Mrs. Enoch good morning, sips a cup of coffee, meets the Lord at his doorstep for his appointed stroll, and at age 365 just walks on up to his celestial home. What a way to go!

I've often wondered what Enoch and the Lord talked about on those daily outings. On the last morning, the morning of Enoch's disappearance, perhaps the discussion goes something like this.

"Well, Enoch," the Lord begins, the hint of a smile playing on the corner of his mouth, "today I've got good news and I've got bad news."

"I want the good news first," Enoch says, playing along.

The Lord pauses. "The good news is that you are going to be mentioned in the book I'm writing," he says at last.

"Really!" exclaims Enoch, his interest rising. "What book is that?"

"People will call it the Bible," the Lord replies. "It's my revelation—my love letter—to mankind. You'll be in it. Of course, it won't be written for several thousand years, and then it will take fifteen hundred more years to complete."

"That *is* good news," Enoch responds. "Thanks! Now what's the bad news?"

"The bad news," the Lord says with a twinkle in his eye, "is that you'll be found primarily in the genealogies."

"What are those?" Enoch asks.

"Long lists of names of ancestors and descendants of the more central characters of my story," God answers with a laugh. "Most readers will rush over them. But don't worry—I'm including you in a special chapter much later in the book."

"Whatever you say," Enoch smiles, "You're the Lord."

"That's my Enoch!" God replies. "Oh, and by the way, I've got some more good news for you!"

"What's that?"

"Let's just keep walking. You'll see."

His Faithful Walk

Enoch is a man known for one thing and one thing only: he walks with God. That's the sum and substance of his legacy. "He was commended," the text tells us, "as having pleased God" (Heb. 11:5). The simplicity of this is arresting, isn't it? Enoch is pleasing to God because of a faithful walk. I love the word *walk* here.

It is frequently used in Scripture to describe our spiritual lives. It is an appropriate metaphor because walking is a step-by-step experience, the way we must live as Christians. The Christian life is not a leap-by-leap lurch; it's a daily, continuous, consistent, and intimate relationship with our creator God.

Enoch's Pilgrimage: A Study in Contrasts

Let's explore Enoch's walk by observing the contrasts between Enoch and Adam, Enoch and Abel, and Enoch and us.

Enoch and Adam

Do not miss the unspoken parallel between Enoch and our first ancestor, Adam. Before their failure, Adam and Eve have a regular evening appointment with God, a standing invitation to walk with him in the cool of Eden's evening (Gen. 3:8). We're never told whether the first human couple ever keeps that appointment, though they likely do. Even after they disobey God by eating the forbidden fruit, God keeps the rendezvous. But Adam and Eve, riddled with the guilt of original sin, hide in fear and shame, desperately trying to cover their nakedness with hastily sewn fig leaves.

When Enoch walks with God, we are reminded of God's appointment with Adam and Eve. God desires to walk with Enoch, like he does with the first couple. The difference is that Enoch keeps the appointment. And what a difference it is!

God always keeps his appointments, even with sinners. He keeps it with Adam and Eve, though they choose to hide. When he finds a willing walker in the man Enoch, this ordinary man and God maintain their daily rendezvous for three hundred years. God keeps his appointment with you too. Always. Are you taking advantage of this choice, divine opportunity?

Enoch and Abel

When we compare Abel and Enoch, we gain fresh perspectives on faith. The two men share a common, singular commitment to God. Both are righteous recipients of God's approval. But in some ways their experiences of faith on this earth are starkly different. Abel is a man who obeys a specific request by God. With Enoch we know of no particular act of obedience, courage, or decision: he just walks with God. Abel is a man who faces a crisis with his brother Cain because he obeys God—at great cost. With Enoch we know of no such crisis: he just walks with God. Abel is a man who surrenders his life for acting uprightly, cut off in his prime from an earthly family or future. With Enoch we know of no such sacrifices: he just walks with God. Enoch lives a long life with many sons and daughters. At the end of it, while walking with God, God takes him. The comparisons are listed below.

Abel and Enoch: A Comparison

Abel	Enoch
• A single act of righteousness	• No known act of righteousness
• Cain murdered him	• God took him
• A short life	• A long life (365 years)
• No children	• Many children
• Though dead, he still speaks	• He walked with God
A man in crisis	*A man of consistency*

Enoch and Us

When I think of Abel and Enoch, I have to ask myself which unlikely hero of faith is harder to imitate: Abel, who makes a righteous choice with fatal consequences, or Enoch, who lives an entire, lengthy life with spiritual consistency. At first impulse, I'm tempted to say Abel. Reading stories of martyrs who make difficult choices to endure agonizing pain, I wonder whether I would have the strength to emulate their courageous faith.

Yet, upon further reflection, my admiration for Enoch's faith grows. The longer I live, the more I appreciate the difficulty of living a consistent, godly life that finishes well. My greatest spiritual challenge is rarely adversity. Usually, it is consistency:

- Consistency in studying God's Word when my schedule is relentless.
- Consistency in prayer when I feel emotionally or spiritually drained.
- Consistency in outreach when I'm fed up "to here" with people.
- Consistency in giving when the needs seem endless and my resources stretch thin.

I always thought spiritual consistency would get easier as I grew older in my faith. I hoped serving in vocational ministry would enhance a faithful walk. But neither age nor professionalism guarantees spiritual success. The keys are character and commitment.

Would I face a faith-threatening challenge with the calm resolve of a Stephen? I wouldn't presume to say. I only observe that God's grace seems to expand during adversity. Nevertheless, my greatest daily challenge seems to be, like Enoch, pleasing God through a faithful walk to the end.

Abel and Enoch are two ordinary witnesses that give expert testimony to a living faith. While their perspectives are far from identical, it is, in fact, the difference in their testimony that is so compelling. Abel, through his acceptable offering to God, provides evidence that living by faith involves obeying God regardless of the consequences. Enoch provides evidence that living by faith involves a daily, continuous walk with God. It means hanging in there. It requires endurance and rewards steady consistency. It is measured not just by starting well but also by finishing strong.

An Applicational Summary

Witness	Principle	Challenge
You and me	Living by faith begins with trust in the God who makes and speaks.	Is our view of God large enough?
Abel	Living by faith requires obedience regardless of the consequences.	Is our faith in God strong enough?
Enoch	Living by faith involves a daily, continuous walk with God.	Is our faith in God steady enough?

Abels and Enochs still surround us. We can learn from, and emulate, their kind of faith. With Abel I ask myself, "Is my faith in God *strong* enough?" With Enoch I ask, "Is my faith in God *steady* enough?"

The pathway of faith will likely involve both crisis and consistency. Abel and Enoch are both charter members of the Hall of Faith, and we can be too. We must prepare for crises and also remember that crisis preparation involves the daily boot-camp regimen of walking continuously and consistently with God.

CHAPTER 4

NOAH:

THE UNLIKELY BUILDER

At Sea on the SS *President Cleveland*

Growing up, I had a powerful urge to see the world. I daydreamed about sailing the seven seas on a tramp steamer, never believing that one day this would really happen.

I hold my brother responsible. Darrell was a medical resident at San Francisco's Presidio hospital. As a college student in Santa Barbara, I had mentioned my wanderlust to my brother. Imagine my surprise when Darrell called with an unexpected question: did I want to become a merchant seaman?

My brother had treated a member of the Marine Firemen, Oilers, and Watertenders Union who was especially appreciative of Darrell's medical skills. This seaman learned of my interest in going to sea and agreed to help (to my mother's everlasting chagrin).

I was to learn what a gigantic favor this was. To be dispatched to a merchant ship, you needed union membership. To join a union required Coast Guard seaman's papers; and to obtain seaman's papers, you had to possess a letter from a union official confirming you had a job. Finally, to receive that letter, you depended on an advocate—a union member in good standing—who would recommend your membership. It sounded to me like a hopeless catch-22.

But this man was true to his word. He patiently guided me for months through the bureaucratic maze, and in June of 1969, I found myself standing on the deck of the SS *President Cleveland*, employed as an engine-room wiper (the engine-room janitor) and ready to sail west for exotic Asian ports.

In a heartbeat, this wet-behind-the-ears college junior was immersed in a cross-cultural experience of gargantuan proportions. I was so disconnected from this segment of society that I went into immediate culture shock.

My youth was a huge disadvantage. To call me callow would be a vast understatement. My WASPish family background was hardly an asset. Growing up in a family that cared for one another (including the brother who got me into this mess) only evoked insults from my crewmates. In particular, my college education isolated me. To most sailors, the more educated you are, the less common sense you have. Unfortunately, I only confirmed their hypothesis with every onboard mistake I made. And, believe me, I made plenty of them.

Most of all, as a Christian I embraced spiritual values that most seamen laugh at. I entered a world where Playboy pinups decorate cabin walls. Since my bunkmates put them there, I couldn't remove them. Vile swearing and crude humor punctuated every conversation. Vulgarity seemed to increase when crewmates learned of my faith. In port, sailors' activities of choice were drinking, strip clubs, prostitution, and fighting. I think there were actually wagers on when I would cave in.

I was a boy in this world of salty men. Longing to fit in, I wondered if it was possible to do so without compromise. Many days I stood alone on deck and asked myself, "What in the world am I doing here?"

An Upright Man in a Corrupt Culture

Can you identify with this feeling of cultural isolation? Noah, our fourth unlikely hero, is certainly a man who can. His uprightness glows against the dark backdrop of a decaying culture. Like a candle in a subterranean cave, the brightness of Noah's testimony illuminates his uniqueness within a world God had chosen to destroy.

How is he able to survive? We'll explore this question by getting beneath the surface. The Bible gives three commendations to Noah, charted below.

Three Biblical Descriptions of Noah

Description	Reference
A righteous man	Genesis 6:9
A herald of righteousness	2 Peter 2:5
An heir of righteousness	Hebrews 11:7

Noah's Profile: A Righteous Man

Noah's Culture

Consider the days of Noah. Noah does not simply inhabit a culture of confusing spiritual trends; he lives in a world that is beyond redemption. God's indictment on Noah's contemporaries stops us cold: "The LORD saw that the wickedness of man was great in the earth, and that every intention of the thoughts of his heart was only evil continually" (Gen. 6:5). Spiritual degeneration is so severe that God, with deep grief, resolves to obliterate them. How does it come to this? Genesis sketches two reasons, as seen in the following chart.

Two Causes of Cultural Collapse: Genesis 4–6

1.	**Spiritual entropy**	• Cain's descendants grow wicked. • Seth's descendants grow weak.
2.	**Spiritual warfare**	• Angelic perversion: sons of God marry human wives. • Human arrogance: God limits human life span to 120 years. • Nephilim violence: giant warriors use their power for evil.

First, spiritual entropy marks the culture. While Cain's descendants flourish as city-builders, they flounder as spiritual leaders. And when we look with hope to the descendants of Adam's third son, Seth, we are deeply disappointed. With the brief exception of Enoch, the Genesis 5 genealogy gives little evidence of a people with vibrant, active faith. The conclusion is frightening: the descendants of Cain grow wicked; the descendants of Seth grow weak.

Second, spiritual warfare intensifies. Here we read puzzling references to the marriages of the sons of God with the daughters of men, the Lord's one hundred twenty-year limit, and the presence of the mighty Nephilim (Gen. 6:1–5). While acknowledging there are many interpretations of this passage, I summarize four of my conclusions as follows:

1. The sons of God are angelic beings who, spurning God's design, marry human women in a particularly depraved example of angelic rebellion. I connect this passage to Jude 6–7.

2. Human fathers and their daughters consent to a marriage union with angels in a misguided and arrogant effort to ensure immortality for themselves and their descendants.

3. God now limits human mortality to one hundred twenty years to frustrate this wicked maneuver toward immortality. Genesis 6:3 is best translated "My life-giving breath will not *abide* in man forever," emphasizing years of life span, not the years until the flood, when the Holy Spirit's restraint of sin would cease.

4. The Nephilim are not the descendants of the unsanctioned, human-angelic union but powerful contemporary warriors. Turning to evil, they intensify the violence and wickedness on the earth during the time when the sons of God and daughters of men marry (Gen. 6:4).

Even if you accept less supernatural interpretations of these verses, the conclusion is the same: the world's evil is so intense and pervasive that God calls down the curtain.

Noah's Character

In the midst of this turmoil, "Noah found favor in the eyes of the LORD" (Gen. 6:8). Little detail is given except for three brief, pointed phrases in Genesis 6:9:

- Noah is a righteous man.
- Noah is blameless in his generation.
- Noah walks with God.

Like Abel, Noah is a righteous man. Like Enoch, Noah walks with God. And above all, Noah is blameless—a man of integrity—in stark contrast to the corruption and violence swirling around him.

There's encouragement here! Do you ever feel that you're lost in the crowd, just part of the masses? Do you wonder whether holding to moral standards or practicing integrity is really worth it, especially when others succeed by bending the rules? Do you doubt that God even sees you? If you ever ask these questions, think of Noah. Amid the multitudes of powerful, ambitious, and self-centered inhabitants of planet earth, God sees Noah. He spots just one man. And Noah finds favor in the eyes of the One who sees all things.

Noah's Calling

The drama of this cultural decline helps us understand God's mingled reaction of grief and disgust at the earth's cultural corruption. That God will judge his wicked world is no surprise. But nothing in the Genesis story prepares us for the breadth of God's mercy. We don't foresee that God's plan of destruction will also provide a way of escape.

Noah is the center of that plan. God tasks him with a project of unfathomable proportions: to build an ark for the salvation of the race. We find no resume that suggests Noah is qualified for such construction; he has no degrees in engineering or seamanship. Does he possess other kinds of leadership experiences: an advocate for social injustice, a defender of the abused, a provider for the poor? The text does not say. We know nothing about his upbringing, his occupation, his source of income, or his social standing. All we know is that when Noah finds favor with God, it is not based on merit, reward, or accomplishment. Rather, "*by faith* Noah, being warned by God concerning events as yet unseen, . . . constructed an ark" (Heb. 11:7).

We do not know how God communicates his warning to Noah or how Noah and his family initially react. Perhaps there is more bad news in the *Mesopotamian Gazette* when Noah sits down with the seven other members of his family for supper.

"What's the matter, dear?" his wife asks as she serves a meal of melons, leeks, and camel cheese. "I know when something's on your mind. Tough day at work again?"

"Yeah, Dad," adds Ham, "you're not your usual chipper self." They all laugh at the irony that their usually serious father would be chipper about anything.

"Well, I don't really know how to say this," Noah begins, "but I talked with the Lord today."

"Really?" exclaims Japheth, the youngest. "How do you know it was God? What does he look like?"

"Hold on," says Shem. "Let Dad explain what he means."

"It's not easy to explain," Noah answers, "but when I met this stranger on the outskirts of the city, there was something about him I couldn't put my finger on. Then he spoke to me, and when I heard his voice, I knew within my spirit it was the Lord."

"C'mon, Dad," interjects Shem. "You've warned us to be skeptical about claims to hear the voice of God.

"Were you frightened?" asks Ham.

"A little," Noah admits, "but his demeanor—his eyes—signaled to me I had nothing to fear. I was more frightened by what he had to say."

"What was it?" asks Mrs. Noah. "I'm sure the Lord isn't one to mince words."

"Yeah, what was it?" interjects Japheth. "Are we going to move again?"

Noah waits a moment before answering. "The Lord shared something of the future with me," he responds with uncharacteristic heaviness. "Not surprisingly, he is both saddened and angry about the state of our world. He plans to destroy all life as we know it with a catastrophic flood."

There is silence around the table for several minutes. Shem's wife begins to weep quietly, and Noah's wife looks at her husband with affection, squeezing his hand. Japheth's wife mouths words to Japheth that are on everyone's mind: "What's a flood?"

Noah breaks the silence. "But there is good news too," he says. "God plans to save the human race by constructing a huge ark—a gigantic boat, I gather—that will withstand the flood of water. The scary thing is that he's asked me to build it."

Immediately everyone speaks at once. Words of skepticism, awe, doubt, and wonder tumble out of their mouths like an avalanche. Finally Shem voices what they all are thinking. "How can the Lord ask this of you, Dad? You have no experience in construction. You can't put a round peg in a round hole!"

Noah looks around the table. "That part is simple," he says with the faintest hint of a smile. "God expects all of you to help."

Noah's Obedience: A Herald of Righteousness

Is God's mission for Noah to build an ark an unusual request? Absolutely! It seems impossible. Is Noah disturbed or confused by it? Probably. But does this matter to Noah? Apparently not. He simply obeys.

Building a massive barge in the middle of a Mesopotamian desert is the obvious expression of Noah's faith. But Scripture emphasizes something more: Noah's godly attitude toward his work. Let's look deeper into three aspects of Noah's divine mission: his sacred task, his enormous task, and his lonely task.

Noah's Sacred Task

People of faith are obedient, and obedient to the end. "Noah did this; he did all that God commanded him" (Gen. 6:22). But Noah's obedience has a spiritual motivation: "In reverent fear [he] constructed an ark for the saving of his household" (Heb. 11:7). In some sacred way, constructing the ark is an act of worship. What does this mean?

God's fingerprints are on this project from start to finish, revealing that every day on the job is a day with the Lord. This shapes our view of work. Work is honoring to God. The skill of a craftsman in building exquisite furniture, the blueprints of an architect realized in a finished home, the precision of a surgeon replacing a heart valve, and the patience of a teacher explaining abstract art to a student, all illustrate the joy and fulfillment of vocation flowing from a grateful heart. Noah shows us that work can be an act of reverence even in the midst of global calamity.

Noah's Enormous Task

Noah's ark, when we take the figures literally, is huge. In cubits it measures three hundred by fifty by thirty. The Hebrew cubit ranged between eighteen and twenty inches. If we take the shorter cubit (eighteen inches), Noah's ark would have measured four hundred fifty by seventy-five by forty-five feet—about half the length of the *Titanic*. God specified that it have three decks, one door, and one window, perhaps running just below the upper eaves. The ark was basically a barge waterproofed with pitch (bitumen); neither keel nor rudder was necessary. Noah's ship had a capacity of 150,000 cubic feet, ample space for thousands of animals and the stores to feed them.

With only Noah and his three sons working, such a project would have taken decades. Some believe the construction lasts one hundred twenty years because of the allusion in Genesis 6:3. I favor a period of perhaps eighty years because God's mission included Noah's sons and daughters-in-law (Gen. 6:18). Noah's sons were not born (let alone grown or married) until one hundred years before the flood (Gen. 5:32; 7:6). Adding twenty years for the sons to grow to adulthood puts the time at about eighty years. But whether the task was a hundred twenty years or eighty, the stamina required to complete this work is unimaginable.

Noah's Lonely Task

Remember, as the only righteous persons on the planet, Noah and his family experience loneliness and alienation like we will never know. There is no local church to attend. No Christian friends to write, visit, or call. No pastor, counselor, or evangelist to drop by now and then to offer a word of encouragement. Noah's family stands alone against the ostracism of their culture.

Noah, as an ordained herald of righteousness (2 Pet. 2:5), also warns his wicked and apathetic neighbors about the impending deluge. Undoubtedly, between the blows of his hammer, he summons them to repent from their wickedness and to join him in the ark. But despite eighty years of preaching, not a single soul responds to the invitation. Not one conversion.

Noah's Legacy: An Heir of Righteousness

What evidence of faith! Noah builds a monstrosity of a boat that seems ridiculous to the world. He does it reverently, as an act of worship, because God tells him to. During the eighty years of building, he proclaims by word and deed that God demands righteousness and punishes rebellion. His testimony condemns his culture and his contemporaries alike (Heb. 11:7). The wickedness of his culture is never clearer than when the eight survivors emerge from the ark and look upon their new world, devoid of any other living soul. Tragically, there is no skeptic alive to learn the important lesson.

How would you describe your culture? Would you call it depraved, wicked, rebellious, or hard-hearted? My own choice would be "godless." While godlessness may involve wickedness, the godless simply don't figure God into their life's equation.

Our challenge, like Noah, is to live in our culture—whether wicked or godless—without spiritual compromise. We can do this in many ways, such as:

- Defining marriage as a life-long union between one man and one woman.
- Understanding a husband's leadership role in the family to exclude absolutely any form of physical, verbal, psychological, or sexual abuse.
- Rejecting definitions of human life that marginalize the unborn, the physically and mentally handicapped, and the elderly.
- Refusing to tolerate racism in the name of civil liberty.

In short, we are called to navigate our culture as "heirs of righteousness."

A Thousand Points of Grace

Years ago, as a young merchant seaman, I discovered it was possible to live uprightly in a hostile culture. I found it unnecessary either to compromise or to become a pariah. In the midst of crises, I experienced points of grace that God provided to encourage me along the way. I met crewmembers who, though not believers, understood my youthful naivety and cut me slack. I encountered sailors who respected my faith and became seekers themselves. In one case, the Lord removed a roommate with whom I was on a collision course by promoting him to a different work schedule and different cabin.

Let's sum up. Creation asks, "Is your view of God *large* enough?" Abel asks, "Is your faith in God *strong* enough?" Enoch asks, "Is your faith in God *steady* enough?" Now, Noah asks, "Is your faith in God *distinct* enough?"

An Applicational Summary

Witness	Principle	Challenge
You and me	Living by faith begins with trust in the God who makes and speaks.	Is our view of God large enough?
Abel	Living by faith requires obedience regardless of the consequences.	Is our faith in God strong enough?
Enoch	Living by faith involves a daily, continuous walk with God.	Is our faith in God steady enough?
Noah	Living by faith will cut against the grain of culture.	Is our faith in God distinct enough?

Do you find yourself cutting against the grain of culture? Congratulations! That means you have spiritual backbone. Remember that God will never overlook righteous people. He will provide points of gracious, guiding light in the midst of cultural and spiritual darkness.

PART 2

THE PATRIARCHS

CHAPTER 5

ABRAHAM:

THE UNLIKELY WANDERER

A European Journey

Hanging on a wall at home, carefully framed and matted, is a small American flag. If you were to examine it closely, you would notice it is weather-stained and tattered. This flag was sewn to a backpack I carried for three months one summer in 1968 while hitchhiking alone throughout Europe. I treasure it as a symbol of an incredible adventure.

This idea of trekking through Europe came in January of my sophomore year. My brother, Larry, who had just been discharged from the Air Force, returned with his family from two years of active service in Germany. They came through Santa Barbara, where I was attending college, and related their rich experiences of the sights and sounds of Europe.

As I viewed their slides that evening, I resolved to travel to Europe myself that summer. So I began to plan. I applied for my first passport, read books on student travel, and researched the places I wanted to visit. I secured a membership card for the International Youth Hostel Association. My most momentous decision was this: I would travel for three months hitchhiking throughout Europe, and I would do it alone.

The challenge of making this dream a reality was, of course, finances. For years my parents taught me to save ten percent of my allowance or other earnings for college. Thanks to their generosity, I hadn't had to touch that account for my college tuition. What better use could there be, I reasoned, than using that college fund to finance a *real* educational experience?

The money was in a custodial account with my mother's name at the top, requiring her approval for withdrawals. So, my voice trembling with anticipation, I called Mom with the exciting news, explaining in detail what I had in mind. She did not share my enthusiasm. She raised, I thought, all kinds of irrelevant and niggling questions about the safety of flying, safety in lodging, and safety of hitchhiking. Hitchhiking especially. She just couldn't leave that one alone.

Then she made a small but ultimately helpful concession. "Well," she finally said, "I'll let you talk to your father." Dad got on the line and listened to my plan, and to my surprise, he thought it was a tremendous idea. "I don't see why you couldn't use some funds from that account," he said. When we ended our conversation, he agreed to send the money and to explain all of this to my mother. Though I could never confirm it, I suspected that my father would have loved to take a trip like this when he was my age.

My journey was the thrilling, mind-expanding experience I hoped for. I flew from LAX carrying a twenty-five-pound backpack with that small American flag sewn on the flap. Landing in Amsterdam, I relied on this backpack and my thumb to travel as far north as Stockholm, as far east as Vienna, as far south as Sicily, and as far west as Dublin. I stayed in hostels, was invited to homes, and slept in barns and open fields. I visited museums and art galleries, hitched with new friends I met on the way, and exited Prague just two weeks before Soviet tanks rolled into town to shut down the country. I returned home just before classes began in September, full of stories and thoroughly enriched. It was the journey of a lifetime.

Abraham, the Unlikely Adventurer

Living by faith is a journey. There are wonders to behold and challenges to overcome. Wise travelers must be problem-solvers, flexible and curious. When they complete their journey, they find themselves changed people, never seeing life the same way again. So it is with the journey of faith.

Abraham, our next unlikely hero of faith, is a wanderer who embarks on an incredible journey. While his quest involves a radical geographical change, it is, most importantly, a spiritual one. His journey of faith occurs in two major stages, summarized in Hebrews 11:8–10. In the first stage Abraham leaves his Mesopotamian home and journeys to Canaan. In the second he journeys through Canaan, dwelling in the land God promises him. The chart below displays these two stages, which we will use as a framework for our exploration.

Abraham's Earthly Journey of Faith

Stage One	Stage Two
Going to Canaan	Living in Canaan
Entry #1: Abraham begins his journey by believing God's Word.	Entry #3
	Entry #4
Entry #2: Abraham continues his journey one stage at a time.	Entry #5
Hebrews 11:8	Hebrews 9–10

Building upon this biographical structure, we will draw from Abraham's nomadic experiences some important principles of faith. I like to imagine that Abraham journals his adventure—as I did my European travels—so we will consider two possible journal entries from Abraham's travels to Canaan. We'll examine the second stage of Abraham's journey and three additional entries in chapter 6.

Journal Entry #1:
Abraham Begins His Journey by Believing God's Word

"By faith," we read, "Abraham obeyed when he was called to go out to a place that he was to receive as an inheritance" (Heb. 11:8). Abraham's first journal entry centers on his knowing, believing, and obeying God's Word.

Knowing and Believing God's Word

The story of Abraham (then named Abram) begins, according to Genesis 11, with God calling Abraham's father, Terah, to lead his family out of Ur of the Chaldees (Gen. 11:31). For that reason, we do not know how God revealed to Abraham that he should leave his remote city of Ur and travel overland to an unidentified location. Does the Lord speak through a vision, appear in a dream, or appear tangibly in theophany as a human form? Although we later learn that God communicates to him in many of these ways, we do not know which method God uses here.

Nor do we know the circumstances from which Abraham and Sarah (then named Sarai) are called. Is Abraham eager to leave or reluctant to do so? Is business booming or busting? Is his social and political influence in the village of Ur on the rise, in decline, or nonexistent? Maybe he has just been elected mayor or voted citizen of the year. Or perhaps some unhappy creditors are beginning to apply legal pressure, making Abraham grateful for an opportunity to skip town.

And where is Sarah in all of this? What does she think about a long camel ride? Is she depressed over leaving her family, her clutch of social intimates, her sewing circle? Or is she the object of merciless gossip (after all, she is beautiful and barren), fed up to her veil with village small-mindedness, and eager to make a fresh start? We simply do not know.

But two things we do know. God calls Abraham, and Abraham knows without question that God has summoned him. As we seek to apply this principle of knowing and believing God's Word, we must remember that Abraham possesses no Bible: no Old Testament, no New Testament, not even a Torah. The Word of God takes a very different form for Abraham than it does for us today. While he may lack the full and complete written revelation of God, God's call is clear, and that is all he needs to know.

Do you ever long to receive God's direct call on your life, like Abraham does? To actually hear God's voice or see God's form? I have these longings. But then I remember that as a New Testament Christian I am blessed in ways Abraham never was. Because of Scripture, I understand clearly God's revelation in his Son, Jesus, and the reason for his death on a Roman cross. Because of the cross, I belong to a new covenant community, the church, which Christ himself built (Matt. 16:18) on the foundation of the apostles (Eph. 2:20). Because of Pentecost, I enjoy the unique, supernatural ministries of the Holy Spirit, who baptizes, indwells, gifts, and fills me. Because of God's grace, I have access to the complete and sufficient revelation in Holy Scripture. So, though I have never heard God's audible voice, I see far more clearly the contours of God's eternal plan of salvation and his purpose for me than Abraham ever could.

Despite these important differences between us and Abraham, the basic application of his journal entry is the same for all of us. We need to design and embrace a strategy for knowing, believing, and obeying the revelation of God that we do possess.

That strategy must include involvement in a thriving local church and attendance at the weekly service. We also need regular, personal nourishment from God's Word. Reading through the Bible each year is one way. Some even read the Bible through in ninety days. I have followed a personal Bible study program in which I select twelve books of the Bible to investigate each year, one a month, from different sections of Scripture.

A strategy may include organized Bible study groups (men's, women's, small group, or evangelistic Bible studies), but ultimately your Bible study should take you deeper. Leading a Bible study or teaching a class is a sure way to immerse yourself in the Word. One goal is to master the basic steps of inductive Bible study: observation, interpretation, correlation, and application. Another is to be familiar with study tools: atlases, Bible dictionaries and encyclopedias, concordances, and commentaries. Of course, if you truly hunger for in-depth knowledge of the whole counsel of God, Multnomah University has a program for you!

Obeying God's Word

Abraham not only hears, understands, and believes God's Word; he also takes that vital step that perfects faith. "Abraham obeyed when he was called to go out to a place that he was to receive as an inheritance" (Heb 11:8). He *obeys*. Let's look at two aspects of obedience: avoiding self-deception and accepting a biblical worldview.

Avoiding self-deception. Abraham's obedience is not inevitable. Abraham could have been inclined to institutionalize God's call.

"Oy vey!" Abraham might have said. "The Lord has spoken and has promised me a land of inheritance someday somewhere, but I'm too busy to leave right now. Can't I obey God when it's more convenient for me to leave?"

"I know," says Abraham after a moment's reflection, "I'll start the Euphrates Chapel of the Epiphany—or perhaps the Camelback Caravan Church—to celebrate God's vision and tell others about it."

But had Abraham remained in Ur, his story would vanish like desert sand in a windstorm. Thankfully he directs his intellectual understanding into obedient faith. Abraham apparently understands the self-deception in being a hearer of the Word but not a doer (James 1:22–25). James describes self-deception as knowing the truth about yourself from God's Word but then deliberately turning away from it unchanged, as a man turns from a mirror and forgets what he looks like. It's hard to imagine something more tragic that this "James delusion."

Accepting a biblical worldview. From our comfortable, twenty-first century perspective, we can easily minimize the magnitude of Abraham's act of obedience; we make journeys all the time to new and exciting places. But Thomas Cahill, pondering Abraham's story in his book *The Gift of the Jews,* makes an astonishing claim: "This particular migration would change the face of the earth by permanently changing the minds and hearts of human beings."*

How is this so? Cahill observes that the religious and philosophical culture of Sumerian Ur—indeed, the worldview of all ancient cultures—is based on a cyclical view of reality. Life is seasonal, predictable, deterministic, and immutable. Like a giant wheel, human experience slowly but predictably plods from summer to winter, planting to harvest, birth to death. The fates, the stars, or the gods control all things; human beings are mere pawns in a divine drama. There is no hope for progress, promise, or change. One survives the mundane, static cycle of life by accepting one's place in the Wheel of Life.

---

* Thomas Cahill, *The Gifts of the Jews: How a Tribe of Desert Nomads Changed the Way Everyone Thinks and Feels* (New York: Nan A. Talese, 1998), 59.

The Sumerian Worldview

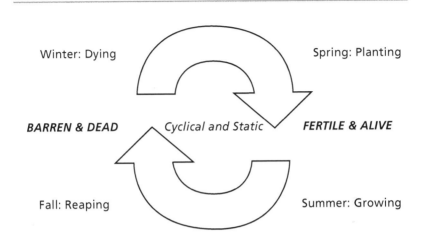

The city of Ur's religious rituals of the moon goddess reflect this worldview. In their ceremonies, king-priests, mounting man-made mountains (ziggurats), reenact the drama of the gods unfolding in heaven. Ascending these high towers, they believe, would bring them closer to the gods. Ultimately they hope to influence the divine cycle just enough to receive another season of fertile crops and another year of pregnant wives.

This explains, in part, the horribly lascivious nature of their religious practices involving male and female prostitution. In the Sumerian worldview, temple prostitution is a symbolic act of fertility that could manipulate the gods to grant fertility to the nation. The Canaanites keep these same practices when Joshua leads the Israelites into the Promised Land some seven hundred years later. It is not surprising that God is so sharp in his warnings against the Canaanites and so severe in his punishment.

This is Abraham's world. He knows these rituals. Perhaps he even believes and practices them. But at one point Abraham is visited by the God who turns both his world and his world-view upside down with a simple offer: "Go from your country and your kindred and your father's house to the land that I will show you" (Gen. 12:1). Certainly, God promises Abraham a future inheritance and a unique covenantal relationship with him. But, as Cahill points out, it is so much more than that. God offers Abraham—and his physical and spiritual descendants right down to the present day—the adventure of a lifetime. The opportunity to take a risk into the unknown. The possibility to get off the great mandala of endless repetitions and to embark on a path with a destination full of hope and promise. God offers Abraham the chance for a change and the opportunity to make decisions that would change history for himself, his family, and his descendants forever.

Cahill summarizes the earth-shaking significance of this as follows:

> So, "Abram went"—two of the boldest words in all literature. They signal a complete departure from everything that has gone before in the long evolution of culture and sensibility. Out of Sumer, civilized repository of the predictable, comes a man who does not know where he is going but goes forth into the unknown wilderness under the prompting of his God. Out of Mesopotamia, home of canny, self-serving merchants who use their gods to ensure prosperity and favor, comes a wealthy caravan with no material goal. Out of ancient humanity, which from the dim beginnings of its consciousness has read its eternal verities in the stars, comes a party traveling by no known compass. Out of the human race, which knows in its bones that all its striving must end in death, comes a

leader who says he has been given an impossible promise. Out of mortal imagination comes a dream of something new, something better, something yet to happen, something—in the future.*

What God presents to Abraham in Ur is a biblical view of history. God's way is a linear, progressive view of reality which sees a purpose to human history because he oversees history and makes certain his promises. History is dynamic, not static. It is filled with hope and promise, not despair. History is also progressive, growing increasingly clearer as God deepens his prophecy with more and more revelation. Humans are participants in this history—not mere pawns—because God enters into covenantal relationship with mankind through the ages. This linear worldview does not begin with Abraham; it originates in Eden with the "Cultural Mandate" (Gen. 1:28–30) and with God's promise that the woman's male seed would someday crush the serpent's head (Gen. 3:15). Nor does it cease with Abraham. This uniquely optimistic worldview influences Christian thought—and Western philosophy—down to the present moment.

The Biblical Worldview

Linear and Dynamic

Human History

Divine Prophecy   Divine Fulfillment

---

* Cahill, *The Gifts of the Jews*, 63.

When God places his call upon your life, how do you react? Do you look at it as an obligation or an adventure? Do you feel duty-bound to obey God but experience very little joy in doing so? If that is your perspective, consider Abraham. This man believes God so much and takes steps of faith so remarkable that he never looks back. And the world, our world, has never been the same.

Journal Entry #2:
Abraham Continues His Journey
One Stage at a Time

Abraham's second journal entry explains the progressive nature of faith's journey. The phrase in Hebrews 11:8 is filled with irony: "And he went out, not knowing where he was going." I know Christians who claim this as their life verse. Aimless and without purpose, they use Scripture to justify complacency. Abraham is anything but aimless. Yet what startles us is that this adventurer is given marching orders with no specific destination. God does not tell Abraham every detail of his sovereign will.

To reconstruct the story, we must supplement the Genesis account with Stephen's Acts 7 sermon. Stephen supplies the important insight that God's call to Abraham comes while he is still in Ur (Acts 7:2–3). In obedience, Abraham, with Terah his father and other relatives, travels up the Fertile Crescent of the Tigris and Euphrates Rivers to Haran. There the party stops and waits. It was only after Terah passes away that Abraham begins the second stage of his journey.

Some scholars suggest from this that Abraham is not completely obedient to God when he leaves Ur. He does not leave his family behind as God asks, they say, and he stops before reaching the land God would show him. Only because of his patience and grace does the Lord extend our unlikely hero a second chance in spite of his halfway obedience.

I disagree. I find no biblical criticism of Abraham on this matter, either in Genesis 12 or in Acts 7. Since it was Father Terah who leads the patriarchal exodus (Gen. 11:31), Terah receives God's call too. Terah and Abraham both obey and journey to Haran. After Terah dies, God reaffirms his call to Abraham (Gen. 12:1–3) for the next stage of the adventure.

But remember the most important lesson here: the life of faith is progressive. God does not all at once tell Abraham everything he will eventually need to know. He only reveals what is necessary for Abraham to take the first step of leaving Ur.

The same is true for us. I must confess there are times I have wished God would reveal his entire plan for my life in detail (preferably on a nice parchment in glowing letters). Usually I long for this at times of key decision. As a young man in college, just after I began dating a beautiful young woman named Jani, I wanted to know the contours of my future life. Specifically I wanted to know whether she was the one! It would have made navigating the hazards of dating so much easier.

Many young Multnomah University students share the same sentiment. "Is the Lord calling me to become a missionary or a businessman?" they ask. "Should I marry this man or not?" "What college major should I choose?" "What vocation should I pursue?" Their motives are sincere—they want to obey the will of God—but they possess the natural impatience of youth to settle the issue and move forward.

Over the years I've become grateful that God does not operate this way. All of us have experiences we never want to repeat. What incapacitating dread might we feel if we foreknew exactly what was coming! I have come to appreciate God's wisdom in the way he progressively unfolds his plan for me.

This principle tells us something about the Bible too. The Bible is less a list of MapQuest directions than a hiking guide and compass. It provides moral principles for the journey and marks the dangers of the road. While showing us the purpose and ultimate destiny of our spiritual journey, the Bible is far more interested in revealing the character of the God who has called us to the journey and the Savior who has provided the grace to endure it. While reassuring us of our destiny, it exhorts us to patience and endurance however the path may twist and turn.

Let the Journey Begin

Mom came to admit that my European summer was immensely beneficial. She even conceded, though with reluctance, that it was worth the money. But she would have smiled when my own daughter, Elise, announced she was going to travel through Europe the summer following her college graduation, despite my expressed hesitations. Elise had heard my story many times and shrewdly calculated that I lacked any rational justification to deny her request. She was right, of course. Now she and I reflect on our shared, enriching experiences.

As men and women of faith, we share an unforgettable adventure with Abraham, the quintessential person of faith in Scripture. The New Testament refers to the faith of Abraham more than any other Old Testament character (see Rom. 4:1–25; Gal. 3:5–9, 15–18; Heb. 11:8–19; and James 2:18–24). In walking the journey of faith, Abraham illustrates how this is the most important experience of our lives, for this journey is an investment in eternity. We walk the road with the High King of Heaven.

Two Applications for the Journey

Principle	Application
1. Faith begins with God's Word.	Know the Book!
2. Faith is progressive.	Be patient!

Let's review. Abraham teaches us that the journey of faith involves two fundamental propositions. First, living by faith begins with the Word of God. That means knowing, believing, and obeying God's Word. Are you spiritually hungry for more knowledge of God? Remember Abraham. Then develop a strategy for understanding the whole counsel of God that we possess. Do you long for a clear calling on your life? Remember Abraham. Then respond to God's call in obedience by taking deliberate steps of faith. Do you sense the despair of the rat race, where life feels like an endless treadmill leading nowhere? Remember Abraham of Ur. Then claim the promises of the Lord of the journey, who invites us to experience the most incredible adventure of our lives with a destiny of hope, purpose, and reward.

Second, Abraham teaches us that living by faith is progressive. Do you sometimes impatiently ask, "Lord, if you'll just tell me what to do, I'll gladly do it"? Remember Abraham. Then practice the biblical truths you already know. Are you sometimes frustrated with the lack of clarity regarding key decisions of life? Remember Abraham. Then thank God he holds your destiny in his loving hand and gives you the strength for each leg of the journey.

CHAPTER 6

ABRAHAM:
THE UNLIKELY WORSHIPPER

The Queenstown Adventure

When our daughter Elise graduated from college in 2004, Jani and I hit upon the ideal graduation gift: a father/daughter adventure in New Zealand. In many ways, the choice was a natural one. Elise and I both share a passion for exciting, on-the-edge activities. New Zealand, we discovered, leads the world in extreme sports.

In this regard the trip was unforgettable. In two short weeks our list of adventures included blackwater rafting in Waitomo, swimming with dolphins in Kaikoura, bungee jumping off the A. J. Hackett bridge near Queenstown, hang gliding off Coronet Peak, ocean kayaking, and celebrating Christmas Eve aboard the *Milford Friendship* amid magnificent fjords and under the night sky's brilliant Southern Cross.

Beyond this, Elise and I share a deep affection for Tolkien's *Lord of the Rings* trilogy and have enjoyed Peter Jackson's epic films many times. We toured the site of Hobbiton, walked the road where the four hobbits escaped the black riders, gazed across the Ford of Bruinen, and stood high above the Anduin River where the Fellowship guided their boats past the mighty Argonath.

Eventually, in Deer Park Heights near Queenstown, we hit pay dirt. Nestled against the backdrop of the breathtaking mountain range appropriately named The Remarkables lay six filming sites from *The Two Towers*, the second film in the series. Amazed, we stood where the refugees of Rohan fled from the armies of Saruman and where Legolas the elf first scouted the Warg riders. Then we came upon the cliff where the mighty Aragorn bravely fought the Uruk-hai before being swept over (apparently) to his death. We could not believe our eyes. As we approached the site, a group of young New Zealanders was already there taking videos of one another acting out the scene. One fellow ran to the cliff and leaped off the precipice, while his mate, playing Legolas, ran to the edge calling, "Aragorn! Aragorn!"

It was at this point that I confess to a small lapse of judgment, because I determined to reenact the scene too. *What better memory to immortalize on videotape?* I thought. With Elise pointing the camera, I ran to the edge. Just before I jumped, I glanced down, wavering at the brink. That drop had to be over eight feet! But those New Zealanders had done it without incident, and so could I. Besides, they were now standing up on the road watching me. No way could I back out now! So I took a second run at the cliff, this time angling toward the left ledge, thinking this to be a shallower drop. With determination, a rolling camera, and an audience, I leaped off.

Later I would reflect that the worst part of this experience was not the sharp pain as my right foot struck that wedge of rock at the base, nor the Christmas afternoon spent in a Queenstown hospital having my ankle coated with plaster, nor the uncomfortable twelve-hour airplane flight home elevating my leg on an open tray table, nor even explaining myself to students and staff upon my post-sabbatical return to Multnomah. No, the worst part had to be the humiliation of asking those young New Zealanders to trek down the hill and carry this crazy, wounded, middle-aged American back up to his car.

But adventures are like that, aren't they? They involve successes and failures, times of great satisfaction and episodes of disappointment. You want to relive the exciting moments where things go well but erase the memories of foolishness and failure. Yet all the experiences create the adventure. In this chapter we will learn that Abraham's journey of faith also involves failure and disappointments, experiences that contribute mightily to his legacy of faith.

Abraham, the Unlikely Immigrant

Living in Canaan

Abraham's journey of faith, summarized in Hebrews 11:8–10, accelerates when he enters the land of Canaan. His experience of living in Canaan adds three other "journal entries" to our diary of Abraham's walk of faith. A chart of all five of these entries is shown below.

Abraham's Earthly Pilgrimage

Stage One	Stage Two
Going to Canaan	Living in Canaan
Entry #1: Abraham begins his journey by believing God's Word. Entry #2: Abraham continues his journey one stage at a time.	Entry #3: Abraham experiences failure. Entry #4: Abraham journeys through barren times. Entry #5: Abraham longs for his eternal home.
Hebrews 11:8	Hebrews 11:9–10

Spiritual Highlights

Three events of Abraham's life in Canaan are spiritual high points. First, Abraham receives God's call from Haran in the first giving of the Abrahamic covenant (Gen. 12:1–3). This covenant is renewed and expanded at least four times during his lifetime (Gen. 13; 15; 17; 22).

Second, God supernaturally renews this unconditional covenant (Gen. 15). After sacrificing the required animals and setting the pieces in two piles, Abraham awaits God's response. At nightfall the Lord appears in a vision of a flaming oven. But instead of passing between the two halves of the sacrifice *with* Abraham, the conventional way of sealing an ancient covenant, God passes *alone* between the pieces, while Abraham watches from the side-lines. "The fulfillment of this covenant depends upon me and me alone," God seems to say.

Third, God, preparing to destroy Sodom and Gomorrah, visits with his friend Abraham and shares a meal (Gen. 18). Before the dialogue in which Abraham presses God to save Sodom if ten righteous people are found, God blesses both Abraham and Sarah as heirs of the promise. It would be hard to identify a more intimate encounter with God in all of Scripture. In the chart below, I have sketched Abraham's spiritual pilgrimage.

Abraham's Spiritual Pilgrimage: Highlights

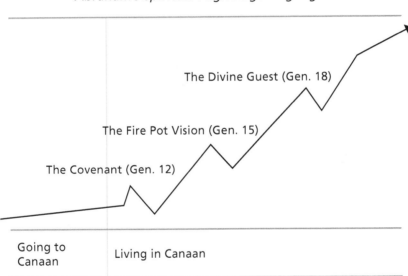

Journal Entry #3: Abraham Experiences Failure

This, however, is only part of Abraham's story. Without contradicting the great faith of Abraham or diminishing his friendship with God, we must acknowledge the times of disobedience too. Consider three spiritual low points in Abraham's walk with God.

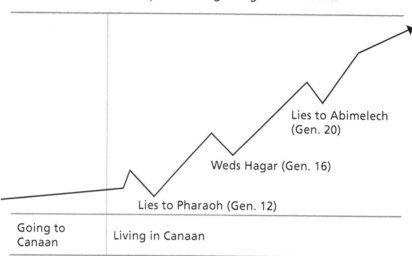

Abraham's Spiritual Pilgrimage: Low Points

Spiritual Failures

The failure with Pharaoh. Abraham's first failure follows on the heels of God's gracious giving of the Abrahamic covenant. Because of a famine in Canaan, Abraham and Sarah travel to Egypt. Some suggest that Abraham's decision to leave Canaan for Egypt is not a selfish act but obedience to a mission-minded God who promises "and in you all the families of the earth shall be blessed" (Gen. 12:3). Personally I am unconvinced, since a prominent Old Testament theme is Israel's responsibility to remain in the land. I believe, rather, that God expects Abraham to depend on him in the land of promise despite any adversity, even famine.

But there is no question that he makes an unrighteous choice in Egypt. Abraham is married to a beautiful woman,

Sarah. Fearing that Egypt's monarch will seize her for his harem, perhaps at the cost of Abraham's life, Abraham crafts the story that Sarah is his sister and persuades Sarah to comply.

Pharaoh does exactly what Abraham fears, taking Sarah into the palace and lavishing gifts upon her "brother." It is only when God sends plagues to Egypt (a prophetic anticipation of the Exodus plagues four hundred years later) that the Egyptian king, understandably angry, returns Sarah to her husband and sends both of them packing. No matter how you nuance it, Abraham blows it big time.

The failure with Hagar. Later, back in Canaan, Abraham takes another wrong turn regarding Sarah's handmaid, Hagar (Gen. 16). Despite God's incredible promise to Abraham of an heir in his old age, Abraham still has no son, and Sarah is barren and beyond childbearing years. It seems that Abraham, like many of us, decides to help God out.

"Well, I know God is in control," Abraham might reason, "but certainly he expects me to do my part."

At Sarah's urging, he takes Hagar the handmaid to be his second wife, and Ishmael is born. Although the text never explicitly states that Abraham sins in doing this, the red flags of folly are all over the place: Hagar's arrogant disdain, Sarah's jealousy, Abraham's insensitivity, the violation of monogamy, and the historical record of long-lasting enmity between the descendants of the two sons. But above all, Abraham's action contradicts God's declaration that the son of promise would be a descendant of Abraham and Sarah, not Hagar.

The failure with Abimelech. A third failure occurs years later when Abraham lies to Abimelech, king of Gerar (Gen. 20).

Sarah is eighty-nine and Abraham ninety-nine when they move to Gerar. An old, familiar dread haunts Abraham. *There is no fear of God in this place,* he thinks, *and the people will kill me to take my beautiful wife.*

In order to protect himself, he resurrects his old story that he and Sarah are brother and sister. Like Pharaoh, King Abimelech seizes Sarah as his wife, and God intervenes, more directly this time. The Lord closes the wombs of Abimelech's household and in a dream warns Abimelech of imminent death if he does not return Sarah to Abraham at once.

Defensively, Abimelech protests that he acted innocently and then demands an explanation from Abraham. Abraham tenders a half-hearted rationalization when he adds, "Besides, she really is my half-sister after all!" Abraham's self-centeredness in jeopardizing Sarah's integrity for his own protection shocks us with its brazenness.

Learning from Abraham's Failures

This brief spiritual overview teaches us some important principles about sin. Let me mention three of them.

First, the temptation to sin often follows spiritual success. The lie to Pharaoh follows Abraham's successful journey to Canaan and God's revelation of the weighty Abrahamic covenant. Similarly, the marriage to Hagar is immediately preceded by God's spectacular reaffirmation of Abraham with the vision of the fire pot. Finally, the lie to Abimelech comes on the heels of God's mealtime discussion with Abraham where God speaks to Abraham as he would a friend and promises Sarah's imminent pregnancy. The lesson is impossible to miss: if you have just experienced spiritual victory, take heed lest you fall.

Second, sin always has consequences, which often lead to further sin. For example, Hagar is Egyptian. Where else would Abraham the Chaldean patriarch find Hagar the Egyptian slave than in Egypt, when Pharaoh gives Abraham many gifts for Sarah, including handmaids (Gen. 12:16)? When Pharaoh runs him out of town, Abraham takes the gifts with him (Gen. 12:20). Wherever her origin, Hagar becomes a spiritual obstacle, a thorn in the household.

Third, sin easily becomes habitual. This is clearly seen in the similarities between Abraham's lies to Pharaoh and Abimelech. Abraham deceives Pharaoh about Sarah early in his walk of faith; he repeats it twenty-three years later.

Some critics of Scripture point to this similarity as proof of the Bible's unreliability. These scriptural passages portray the same event, they say. One ancient author wrote his version about Pharaoh, another about Abimelech. Then, much later, an editor with access to both stories mistakenly treated them as different events, weaving them into our present Genesis narrative.

There are many weaknesses of this theory, but the most significant one is common sense. These critics assume that a man of faith like Abraham would not commit the same sin twice. But experience shows that nothing could be further from the truth. Where fear and self-preservation are at stake, people default to the strategies, lies, and deceptions that have been successful in the past. The "sister lie" was becoming a habit.

So, let me state a principle: the journey of faith may involve failure. Please do not misunderstand me to say this excuses sin. Sin is a tragic, rebellious disregard of God's holy character and holy word. Therefore, the consequences of sin are serious and painful. Rather, I say this to encourage us. We can still be men or women of faith despite sin and failure. If Abraham can be the prototype of faith in the New Testament even with these failures, we can rejoice that God will not abandon us when we succumb to moral and spiritual temptation.

Have you ever done anything that you believe God could not, or would not, forgive? I am not asking a theological question; I am asking a personal one. Do you really believe the Scripture that proclaims, "He is faithful and just to forgive us our sins and to cleanse us from *all* unrighteousness" (1 John 1:9)?

On the other hand, has someone ever offended you in a way that you find impossible to forgive? The pain of marital infidelity, bitter divorce, physical or sexual abuse, financial scams, or other violations of trust seems insurmountable. But the same God who grants unconditional forgiveness to us expects us to extend it to others.

Like many of us, Peter attempts to invent an acceptable algebra for forgiving others (Matt. 18:21–22). "Lord, how many times shall I forgive my brother when he sins against me?" he asks Jesus. "Up to seven times?"

"Not seven times," Jesus answers, "but seventy times seven."

And just when Peter calculates he can clobber his brother at the four hundred ninety-first violation, Jesus silences him with the difficult parable of the unforgiving servant (Matt. 18:23–35). The Lord's point is crystal clear. There is no statute of limitations on forgiveness. If you're counting, you're not forgiving, because while people of faith are not perfect, they are forgiven—and forgiving—people.

Journal Entry #4:
Abraham Journeys through Barren Times

It is natural to read the Abraham story with the sense that Abraham hears God's voice, dines with him face to face, and witnesses eye-popping miracles almost daily. But Abraham's history, like so many other biblical accounts, is telescoped. The events included in the narrative are not exhaustive but selective. They advance the story and underscore key spiritual truths. Because of this, there are significant chronological gaps in the story.

To see this, it is helpful to view the three periods of Abraham's life. The Genesis story is explicit about the age of Abraham at the beginning and end of these three periods, enabling us to establish a helpful time frame.

Abraham's Spiritual Deserts

Era	Era of Lot and Eliezer	Era of Ishmael	Era of Isaac
Beginning event	Travels to Canaan	Ishmael's birth	Isaac's birth
Abraham's age	75 years (Gen. 12:4)	86 years (Gen. 16:16)	100 years (Gen. 21:5)
Concluding event	Ishmael's birth	Isaac's birth	Abraham's death
Abraham's age	86 years (Gen. 16:16)	100 years (Gen. 21:5)	175 years (Gen. 25:7)
Total years	11 years	14 years	75 years

The three eras of Lot and Eliezer (eleven years), Ishmael (fourteen years), and Isaac (seventy-five years) exist because these individuals stand at center stage during these phases of Abraham's life. In all likelihood Abraham considered each person his heir during that era. Though the text never says so explicitly, Abraham surely intended Lot to be his heir until they parted company (Gen. 13:8–12). Eliezer of Damascus, Abraham's servant, is his designated heir (Gen. 15:3) until Ishmael is born. And though Abraham desires Ishmael to be accepted by God as his heir (Gen. 17:18), Isaac becomes the heir of promise when he is born (Gen. 17:21).

God is active in each period, but close inspection shows there are many years of silence. Look, for example, at the Ishmael era. God appears only in the final year of the period, one year before the birth of Isaac when Abraham is ninety-nine. The reference to Ishmael's birth when Abraham is eighty-six (Gen. 16:16) is only one verse away from God's next appearance to the patriarch at ninety-nine years of age (Gen. 17:1). For the first thirteen years of Ishmael's life, there is no recorded divine intervention. There is no theophany, no miraculous desert visit, no nothing!

What does Abraham think? He has abandoned his familiar home in Ur to enter an unknown desert land. He relies on the God who guides him, instructs him, protects him, promises him, and provides for him every step of the way. But then, after Abraham makes an ill-advised decision, the curtain of silence falls.

Year one passes without a word. Where is the Lord? Years two and three run their course. No revelation from God except the memory that he promises this land to Abraham and guarantees him an heir. Years five, six, and seven recede into history. No Bible to read. No church to attend. No Christian radio. None of the things available to us to nourish our souls. Eight, nine, ten years expire. Where *is* God, anyway?

"Has God abandoned me?" Abraham might have asked. "Why did I ever leave home in the first place? Was it really God's voice I heard, or was it only the wind, a vision as elusive as a desert mirage?"

The text is silent except to report that Abraham faithfully stays in the land, ready to hear God's voice when he speaks thirteen years later. Whatever his feelings and thoughts, he continues to walk by faith.

Has this ever happened to you? Sometimes the heavens are brass, and our prayers don't seem to penetrate the ceiling. Worse, everyone around us rejoices in their intimacy with God. To reclaim that lost intimacy, we examine our life, confess all known sin, and ask, "What's wrong with me?" We follow all the formulas: stay connected with other believers, study the Word, and fine-tune our prayer life. But with all the adjustments in spiritual disciplines, it just seems God is absent.

If you can identify with this, congratulations! You're on the journey of faith. I believe God brings every one of us through the desert, through spiritually barren times. This may result from spiritual failure on our part, true enough. But just as often it does not. Moses herds sheep in Midian for forty years. The new generation of Israelites destined for Canaan wanders in the Sinai for forty years until the old generation passes on. Elijah, fleeing from Jezebel, travels through the wilderness to Horeb for forty days and nights. Jesus is tempted in the wilderness for forty days.

God brings those experiences to us for reasons he alone knows. His purposes, though often mysterious, are always wise, generous, and beneficial. So be faithful. Be obedient. Hold on.

God will draw close again, having walked you through the barren times for his purpose.

Journal Entry #5:
Abraham Longs for an Eternal Home
Abraham's Earthly Career

Two words describe Abraham: *wanderer* and *worshipper*. Correspondingly, two repeated construction projects head his list of priorities. Wherever he journeys in Canaan, he pitches a tent and builds an altar.

Abraham is a wanderer. We spoke of his unlikely journey to Canaan in the previous chapter. But even when he arrives in Canaan, he remains a wanderer. He travels frequently in the early years: from Haran to the oak of Moreh at Shechem (Gen. 12:6); from Shechem to a spot between Bethel and Ai (Gen. 12:8); then to the Negev, where famine hits (Gen. 12:9–10). After his hiatus in Egypt, he returns to the Negev (Gen. 13:1) and resettles between Bethel and Ai (Gen. 13:3), where strife with Lot leads to a parting of ways. Because of that parting, Abraham moves near the oaks of Mamre in Hebron (Gen. 13:18), where he lives until Isaac is conceived. Isaac is born when Abraham and Sarah live in Gerar (Gen. 20:1; 21:2) at a place later called Beersheba (Gen. 21:31). Abraham remains there until he is buried in Machpelah (Gen. 25:9).

As a wanderer, Abraham always dwells in tents. Throughout his long life, and despite his immense wealth, he never owns a piece of property to build a home. The only acreage he finally purchases is the cave of Machpelah, negotiated from Ephron the Hittite, to bury Sarah (Gen. 23:8–20). Indeed, "by faith he went to live in the land of promise, as in a foreign land, living in tents with Isaac and Jacob, heirs with him of the same promise" (Heb. 11:9).

Why is this? Perhaps Abraham wishes to avoid the wickedness of the urban life characterized by Sodom and Gomorrah that so ensnared Lot (Gen. 13:12–13). Maybe he seeks mobility to walk the "length and breadth" of the land that he and his descendants would one day possess (Gen. 13:17). To the end of his days, Abraham is still walking the property. But his motive is deeper: "For he was looking forward to the city that has foundations, whose designer and builder is God" (Heb. 11:10). Abraham views life from an eternal perspective. That's why his final journal entry might read, "I long for my eternal home." He realizes his ultimate home is to be found not in contemporary Canaan but in a celestial city.

Abraham is also a worshipper. Everywhere he goes he builds an altar. The altars at Shechem, Bethel-Ai, and Hebron are where Abraham calls on the name of the Lord and, apparently, where God speaks to him.

Abraham's Heavenly City

Just what is this city with foundations, the object of Abraham's earthly wandering and worshipping? The Bible is explicit on the city's identity and appearance.

And he carried me away in the Spirit to a great, high mountain, and showed me the holy city Jerusalem coming down out of heaven from God, having the glory of God, its radiance like a most rare jewel, like a jasper, clear as crystal. It had a great, high wall, with twelve gates, and at the gates twelve angels, and on the gates the names of the twelve tribes of the sons of Israel were inscribed—on the east three gates, on the north three gates, on the south three gates, and on the west three gates. And the wall of the city had twelve foundations, and on them were the twelve names of the twelve apostles of the Lamb. (Rev. 21:10–14)

What a city! What a faith! Abraham possesses an eternal perspective, grasping that this life is not all there is. For Abraham, his true citizenship is not in earthly Palestine. He registers his permanent address in the New Jerusalem.

Where is our citizenship? Do we seek the eternal city, with twelve gates and twelve foundation stones, in which all the children of the Lamb someday will reside? If we do, we will approach this present life very differently.

An eternal perspective will affect the way we think. Theological problems like sin and suffering do not disappear, but they take on a different hue when we are confident of a glorious, eternal life that will render our present suffering only a shadow.

An eternal perspective will affect our politics. While we must seek social justice in our present world, the hope of an eternal home reminds us that creating a theocracy on earth today is not part of the Great Commission.

An eternal perspective will affect our evangelism. We can proclaim the good news with power and confidence because, like Abraham, we have genuine hope to offer. Ours is a hope in an eternal destiny, in a real city, in a victorious Savior on a magnificent throne. He will bid us join him in a banquet feast beyond our wildest dreams and commission us to serve in the court of heaven's King.

Abraham's Legacy

Although the Hebrews 11 registry is not yet finished with Abraham, we close our two chapters on Abraham's journey and adventure of faith with a summary of the five principles we have gleaned.

Five Applications for the Journey

Principle	Application
1. Faith begins with God's Word.	Know the Book!
2. Faith is progressive.	Be patient!
3. Faith may involve failure.	Repent and endure!
4. Faith passes through the desert.	Stay the course!
5. Faith longs for home.	Look toward heaven!

First, the journey of faith begins with the Word of God. Know the Book. Develop a strategy to enrich your knowledge and application of the Bible. Then obey it and integrate it into your experience.

Second, the journey of faith is progressive. Be patient. That God does not reveal all the details of your life is a blessing, not a curse. Develop spiritual endurance sitting in God's "waiting room."

Third, the journey of faith may involve failure. Repent and endure. Identify areas of your life that need restoration with the Lord and with others. Relying on the biblical promises that God's forgiveness is absolute, leave your burden of guilt at the cross once and for all, and move on in faith today. Pray that the Holy Spirit will subdue those areas of life that displease God. Extend to others the same forgiveness that God has extended to you.

Fourth, the journey of faith passes through the desert. Stay the course. In the middle of a spiritual wasteland, strive to maintain spiritual discipline. Do you sense distance from God? Don't give up, hang in there, and encourage others.

Fifth, the journey of faith longs for home. Always look toward heaven. Remember that old spiritual, "This world is not my home; I'm just a-passin' through." Keep your perspective on heaven, not earth; on the eternal, not the temporal. Like the character Christian in John Bunyan's *The Pilgrim's Progress*, keep your feet on the path, but fix your gaze toward the celestial city. Remember that your citizenship is in an eternal city with foundations.

CHAPTER 7

SARAH:

THE UNLIKELY PARTNER

A Parental Partnership

My mother and father enjoyed a wonderful marriage for over sixty-two years. Part of the reason for their success was that they shared so much in common.

Both had deep roots in rural America. Dad was born in Somers, Montana. He fondly recalled winters ice-skating on Flathead Lake and summers horseback riding in old-growth forests on a rugged homestead. Mom was born in Gifford, Idaho, about thirty miles east of Lewiston. She spent her early years, like most farm girls, hard at work in the kitchen, the garden, the creamery, and the barn. The two met at Gifford High School in Idaho, where a romance began to blossom.

Both loved learning and ideas, and they decided, despite seeming insurmountable odds, to enroll at the University of Idaho. Like many students today, they crammed the four-year bachelor's program into six. By their sophomore year they were married, and they took a year off to teach school in tiny New Meadows, Idaho. Mom taught home economics; Dad served as principal, teacher, and boys' basketball coach.

They shared other values too: deep faith in God, hard work, love of family, a hunger for God's Word, and an openness to new experiences. But they were also different. Outgoing and talkative, Mom was the family initiator, party coordinator, and sun around which the rest of us orbited. She was a tireless advocate for her kids, quick to correct, quick to punish, and quicker to forgive. Dad, introverted and taciturn, was a conscientious breadwinner and a dignified man whose few words rang with authority when he uttered them. He unfailingly supported Mom's many initiatives.

They did not always see eye to eye. In Idaho Dad, a biology major who loved nature, somehow got it into his head to become a physician. Mom, content to be the wife of a high school principal, urged him instead to settle into a satisfying and rewarding career in secondary education.

The resolution of their vocational visions was classic. Before signing a teaching contract, Dad accepted a summer job on a fire lookout station in Oregon. Throughout the long, lonely summer, he reflected and prayed about their divergent desires and returned home with his decision to remain a principal. "I've carefully weighed the options," he announced to my mother earnestly, "and I've decided what I want to do."

Mom interrupted him before he could continue. "I've been thinking about it all summer too," she said. "You must follow your dream of medical school!"

As I matured into adulthood, married, and became a father myself, I grew to appreciate my parents' solid partnership. I discovered faith and families are forged in partnership. There is no better illustration of this than our next unlikely hero of faith, Sarah.

Sarah's Snapshot: A Woman for the Ages

Sarah is an unlikely hero of faith for many reasons. A primary one is that she is a woman in a male-dominated culture. People often ignore the rich biblical examples of women of courageous faith, but this is not true of the author of Hebrews. In the roll call of sixteen named biblical heroes, two women—Sarah and Rahab—receive primary attention. And Sarah, without question, is the grand matriarch of this roster.

Hebrews presents a stunning snapshot of Sarah as a woman with unmistakable faith. In just two verses (Heb. 11:11–12), we glimpse Sarah's earthly life of faith in God and her eternal legacy beyond the Genesis story. These two aspects of Sarah's story are displayed in the table below.

Sarah's Hebrews 11 Snapshot

Sarah's Earthly Life	Sarah's Eternal Legacy
Her partnership with Abraham	Her partnership with God
The promise of a son: Isaac A miracle boy An amazing faith	The promise of a people: Israel An unlikely seed An unlikely nation

The faith of Sarah	The faithfulness of God
Hebrews 11:11	Hebrews 11:12

Sarah's earthly life, as recorded in Genesis 11–23, focuses on God's promise that Sarah would miraculously bear a son. The author notes the *consequence* of her faith. She was able to conceive and bear Isaac at ninety years of age, long past the normal age of childbearing. Hebrews also highlights the *content* of her faith. She believes God to be faithful to his word.

Sarah's eternal legacy extends beyond the grave. In the Hebrews 11 snapshot of Sarah's future inheritance, the spotlight shifts to the Lord's faithfulness in fulfilling the promise to Sarah in the generations that follow. Sarah would not only become the mother of the child of promise (fulfilled in Isaac); she also would be the matriarch of a nation (fulfilled in Israel).

True enough, Sarah's legacy must be viewed through her partnership with her husband. But the same is true of Abraham. While Abraham prays for Ishmael's acceptance, God chooses Isaac because the Abrahamic covenant will be fulfilled through Abraham and Sarah. The story illustrates the importance of the *partnership* of faith. On earth, Sarah is Abraham's partner. For eternity, she remains the partner of God.

Sarah's Portrait: Three Faces of a Princess

Sarah is sometimes treated as an historical footnote, a colorless figure living only in the shadow of her husband, Abraham. That seven long verses in our passage are devoted to Abraham

(Heb. 11:8–10, 12, 17–19), with Sarah mentioned in only one (Heb. 11:11), underscores the perception.*

This viewpoint of Sarah is an eclipsed one. Details about her life and character, not to mention her role in fulfilling the Abrahamic promise, are woven into virtually every episode of the Genesis narrative.

To unlock the facets of her life, we shall consider three biblical descriptions of Sarah: beautiful, barren, and blessed. Around each of these terms are events and decisions that highlight the perils and joys of this partnership of faith, summarized in the chart below.

A Portrait of a Princess

Description	Event	Strategy
Beautiful	Pharaoh's Harem Abimelech's Harem	Abraham's "Sister" Strategy
Barren	Birth of Ishmael	Sarah's "Surrogate Wife" Strategy
Blessed	Birth of Isaac	God's "Supernatural Son" Strategy

Sarah Is Beautiful

First, Sarah is described in terms of her outstanding physical beauty (Gen. 12:11, 14). Her beauty is significant in the stories with Pharaoh (Gen. 12) and Abimelech (Gen. 20), which we considered in the previous chapter about Abraham.

---

* Surprisingly, the popular New International Version (NIV 1984) begins this one verse, "By faith Abraham," despite the fact the alternative reading, "By faith Sarah," reflects the clear structure of the Greek text. The better translation is preferred in other versions such as the ESV, NASB, and KJV. The 2011 NIV corrects their earlier weaker reading.

Beauty is a universal value. People of every culture strive for it, and few would doubt its emphasis in American society. If you happen to be attractive, we are told, you've got it made. It is no different in the Ancient Near East. By this criterion of success, Sarah should be on top of the world. But sometimes one's greatest asset can become one's greatest liability.

In Egypt Sarah's beauty becomes a bartering commodity between the powerful Pharaoh and the ambitious Abraham. Her physical beauty must be incomparable, since Abraham, the court officials, and Pharaoh all acknowledge it (Gen. 12:11, 14). And Sarah is sixty-five years old during the Egyptian episode while Abraham, ten years older, is seventy-five (Gen. 12:4).

Abraham displays his callous disregard for Sarah's moral purity and physical protection by concocting his "sister" strategy. His self-centered rationale for the lie is vividly apparent in the two phrases: "that it may *go well with me* because of you, and that *my life may be spared* for your sake" (Gen. 12:13).

And what is Sarah's reaction? The story is silent on her opinion of her husband's plan, her fears upon entering the harem, and her first words to Abraham when they reunite. Nor is there a hint of rebellion, recrimination, or betrayal on Sarah's part; it is the Lord, not Sarah, who reveals the truth to Pharaoh by sending plagues. Sarah is courageously loyal to Abraham. Perhaps at this point in her spiritual journey her faith that God would deliver them is as weak as Abraham's. Likely, she believes both of them are doomed unless she agrees to the plan. But she never divulges their secret to the king, even when her husband's motives stink of selfishness and she alone will bear the cost of sacrificed virtue.

In the Abimelech story, Abraham's failure is far worse. Two elements are the same: the family traveling to a land of a pagan king, and Abraham's "sister" strategy to protect himself. Sarah, now nearly ninety, is still a bargaining chip in the struggle between two men. Though no explicit mention is made of her beauty, the implication is that Sarah is desirable for Abimelech's harem.

The new and critical element to this story is the time frame, occurring some twenty-four years after Egypt. The encounter with Abimelech occurs in the year between God's promise that Sarah would have a son (Gen. 18:10) and Isaac's birth (Gen. 21:2). In light of that imminent fulfillment, Abraham's behavior is unconscionable. It has scandal written all over it. Not only does Abraham put his wife and his marriage in moral jeopardy for his own preservation; he risks casting permanent doubt on Isaac's true parentage. What if Abimelech indeed has sexual relations with Sarah as Abraham's strategy allows? When Sarah becomes pregnant and gives birth to Isaac in subsequent months, every generation down to the present would wonder whether Isaac is really Abraham's son. The world would always question whether God keeps his word.

For this reason the narrative, unlike the Pharaoh story, takes extraordinary care to demonstrate that Sarah is completely untouched by Abimelech. Abimelech protests, and God agrees, that he has a clear conscience and clean hands (Gen. 20:5–6). God says that he prevents Abimelech from sinning by touching Sarah (Gen. 20:6). Abimelech atones for Abraham with one thousand silver shekels to vindicate Sarah publicly (Gen. 20:16). And God, after closing the wombs of all Abimelech's household (*no one* was getting pregnant), restores their fertility (Gen. 20:17–18).

Why all this precaution? Because the Lord wants it crystal clear that Isaac is the son of Abraham through Sarah. Period. When God makes a promise, he keeps it.

Sarah's courageous loyalty is remarkable. She likely had no recourse in the midst of these events. What's incredible is that in the years that follow she remains in loving partnership with a husband who so ill-uses her.

Sarah Is Barren

The second description of Sarah is her barrenness—as strongly a pejorative condition in her culture as beauty is an asset. Sarah is first introduced as Abraham's wife with the words "Now Sarai was barren; she had no children" (Gen. 11:30). That Sarah had borne no children, either because of barrenness or old age, is mentioned a half-dozen times in the narrative. Her barrenness makes her an unlikely hero of faith because fruitfulness is often mentioned in Scripture as a sign of God's favor.

Sarah's barrenness creates a dilemma for the family. First, God promises that from Abraham will emerge a great nation (Gen. 12:2). Then, after Abraham and Lot separate, God reaffirms the promise that the land will forever belong to Abraham's offspring, who will be as numerous as the dust (Gen. 13:15–16). Later, God reveals that a son from Abraham's own body will be his heir, not Eliezer of Damascus (Gen. 15:4), and his descendants will inherit the land (Gen. 15:18). These promises come to Abraham over a ten-year period (Gen. 16:3), and up to this point it is not explicit that Abraham's heir must be born of Sarah.

This must have put Abraham and Sarah's marriage into considerable tension. Imagine what happens next. Perhaps Abraham, returning from yet another conversation with the Lord about his many offspring, can't make things add up. Abraham sinks into a funk.

"Why does God keep telling me this?" he snaps at Sarah. "He knows you can't have children. Never have; never will. If God wants me to have a son so bad, why doesn't he give me a wife up to the task? God knows I've done all I can do. I brought Lot from Ur to be my heir. I've designated Eliezer. But he'll have none of it. What's a man to do?"

I suspect that Sarah, like any loving wife, wants her husband to be happy but wishes he would quit whining. Since she is a can-do woman who is good at fixing things, she formulates a plan—the "surrogate wife" strategy. In this ploy, apparently common in Ancient Near Eastern culture, a barren wife presents her handmaid to her husband as a surrogate to bear a child in the mother's name. This requires taking a second wife.

So Sarah presents Hagar to Abraham, who offers no objection. He takes Hagar as his wife and consummates the marriage. Almost immediately Hagar becomes pregnant and trouble begins. Knowing that fertility is valuable coinage, Hagar becomes proud. She despises her mistress, Sarah, who mistreats her. Abraham is passively complicit. When the pregnant Hagar flees to the desert, God encourages her with a promise about her son and enjoins her to return to Abraham's household.

Here we must admit that the loyal Sarah is misguided in attempting to assist God. Her strategy causes endless amounts of trouble, even to the present day. We learn two things from this. First, though their partnership faces tremendous stresses, Abraham and Sarah remain committed to each other despite the self-centeredness of Abraham and the misguided interference of Sarah. Second, their failures do not invalidate God's promises. God's Word is not based on our faithfulness nor cancelled by our faithlessness; it is founded on the eternal God who is faithful and true.

Sarah Is Blessed

The final biblical description is Sarah's blessedness. Sarah's blessing culminates in the birth of Isaac: God's "supernatural son" strategy. When the Lord specifically promises that the heir will come through Sarah, he blesses Sarah twice: once in the blessing of becoming the mother of the son of promise; the other in the blessing of becoming the matriarch of the nation (Gen. 17:15–16). This is also the first giving of the son's name, Isaac (Gen. 17:19). Later, God repeats this promised blessing in Sarah's hearing, adding the detail of its imminent fulfillment within the year (Gen. 18:10–15).

To underscore the importance of this divinely approved partnership, God authorizes a double name change (Gen. 17:5, 15). Abraham, originally named Abram (the exalted father), is now Abraham (the father of multitudes). Sarah's name is changed from Sarai to Sarah. Since both her names mean "princess," the meaning of the name is less significant than the fact that God changes it. It is as if God renames Sarah to raise her stature in the covenant right up to that of Abraham. Indeed, they are partners in the Abrahamic covenant.

Isaac's name, meaning "laughter," is also significant to the fulfilled blessing. His name recalls three episodes of laughter. Before his birth, both Abraham (Gen. 17:17) and Sarah (Gen. 18:12) laugh in disbelief at the notion of having a child. But when Isaac is born, Sarah christens him with the laughter of joy (Gen. 21:6–7).

Sarah's Impact: Four New Testament Tributes

As contemporary pilgrims of faith, how can we display the faith of Sarah? Consider the four ways in which the New Testament describes her legacy.

Four New Testament Tributes

Reference	Description	Significance
Romans 9:8–9	A blessed woman	She receives the promise by grace, not ability.
Hebrews 11:11	A faith-guided woman	She believes God despite impossible odds.
1 Peter 3:6	A loyal woman	She calls Abraham "lord," showing respect.
Galatians 4:22–23	A free woman	She illustrates the freedom of grace.

The apostle Paul confirms Sarah's unmerited blessing (Rom. 9:8–9). Consistent with Roman's theme of justification by faith alone, Sarah is a woman who receives the marvelous promise of God not by works but by faith. What a reminder to us that all the blessings we receive come graciously from the hand of God, not as payment for our own efforts. Blessing is unmerited, unearned, and graciously given, just like Sarah's unlikely motherhood at age ninety is a miraculous gift of God.

Hebrews highlights the immensity of Sarah's faith (Heb. 11:11). She believes despite impossible odds. This legacy is true despite the inconsistency of Sarah's faith. At times her faith seems to falter: when she suggests her husband raise up an heir through Hagar, and when she laughs incredulously at God's promise that she, a ninety-year-old matriarch, would bear a son. Those important incidents are not mentioned by the writer to the Hebrews. The passage suggests that what really counts is that God considers Sarah faithful and worthy to bear the son of promise for the fulfillment of his plan.

The apostle Peter focuses on Sarah's loyalty (1 Pet. 3:6). In a passage describing the relationship between husband and wife, Peter cites the example of Sarah, a woman who loves her husband with unstinting loyalty, showing him respect and honor. Knowing the flaws in Abraham's character makes Sarah's example even more powerful.

Finally, Paul portrays Sarah as the prototype of God's gracious freedom from the Law (Gal. 4:22–23).

Sarah is a remarkable woman. She recognizes that the life of faith is a twofold partnership: a horizontal partnership with her husband and a vertical partnership with God. She is loyal to Abraham and respectfully calls him "lord," even when he puts her in moral jeopardy because of his own selfishness. Sarah is no shadow, no cipher. This woman of faith, a prototype of obedience to God and still beautiful to kings at age ninety, enjoys the richness of God's grace to conceive a child that makes her laugh.

Yet Sarah's story of faith raises questions about how we should live in partnership today, especially with flawed people and insensitive spouses, and also amid adversity that seems overwhelming. We will address these questions in the next chapter.

CHAPTER 8

SARAH:

THE UNLIKELY EXAMPLE

Contemporary Questions of Sarah's Faith

The survey of Sarah's life in the previous chapter suggests two important principles of faith: partnership and contentment. These principles are universally true in relation to faith and are applicable to men and women of faith everywhere. But a moment's reflection reveals some serious questions about what Sarah's partnership with Abraham means for us and whether her behavior is the kind we should emulate today. The principles and questions are listed in the following chart.

Sarah's Principles of Faith

The Principle of Partnership	The Principle of Contentment
Living by faith means walking in partnership.	Living by faith will fulfill one's deepest longings.

The Questions of Partnership	The Question of Contentment
What if I remain single?	
Should a wife always obey her husband?	Will my deepest longings always come true?
Will God always deliver me?	

The Principle of Partnership

The first principle is that living by faith means walking in partnership. While both Abraham and Sarah possess individual faith, their faith experiences are inseparably linked. The couple's partnership is highlighted in several passages where Abraham travels "with his wife" (Gen. 11:31; 12:5; 12:20; 13:1). This principle raises some important questions.

The question of singleness. One question is, what does this mean if you are single? The answer is that we all experience a web of relationships on our journey of faith, including two (and for married people three) partnerships.

First, every believer, regardless of marital status, lives in partnership with God. There is no life of faith without a vertical relationship with the Lord. The writer to the Hebrews makes this profound point about Sarah in the phrase, "she considered *him* faithful who had promised" (Heb. 11:11). Both Abraham and Sarah are in relationship—a partnership—with the living God. For all of us, the life of faith starts here.

Second, all men and women of faith enjoy a network of partnerships with other believers. In Abraham's day this involves the clan or family under the direction of a patriarch. In Moses' day the Israelites participate in a national and spiritual identity through the old covenant, the Torah. Since the cross of Christ, followers of Jesus enjoy partnership with one another through the new covenant, with Christ as their head. We live in community, members of one body, interdependent on one another. The New Testament, contrary to some traditions, lends little credence to solitary monasticism.

Third, for many there is the one-flesh partnership with one's spouse. This partnership, ordained by God in the Garden of Eden, directs the first human couple to fulfill the cultural mandate of subduing and replenishing the earth (Gen. 1:28–30). Sarah, with her husband Abraham, walks the path of faith in this kind of partnership.

Yet Jesus is clear that some people are given a gift of celibacy (Matt. 19:12). Paul even recommends the celibate life to the Corinthians in light of a present crisis (1 Cor. 7:26). Single men and women are not second-class citizens in the kingdom of God. God provides a web of partnerships for single Christians who walk the path of faith.

The question of obedience. The nature of Sarah's marriage partnership with Abraham raises a second question relevant to our contemporary culture: Is it right for a woman to always obey her husband, particularly if he directs her to do something illegal or immoral? Abraham twice asks Sarah to lie for him (posing as his sister, not his wife) and twice to submit to the possible sexual overtures of another man. Is the godly response to obey one's husband (or wife) without question in such a situation, even if the command is contrary to God's standard of righteousness?

The answer is clearly no! Certainly the Bible says, "Wives, submit to your husbands, as to the Lord." Both Paul and Peter command this (Eph. 5:22; Col. 3:18; 1 Pet. 3:1). I do not wish to dilute the meaning of "submit" in these passages, but I would point out two important qualifications.

First, we must not ignore the condition "as to the Lord." True, the command for wives to submit implies that God has given husbands a qualified authority over the family, holding them accountable for the family's spiritual health. But since God does not ask men or women to act contrary to his word, a husband who commands something immoral cannot expect a wife to obey him "as to the Lord." His immoral command negates the principle of divinely granted authority.

Second, and more importantly, there is an important difference between submission and obedience. Submission is the respectful deference to others in authority, while obedience is doing strictly what one is commanded. Submission captures the attitude of respect and loyalty; obedience depicts specific compliant action.

The Bible clearly distinguishes submission and obedience in such human relationships as civil government. For example, when Daniel is commanded by King Darius not to pray to anything else on pain of death, Daniel immediately opens his window toward Jerusalem and talks to God (Dan. 6:10). Daniel is always respectful of Darius, but he does not—could not—obey his decree. Paul and Peter also instruct us to be submissive to governmental authorities (Rom. 13:1, 5; 1 Pet. 2:13), but they clearly do not intend absolute obedience. When the Sanhedrin commands Peter and the apostles to quit preaching, Peter respectfully refuses, responding, "We must obey God rather than men" (Acts 5:29). The apostles reflect Jesus' distinction between the ultimate authority of God and the derived authority of human government when he tells the scribes, "Render to Caesar the things that are Caesar's, and to God the things that are God's" (Mark 12:17).

It is possible, then, to be submissive (respectful) to authority and at the same time disobey a particular command that violates the Word of God. The opposite is also true. It is possible to be obedient (follow the letter of the law) but unsubmissive (disrespectful) to authority. Scripture commands submission.

Let me ask this plainly. If a husband commands his wife to do something immoral or illegal (e.g., lie, steal, or cheat), is the godly Christian wife obliged to obey? Absolutely not. But should she be submissive and respectful? Without question.

This has a profound implication for husbands too. For how does a man earn his wife's love, loyalty, and respect? He does it, Paul tells us, by loving his wife as Christ loves the church (unconditionally, self-sacrificially) and as he loves his own body (protecting, caring, and nourishing it, Eph. 5:25–30). That is God's design. When a husband perfectly loves his wife, she will respect him and submit to him with no questions of conscience. As a wife fully respects and honors her husband, his love for her intensifies all the more.

The question of deliverance. A third question is, does God guarantee my physical protection? If I am loyal to my spouse and faithful to God, will God always deliver me as he delivers Sarah from Pharaoh and Abimelech, protecting her virtue and honor? The answer to this question is also no. Though God intervenes for Sarah (for covenantal purposes discussed above), he does not promise to protect us from all physical dangers and evils of this world. In fact, countless men and women who faithfully follow God experience torture, jeering, flogging, imprisonment, destitution, persecution, and death for their faith (Heb. 11:35–38). God does not promise an easy life, a safe life, or a secure life on this earth. What he does is infinitely more valuable—he guarantees eternal life in his Son.

The Principle of Contentment

The second principle from the life of Sarah is that living by faith will fulfill one's deepest longings. Sarah's deepest longing is to bear a child. Beyond all reason, beyond all time, beyond all ability, beyond all hope, and almost to the point of absolute despair, the miracle boy is born. God makes good on his word. Sarah's deepest longing is fulfilled, and she is content to the end of her days. The benevolence of God shown to Sarah is a timeless attribute. We see it promised by Jesus when he says, "I came that they may have life and have it abundantly" (John 10:10).

But the question here is, will *my* deepest longings come to pass? Aren't there abundant examples in Scripture and life where this doesn't seem to stand? Yes, there are. That is why this principle must be understood in terms of four qualifications, each necessary to avoid commonly held misunderstandings about God's plan for our growth and maturity. These four qualifications, along with their common misunderstandings, are listed in the following chart.

Faith's Deepest Longings

Four Qualifications	Four Misunderstandings
1. The temporal qualification: *They are not fulfilled immediately.*	1. God does not have larger purposes in view.
2. The procedural qualification: *They are not fulfilled easily, without struggle.*	2. God is unconcerned about refining us through adversity.

3. The perceptual qualification: *They are not fulfilled as understood initially.*	3. Our human perspective is exhaustive, not limited.
4. The eternal qualification: *They may not be fulfilled fully in this lifetime.*	4. There is no future, ultimate destiny.

First, there is the *temporal* qualification. Although God will fulfill our deepest longings, he makes no promise to fulfill them immediately. In fact, very often he does not. Many times we fail to understand that our all-wise and all-good God has larger purposes in view and may postpone fulfillment for many reasons. Some reasons include our own destinies, but many involve the intertwining purposes of the rest of God's creation, both terrestrial and celestial. God is not only the God of Sarah and Abraham; he is the Lord of Pharaoh, Abimelech, Lot, Melchizedek, the five kings of the plain (Gen. 14:8), and the cities of Sodom and Gomorrah too.

Second, there is the *procedural* qualification. God's promises are not always fulfilled easily, without struggle; adversity is often part of the divine equation. It is easy to forget that the refining process of maturity takes time, isn't it? We focus on the outcome, the result God promises to deliver in the end. But God governs the process too. As the divine Potter working with stubborn human clay, the Lord understands that adversity over time molds us into what he intends for us to become. To cultivate the spiritual fruit of patience, self-control, and peace, he employs the pruning shears of adversity. The Lord determines that Sarah and Abraham would produce a healthy heir named Isaac, but the quarter-century of lessons ripen their faith and deepen their love.

Third, there is the *perceptual* qualification. God satisfies our deepest longings, not as we initially perceive them but as he ultimately defines them. That's because even as believers we battle mixed motives. While we desire to obey the Lord's will, the carnality and self-centeredness of our fallen human natures intrude. God's promise to shape us into the image of Christ (Rom. 8:29) requires that our human desires and motives align with his. At the end of this process we discover that our passions, now harmonized with God's, correspond with what is truly best for us.

Finally, there is the *eternal* qualification. God will fulfill our deepest longings, but not always in our earthly lifetime. How often we forget that our ultimate destiny is to live forever in God's presence! We must resist the worldly philosophy that shouts, "This is all there is!" Our life stories do not end at death. Death is simply the transition from boot camp to active service. Though Sarah experiences the earthly fulfillment of bearing her son, she also knows God's promise transcends her 127-year sojourn on planet earth. God has so much more in store for Sarah. He does for us too.

Dr. John Mitchell, founder of Multnomah School of the Bible, and his wife, Mary, illustrate the principle of contentment. The Mitchells never had children of their own. One chapter in John Mitchell's biography, *The Lion of God*, discusses the couple's desire for children and Mary's sorrow that she was unable to have any. Throughout their lives and their long ministry at Multnomah, God fills that longing with thousands of "children," young students whom John and Mary Mitchell "adopted" as their own kids.

If you asked Mary at the end of her life, "Did God fulfill your deepest longings?" she would likely have said, "Yes." The Lord redefined and refocused her longings, fulfilling them in ways greater than she ever anticipated. Thousands even today, long after the Mitchells' graduation to heaven, still call them Uncle John and Aunt Mary.

The life of faith will fulfill your deepest longings, but it is a process that requires time plus the sandpaper of adversity. Like Sarah and many others, we will encounter delays and obstacles. But we know that God is working in us (Phil. 2:13), and having begun that good work in us, he will carry it to completion in Jesus (Phil. 1:6).

CHAPTER 9

ABRAHAM:
THE UNLIKELY BELIEVER

A College Crisis

More often than not, young people raised in a Christian home have a crisis of faith during their late teens or early adult years. This shouldn't surprise us. The faith we were handed down from our parents, our pastors, our youth leaders, or our camp counselors must become our own.

My mother came to faith as a teenager after a preacher on the revival circuit came through town. Her conversion was genuine, and she decided that she would present her children with the good news much, much earlier. When I was very young, Mom made me vividly aware that I was a sinner facing an eternity without God. This was not hard for her to do, especially when I had been particularly disobedient. She explained that I could go to heaven and have eternal life simply by asking Jesus into my heart. So I did!

My Christian upbringing was not a source of rebellion for me. Educated in private Christian schools, I never felt the draw to drift from my faith, despite having classmates who didn't accept their parents' belief system.

After graduating from high school, I enrolled at Westmont College in Santa Barbara, California, where I experienced a significant turning point in my walk of faith. It began in my required Old Testament class, where freshmen were exposed to higher critical views and evangelical responses to these criticisms. For the first time I learned that there were many intelligent scholars who neither believed the Bible nor the God of the Bible. To compound my confusion, one day our professor debated a secular religious studies professor on the reliability of Scripture. It was a cordial, irenic debate, but this scholar's assertions and claims shook me greatly. That my professor brilliantly answered his arguments and supported the trustworthiness of Scripture only slightly eased my anxiety. I wondered how I would ever be able to respond to such incisive, brilliant critiques of my faith.

That's when it hit me. I never would be sharp enough on my own. I had to decide whether I would consider God and his Word trustworthy even if I lacked the answers to every question. Such a decision was not a leap in the dark because history is littered with discarded critiques of the Bible's reliability, critiques that have been soundly refuted by insights from archeology, historiography, linguistics, and textual criticism.

In my dormitory room that evening, I made the personal and humbling decision to believe that God has the answers even if I do not. "Father," I prayed, "I place my intellect, such as it is, under the authority of your Word, not over it." My crisis of faith passed, and I have never been the same.

Abraham's Unbelievable Test

By many standards my crossroads experience is extremely tame. You may have experienced overwhelming tsunamis of doubt that shook you to your core. But whatever any of us has experienced, it is unlikely that our faith will ever be tested with the severity that Abraham endures. Abraham's crisis of faith is so profound that the author of Hebrews returns to Abraham and this single story to address it (Heb. 11:17–19).

Again, Abraham takes us by surprise. We have come to see Abraham, the unlikely wanderer and the unlikely worshipper, as a spiritual man in process. A colossus of faith, Abraham also has feet of clay. He twice places his wife in moral jeopardy, he caves in to bigamy, he appears passive to the conflict within his own household, and in favoring Ishmael he seems willing to settle for second best. So, when we read that God tests Abraham, we naturally fear the worst.

The surprise is that Abraham endures this test with absolutely no hint of hesitation, deliberation, self-questioning, bitterness, anger, or doubt. Not once does he complain to God or even offer a polite objection. Instead, he passes this test with flying colors.

It is this almost otherworldly response I wish to examine in this chapter. But first we must walk this trial with Abraham, wearing his sandals so to speak, to fully appreciate the significance and intensity of the event. The narrative of Abraham's great test unfolds in Genesis 22:1–14. Like a short play, the story develops simply yet powerfully in four scenes.

Scene One: The Test Initiated
The Timing of the Test

We arrive at the closing chapters of Abraham's life. He takes great leaps of faith since God first calls him at age seventy-five. He and Sarah undertake the arduous journey from Ur to Haran to Canaan; and then, after entering Canaan, they travel throughout Palestine, moving from place to place. Abraham resolves many of the conflicts in his life. His relationship with Lot is finalized. Hagar and Ishmael leave Abraham's household under the blessing of God. Isaac, the son of promise, is miraculously born and thrives. Abraham makes peace with his neighbors, including Abimelech. He is nearing the ripe old age of 120 years, a time when a patriarch like Abraham should relax.

That's why we are shocked at what happens next. God tests Abraham. While we will raise and answer many questions in this chapter, the *fact* of this divine testing is not one of them. The Genesis record makes it crystal clear that God initiates this event and that it is a real test. And the test itself, stated in terse words, could not be plainer.

"Take your son," God tells Abraham, "and offer him as a burnt offering on a mountain I'll show you once you're on your way. And Abraham, you know the son I mean. It's not Ishmael. It's your only true son by Sarah, your miracle boy, the son you dearly love, the child of promise. It's Isaac. Do it now!"

Objections to the Test

Abraham could present a half-dozen moral, practical, and theological reasons to the Lord as to why this was a bad idea. The underlying theme of all these objections is the character of God. Let's examine three questions about God's character.

First, doesn't God know what will happen? Abraham might wonder why an all-knowing, omniscient God would need to test anyone at all.

"Since God knows everything—past, present, and future," Abraham could have said, "why does he need to test me? What would God learn about my heart, my faith, or my character that he doesn't already know? Since this is a real test, isn't God being inconsistent with his all-knowing nature in giving it?"

One answer lies in distinguishing between tests to discover knowledge and tests to confirm authenticity. When I give a theology exam, for example, my purpose is to discover something I do not know, namely, how much theology my students have learned. But when an assayer tests a nugget of gold for quality, he often has a clear idea of the nature of the nugget. He performs the assay test both to authenticate the gold for another and to purify the sample by removing dross. (See Ps. 66:10; Prov. 17:3; Jer. 9:7; and Zech. 13:9 for passages where God's refining and testing processes go hand in hand.)

God's test of Abraham is more like an assay test than a theology exam. His goal is not discovery but confirmation; its effects are less for God than they are for Abraham (and us!). This conforms to the New Testament purpose of testing, where tests and trials are means to refine and perfect our faith (James 1:2–4, 12), and where divine discipline confirms rather than questions God's love for us (Heb. 12:5–6).

Second, doesn't this make God the author of evil? Abraham could easily have questioned the fundamental righteousness of God. The Lord seems to be asking Abraham to do something he has specifically prohibited his people—indeed, all people—from doing.

"But Lord," we can imagine Abraham saying, "you're asking me to murder, to take the life of an innocent person, Isaac. All children of Adam know that Cain's murder of Abel was despicable, and all children of Noah remember that murdering another human being made in your image is nothing less than attacking you (Gen. 9:6). So, how can you ask me to do the very thing you have prohibited all of us from doing?

"Furthermore," Abraham might add after catching his breath, "you're asking me to make a human sacrifice, something the Canaanite worshippers of Molech do that you find particularly abhorrent. How can you ask this? Plus, you're asking me to kill my own son. How could you be so cruel, so mean-spirited?"

While the emotional objections of "mean-spiritedness" are valid, they pale beside the real issue here: How can a righteous God command murder?

The answer, from a purely ethical standpoint, is simpler than many think. It's rooted in the fact that God is the creator of all that lives. As Creator, he who sovereignly gives life also has the sovereign right to take life, or permit the taking of life, at any time and in any way he chooses. For us humans, however, the unjustifiable taking of life is prohibited and morally wrong because we neither create nor own life. Murder, therefore, is a moral category that applies to us but never to God.

In fact, God takes life all the time, and he will take the life of every person in the history of mankind until the end of time. Further, God as the Creator can use any means he chooses for the taking of life. Later, for example, he will command Israel to destroy the wicked Canaanites. So there is no moral restriction on God to use Abraham as his instrument. And because God is not asking Abraham to sacrifice to Molech, the issue of paganism is beside the point.

Questions of God being mean-spirited are not about the test's morality but about the test's intensity. For example, the test would be less severe for Abraham if God had required him to offer a Sodomite, or Lot, or even Ishmael. The command to offer Isaac instead of Ishmael does not change the moral question; it raises the intensity of the test to the level that God's wisdom requires.

The third question is, does this mean that God goes back on his word? Abraham's strongest objection might well be to challenge the truthfulness and faithfulness of God to his word.

"Wait a minute, Lord," Abraham could say. "You promised that only through Isaac will your eternal covenant be fulfilled. I would have been content with Lot or Eliezer, as you know. I even tried to help you out by fathering Ishmael, and you would have none of it. You insisted it must be through Isaac, the son of Sarah, that a nation will arise whose numbers exceed the sands of the sea and the stars of the sky. If you go through with this, Lord, you will have ordered the killing of the one person through whom your promise can be fulfilled."

Then Abraham might play his trump card. "Insist on this," he could add, "and your reputation among the nations as a God who keeps his promises will be dashed forever!"

We will examine this important objection later. For now, the remarkable thing to note is that none of these objections appears in the story. Rather, Abraham rises early the next morning, assembles his company and caravan, and is on his way. There is no suggestion that he even awakens Sarah as he begins his pre-dawn journey. Whether he does this to avoid a confrontation with his wife, as some suggest, we will never know. All we are told is that he firmly and intentionally takes that first step of obedience: he sets out.

Scene Two: The Test Extended

Abraham and Isaac, accompanied by two young servants, head out on the three-day journey to Mount Moriah. On the third day Abraham sees the place from a distance and instructs the servants to stay behind with the animals. He asks Isaac to shoulder the wood while he carries the fire and the knife. As they walk together, Isaac breaks the silence with a question the old patriarch had probably expected—and dreaded—for three days.

"Dad, you've always been a careful planner, especially when it comes to overnight camping," Isaac begins. "But I think you may have forgotten something."

"And what is that?" Abraham says, not daring to look his son in the eye.

"Well," Isaac answers slowly, "I'm carrying the wood, and you've got the fire and knife. But where's the sacrificial lamb?"

"Don't worry, my son," Abraham responds, trying to keep his own lack of conviction out of his voice. "God will provide for himself the lamb for the burnt offering." The questions stop; father and son walk on together.

Sometimes I wonder if the toughest part of the trial is that Abraham has three days to think about it. Three days to mull over all the theological, moral, and covenantal objections to God's command. Three days to think, *What a terrible plan! I cannot—no, I will not—go through with this.* Three days to turn around. And yet over the three days on the road to Moriah, Abraham remains firm.

There is surprising warmth to this otherwise bleak scene. Twice we read, "So they went both of them together" (Gen. 22:6, 8). Abraham enjoys the company of his son even in these final, excruciating steps up the mountain.

Isaac is probably a teenager. I had a picture book of Bible stories as a boy that included this story, and Isaac was depicted as a little boy of about seven, complete with blond curls and a cute face. In fact, I thought he looked like a little girl! This familiar caricature is very wide of the mark. The biblical word for "lad" used of Isaac is not the usual word for a toddler or young child. It can denote someone in their teenage years, old enough to endure a three-day hike and strong enough to carry a load of wood up a mountain. Isaac is smart enough to figure out something weird is going on.

The two walk on together. I wonder what Abraham, over three days with his heart breaking, said to his son. Without letting Isaac know his intentions, Abraham may have opened up to Isaac like never before. Here we glimpse a man of deep human love for his son and with a faith strong enough to obey a divine command that seems designed to crush his soul.

Scene Three: The Test Intensified

In scene three, father and son arrive at the summit site for the sacrifice, where Abraham builds the altar and arranges the wood that Isaac has carried on his back. Then, after binding his son and laying him on the altar, the old patriarch unsheathes his knife.

Both people in this scene display remarkable faith. Isaac certainly does. In my Bible picture book, little girlish Isaac is laid on the wood of the altar. What a pale depiction of the real story! Isaac is old enough to say, "Hey, Pops, you can do whatever you want for God, but I've got one question for you. How are you gonna catch me? I'm outta here!" But he doesn't. He submits to his father's wishes. I imagine Abraham does most of the talking now, probably through tears.

"Isaac," he might say, "God considers me his friend, but he spoke to me clearer than ever. He made it possible for you even to be born, beyond our wildest dreams. He directed us to this land and has been true to his promises time and time again. Now, since he has commanded this sacrifice, I have no choice. This is what I must do." And teenage Isaac submits to his father.

Abraham, too, displays remarkable faith. There is no question of his intention; the real question is his motivation. What urges him to go through with it? We know he trusts God and desires to obey him. But what about the objection to God's truthfulness we raised earlier? How does Abraham harmonize God's sovereign right to command the sacrifice of his son with God's unfailing and faithful promise to keep his word no matter what?

Lord, Abraham must have thought, *are you sure about this? This doesn't just make you a murderer. Won't this make you a liar as well?*

The Genesis account gives little insight into Abraham's thinking, but our Hebrews passage does. Abraham "considered that God was able even to raise [Isaac] from the dead," the writer tells us (Heb. 11:19). Incredibly, Abraham reasons from the doctrine of resurrection.

When I go through the horror of slaying my son, Abraham may have thought, *God can raise him from the dead. Of course! He'll bring Isaac back to life and keep his word about his eternal covenant in one stroke. And I'll see my son, I'll see Isaac, again.*

I still wonder how Abraham could have conceived of a resurrection. After all, no resurrection occurs prior to Abraham. But we detect a subtle hint in the Abimelech story in Genesis 21. At the end of a series of trust-destroying incidents, Abraham and Abimelech make a peace treaty in Beersheba. When it's over, Abraham plants a tamarisk tree and calls on the Lord, using his name "El Olam," which means the everlasting God or the God of eternity. The tamarisk tree, probably a type of evergreen juniper, seems to convey the idea of an everlasting treaty. Perhaps as Abraham is wondering whether a covenant with the wily Abimelech would last very long, he reflects that the eternal God would keep his covenant forever.

When the test comes, Abraham might reason that El Olam, the eternal God, the giver and taker of life who is unaffected by death, could easily raise someone from the dead.

This hardly lessens the intensity of the test, though. Abraham still has to go through with it. And what if he is wrong about God? This is where the theological rubber meets the everyday road of reality. The patriarch still must take the knife and plunge it into the heart of his son. Yet his faith in a sovereign, righteous, truthful, and faithful Creator stands firm. He brings down his arm.

Scene Four: The Test Completed

Many Renaissance paintings portray this final, captivating scene. Most artists, like Rembrandt, show the angel of the Lord actually grabbing Abraham's knife-wielding arm. All the paintings make it clear that Abraham fully intends to kill his son and that God stops him in the nick of time.

God provides a lamb for the sacrifice, as Abraham foretells to Isaac, when the patriarch spots a ram caught by its horns in a thicket. After Abraham offers the ram in place of Isaac, God reaffirms his great covenant, expanding it with new promises and new provisions.

The story closes with a beautiful picture of substitutionary atonement, of God's faithfulness, righteousness, and truthfulness in the enlarged Abrahamic covenant. But for me the most important words are found in God's warm and loving affirmation, "Now I know that you love me." Abraham knows this in a startlingly new and deepened way too.

A Theology of Testing

I hope that you and I never have to go through this kind of test. But we cannot avoid the subject of testing, because it affects us all. Consider five axioms of God's testing in life as charted below.

A Theology of Testing: Five Axioms

1. Testing is certain (James 1:2)

2. Testing is purposeful (James 1:3–4)

3. Testing is distinct from tempting (James 1:13–15)

4. Testing is painful (Matt. 6:13)

5. Testing is appropriate (1 Cor. 10:13)

   • To human experience

   • To individual capacity

   • With a divine escape plan

Testing Is Certain

Though the timing may be uncertain, testing itself is inevitable. "When you encounter various trials," James says in effect, "chalk it up to something that brings joy" (James 1:2). James does not say *if* you encounter trials, but *when*. Be prepared for trials. Reflect on biblical and personal examples of faithful women and men, like Abraham, who endure severe testing. Examine the Scriptures for resources that will prepare you for when it comes.

Testing Is Purposeful

In testing, God has a grand outcome in mind. "Please know," James adds, "that the testing of your faith produces endurance. And the result of your endurance is maturity. You will lack nothing!" (James 1:3–4). Job, Moses, David, and Elijah could all testify that this is true. Since it is purposeful, testing is neither random nor accidental. It is designed to make us complete in Christ. I long for the Lord to say that I am perfectly mature, completely equipped, lacking nothing. I imagine all of us want that. The path from here to there involves testing.

Testing Is Distinct from Tempting

The word for "tempt" and "test" is the same in the Greek New Testament. We commonly translate them differently according to clues in the context. *Test* refers to external trials or adversity, while *tempt* refers to the internal, sinful desires of our base appetites. James underscores this when he admonishes us to rejoice when tests come, but never to attribute sinful temptation to God (James 1:13–14). God tests us to shape us, but he never tempts us to sin since that is contrary to his character. The Abraham story does not contradict this axiom; it affirms that God tests us for our benefit.

Testing Is Painful

Whether we face tests, trials, or temptations, they are never fun. James admonishes us to rejoice in the midst of trials not because they're pleasant but because they're beneficial.

Jesus understands both the purpose and the pain of testing. He experiences the fierce brunt of Satan's testing in the wilderness. Mark's account informs us that the Spirit "drove" Jesus into the wilderness to be tested (Mark 1:12) but makes it clear that it is Satan, not God, who tempts him to sin. Jesus' commentary on this experience is found in the Lord's model prayer.

"Lead us not into temptation," Jesus instructs his disciples to pray, "but deliver us from evil" (Matt. 6:13). Jesus affirms both that the Spirit may lead us to places of testing and that testing can be severe. But he suggests that we should pray, "Lord, please do not lead us into places of testing or temptation. But if this is your will, as it was for Jesus, please give us the strength to resist the evil one, just as Jesus rebuffed Satan's temptation in the desert."

Testing Is Appropriate

"No temptation has overtaken you," Paul says, "that is not common to man. God is faithful, and he will not let you be tempted beyond your ability, but with the temptation he will also provide the way of escape, that you may be able to endure it" (1 Cor. 10:13). Testing is appropriate in three ways.

First, it's appropriate to human experience. It is a small comfort that others experience similar tests. It is an immense consolation that Jesus feels the full brunt of testing.

Second, it's appropriate to individual capacities. Since tests are purposeful, it makes sense that God would design them with our individuality in mind. He tailors tests to our capacities and supplies the resources we need. God knows that Job could sustain the worst physical calamity Satan could muster. God knows that Abraham developed a faith robust enough to offer Isaac. And he knows you and me. He calculates our capacity to withstand trials better than we ever can and devises an unwritten curriculum that brings us to complete maturity.

Finally, testing is appropriate because of God's escape plan. "With the temptation," Paul tells us, "God provides a way of escape." What a great comfort! Remember, God does not promise that we will escape the test; countless men and women have died at the hands of evil men while standing firm for their faith. Nor does he promise we will pass the test; many believers succumb to sinful appetites. No, the promise is not deliverance from the trial but escape from failure in the trial. "God provides a way of escape," Paul says, *that you may be able to endure it.*" We can experience a test, but we need not fail. Like Abraham, we have the choice to be obedient, and to emerge stronger and more faithful in the end.

Abraham's Unlikely Faith

Abraham is thoroughly tested by God, and this "friend of God" passes with flying colors. He seems every bit a man with unlikely, almost unbelievable faith. He shows no hesitation, no theological wrangling or complaining, no procrastination, and no questioning of God's motives. But remember! On Mount Moriah we see in Abraham a prototypical "James 1" man, a man who walked the path of faith with God for nearly fifty years and has already experienced various tests. He has scored both successes and failure. But here he stands as an example of a man with faith made complete through trials and honed by endurance. We can have faith as mature and complete as Abraham's.

CHAPTER 10

ISAAC:

THE UNLIKELY HEIR

My Family Heritage

I am blessed exceedingly with a strong Christian family heritage, from both my mother and father. Because Mom was so outgoing, Dad often remained in the background. Nevertheless, he was a man of deep spiritual convictions.

One project Dad took upon himself I will never forget. He created a small, black, loose-leaf notebook filled with Bible verses arranged in a topical system of his own devising. It had twelve themes, including human sin, salvation, the Savior, and the blessed hope. The last half of the notebook contained key passages like Psalm 23 and Isaiah 53, which he felt every Christian should memorize.

Many a Sunday afternoon passed with Dad sitting in front of an old, portable Royal typewriter, pecking out these verses letter by letter. On small, white slips of paper that would fit his note-book, he typed an original with three carbon copies; he wanted each of us kids to have our own. You can imagine how painstaking and slow this was. He probably would never have finished if he had not hired our neighbor, a professional typist, to finish the job.

Long before the project was complete, we memorized many of these verses as we sat around the kitchen table. I eventually received my own copy of Dad's notes on March 9, 1972, just before embarking on a sea voyage. Mom wrote an inscription to me on that date, and I cherish the collection today.

Another memory underscores my family heritage. In 1994, when Dad passed away, the family asked me to speak at his memorial service—one of the consequences of being the only seminary graduate in the family. As I looked through Dad's personal effects in preparing the eulogy, I came across his Bible. Inside the front cover he kept a record of the Bible books he had been reading the past four years. I was fascinated by what I saw. In the four years since Mom died, Dad recorded reading only four books of the Bible: Genesis, Job, Matthew, and Romans. But he read this four-book cycle again and again.

I've wondered about that pattern from time to time. Though I will never be certain of Dad's rationale, the central importance of these books is undeniable: Genesis, the book of origins, contains the fundamental themes of all biblical revelation; Matthew, the Gospel of Jesus' Galilean ministry, portrays him both as King of Israel and Savior of the world; and Romans, the towering theological epistle, unfolds the gospel of justification by faith alone in all its splendor. As to Job, I suspect he read it for perspective on his grief over the sudden death of his beloved Esther.

Isaac, the Unlikely Child of Promise

Family heritage is something Isaac and I share in common. Dr. B. B. Sutcliffe, one of the founders of Multnomah School of the Bible, penned a brief letter which my mother pasted in my baby book.

"Dear Daniel Ralph," he wrote to me. "I want to heartily commend you for your wisdom in your choice of parents. Their God will be your God, and the Lord Jesus be to you what he is to them." From a human standpoint, that could well apply to Isaac.

"Congratulations, Isaac, on being the son of Abraham, God's friend," Genesis seems to say. "Wisely, you have chosen Sarah, Abraham's partner in faith, as your remarkable mother!"

Isaac's greatest accomplishment seems to be being Abraham's son. Beyond that, Isaac appears unimpressive. He is different from his father, with accomplishments that are meager by comparison. Isaac is more passive, gentler. He experiences none of the challenges of Abraham. If Abraham is the pioneer, Isaac is the settler. If Abraham is the entrepreneur, Isaac is the executive. If Abraham is an initiator, Isaac is a maintainer. In Isaac we see a man with a sense of security, a peacefulness. When he makes decisions, his record, like all of ours, is spotted. Even his patriarchal blessing, which earns him notice in Hebrews 11, is a mixed compliment.

Isaac's faith is not necessarily superficial. We know from the biblical record that it is genuine. But Isaac expresses it differently, and once again we are reminded that Isaac, the heir of Abraham and of the divine promise, is an unlikely hero too.

Let's examine Isaac by consulting three reference materials: his earthly biography that summarizes the major events of his life (Gen. 21–27; 35), his spiritual ledger that recounts six key events (Gen. 26), and his divine epitaph that states the Lord's final assessment of his faith (Heb. 11:20).

Isaac's Earthly Biography

Highlights of Isaac's Life

It is not difficult to recap the major events of Isaac's life. Isaac is God's miracle boy. His birth (Gen. 21) is supernaturally predicted on several occasions. His extraordinary beginning highlights God's supernatural intervention in the relationship of Abraham and Sarah, who, beyond all hope, wait twenty-five long years for this prophecy to be fulfilled. The story of Isaac's sacrifice (Gen. 22) focuses less on Isaac than on Abraham's faith, although Isaac's submission to his father must not be missed. When Sarah passes away (Gen. 23), Isaac mourns his mother's death until he marries Rebekah some four years later.

Isaac's union with Rebekah is an arranged marriage (Gen. 24). Abraham sends his trusted servant, likely Eliezer who is unnamed in this chapter, back to the city of Nahor to find a wife for Isaac. After meeting Rebekah and her brother Laban at a divinely appointed rendezvous, Eliezer persuades Rebekah to travel to distant Canaan with a stranger to marry a man she's never met. Nevertheless, from what we can tell, theirs is a solid marriage. Isaac is the only one of the three patriarchs that marries only once. And Rebekah, though possessing a questionable value system, seems to be a woman of faith, aware of God's covenant promise.

Twenty years later, at sixty years of age, Isaac fathers his twin sons Esau and Jacob (Gen. 25). While Isaac seems to be a peaceful man, his boys are anything but, fighting even in their mother's womb. As a patriarch Isaac lives his entire life in the land of Canaan, making crucial moral decisions that often parallel his father's choices (Gen. 26). And when he is well past the century mark, likely anticipating his death with dimming eyesight, Isaac decides to bestow his patriarchal blessing on his twin sons (Gen. 27). Finally, Isaac passes away at age 180, living the final years of his life where Abraham lived (Gen. 35). These events are charted below:

Isaac's Biographical Sketch

Reference	Event	Description
Genesis 21	Isaac's birth	God miraculously gives Abraham and Sarah a son.
Genesis 22	Isaac's sacrifice	Abraham shows remarkable faith; Isaac shows remarkable submission.
Genesis 23	Isaac's mother's death	Sarah dies; Isaac mourns four years.
Genesis 24	Isaac's arranged marriage	Eliezer brings Rebekah from Laban's house to be Isaac's bride.
Genesis 25	Isaac's twin boys born	Esau is the firstborn; Jacob is born holding Esau's heel.
Genesis 26	Isaac's life in Canaan	Isaac makes five moral decisions.
Genesis 27	Isaac's patriarchal blessing	The blessing of Jacob and Esau has far-reaching implications.
Genesis 35	Isaac's death	He dies at age 180.

Two Inferences about Isaac

We can infer two things about Isaac from this biographical sketch. First, he remains very close to his parents. Thirty-six when his mother dies, Isaac mourns four years for her until he marries Rebekah at age forty. Abraham dies forty years after Sarah's death, making Isaac seventy-six years of age before he is bereft of both his parents. Some might call Isaac a mama's boy. Maybe that's what Ishmael told the servants when he returned for the occasional family reunion.

"The kid just can't cut the apron strings, can he?" Ishmael might have sneered. "Still hanging around the house at thirty. He'll never marry because no woman will ever dote on him like his mother. Well, they deserve each other. I never much cared for the old lady anyway!"

Others may have considered him a spoiled rich kid who was successful only because he enjoyed the favor, protection, and finances of his wealthy father. Perhaps Abraham's six sons by his concubine Keturah shared this opinion.

"Gifts? Dad only gives us gifts?" they may have complained to one another when Abraham sent them away (Gen. 25:6). "That spoiled brat Isaac is going to get everything when the old man dies. Too bad he doesn't have his guts or smarts. Two-to-one he spends himself into poverty within a year of Dad's death!"

Second, Isaac is comfortable to let life happen to him rather than make life happen. The events of his life up to Genesis 26 suggest that he is a passive man. For example, Isaac submits to his father's will on Mount Moriah, while Lot or Ishmael probably would never have acted this way. Also, Isaac is in no rush to marry. Unlike Esau or Jacob, he does not take the initiative to choose a wife but is willing to let his father pick one from distant relatives.

A Rich Family Heritage

Isaac's life illustrates the important principle that the life of faith is strengthened by a strong family heritage. Did Isaac always value this heritage, or did he resent living under the shadow of his powerful, prestigious father? Did he ever grow weary of hearing the story of his miraculous conception or the humorous origins of the name Isaac?

"Why couldn't they have named me something nobler, like Eliezer?" he could have said to himself, "instead of my ridiculous name, 'Laughter'? Every time I'm introduced to another Bedouin chieftain or caravan camel driver, I have to endure that boring story again!"

What did Isaac think when Ishmael came up in conversation, perhaps as part of an old, continuing argument between his mother and father?

Sometimes I think Dad still prefers that wild man Ishmael to me, he could have thought. *The next time Dad mentions it, I'll let him know some of the ways that son-of-a-slave tormented me without his knowing.*

The Genesis narrative explores little of Isaac's inner thoughts, but there is every indication that he valued this heritage rather than scorned it. He obeys his parents, honors them, loves them, and emulates them.

Isaac's Spiritual Ledger

Aside from a strong family heritage, is Isaac a man of faith on his own? Does faith guide his moral choices? To answer these questions, we must look at six events in Genesis 26. Together they weave a tapestry that provides an insightful portrait of his faith and choices as an adult.

Six Defining Events

The famine (Gen. 26:1–6). Sometime after Abraham's death, another famine engulfs Canaan. This time God is clear that Isaac should not flee to Egypt but stay in Canaan where the Lord will provide for him. This incident has a familiar ring because years before Abraham also faces a famine upon entering Canaan (Gen. 12:10). He heads to Egypt with his family with dire consequences. Not Isaac. With the Lord's clear instructions in his mind, and perhaps with the memory of his father's ill-advised choice, Isaac obeys. He heads westward in Canaan to the coastal plain of the Philistines (Gerar), where Abimelech is king. One credit for Isaac!

The wife crisis (Gen. 26:7–11). Immediately, another familiar incident occurs. When the men of Gerar take an interest in the beautiful Rebekah, Isaac lies about their relationship. "She's my sister," he tells anyone who will listen. Fearing for his life among this godless crowd, Isaac reverts to the same ploy Abraham twice uses in similar circumstances. In fact, Abraham's second incident also occurs in Gerar with King Abimelech, likely the father of the king during Isaac's visit. The fruit doesn't fall far from the tree, does it?

How Isaac's ruse lasted as long as it does with two twin boys running around is a mystery to me. But finally Abimelech, with understandable anger, exposes it. Isaac has no "half-sister" explanation. He simply admits his own naked fear. Surprisingly, Abimelech allows Isaac and his family to stay, sternly warning his people to keep their hands off. A debit in Isaac's ledger for this one!

Growing prosperity (Gen. 26:12–16). Despite Isaac's fear-motivated lie, God blesses Isaac in Gerar. Isaac remains there long enough to cycle through at least one full year of planting and harvest. God rewards him with a hundredfold return on his crops, a supernatural bounty. Isaac's flocks and herds multiply, and he moves from possessing riches to being wealthy.

Such prosperity in godless Gerar, however, incites envy. Abimelech, perhaps out of personal jealousy and political interest to prevent open conflict, banishes Isaac and his household from the land.

Parallels with Abraham emerge again. Material prosperity is evidence of God's blessing on Abraham (e.g., Gen. 13:2; 14:22–23), and it leads to conflict with Lot. Just as Abraham avoids hostility with Lot by giving him the choicest land, Isaac averts confrontation with Abimelech by leaving the region in peace.

The water-rights feud (Gen. 26:17–22). Peace between Isaac and Abimelech's people is short-lived. Vast herds require sufficient water, and water wells in the Valley of Gerar are as highly valued as oil wells in West Texas!

The mean-spirited Philistines begin the water-rights feud by plugging Abraham's wells (Gen. 26:15, 18). They don't take them for their own use; they seek to prevent others from using them. Without a fuss, Isaac reopens them and renames them in honor of his father.

Then, discovering a valley spring, his servants dig a new well. When the Philistines contest it, Isaac, instead of fighting, names the well "Contention" (*Esek*) and moves on to another spot to dig. The Philistines grab this one too. Isaac names this well "Enmity" (*Sitnah*) and, avoiding conflict a second time, moves again to a new site. This time the Philistines leave Isaac alone, and he names the well "Room" (*Rehoboth*), because the Lord has made room enough for all to dwell peacefully.

Was Isaac a coward? Absolutely not! A man of his means undoubtedly had the legal right and the military might to defend his claims. He chooses the more difficult and courageous path of peace. Score three credits for Isaac!

The renewed covenant (Gen. 26:23–25). Apparently God honors Isaac's choices, because he renews the Abrahamic covenant to Isaac at Beersheba. This is God's second renewal of the covenant to Isaac (the first is Genesis 26:2–5), and both renewals appear as God's response to Isaac's faithfulness. Isaac does two things highly reminiscent of Abraham, the wanderer and the worshipper: he builds an altar, and he pitches his tent while his servants begin digging another well. He truly is his father's son while remaining his own man.

The Abimelech agreement (Gen. 26:26–35). Further affirmation of Isaac's stature comes, finally, from the shifty Philistines. King Abimelech sues for peace.

"We cannot deny God is with you, Isaac," Abimelech says magnanimously. "Let's agree to a lasting peace. Promise not to harm us in any way, just as we have never defrauded you."

Isaac is understandably suspicious of Abimelech's motives, but he knows God is the source of his blessing. So he agrees to this shaky covenant, throwing a feast and sending the Philistine party away in peace.

Is Isaac a doofus? I doubt it. He knows the kind of man Abimelech is, and he learns from Abraham that the covenants of the kings of Gerar are worth no more than the breath that carries their words. Abraham's plugged water wells testify to that. But, with the promise of the God of Israel ringing in his ears, Isaac cuts a covenant with Abimelech. He trusts only in God. As an ironic postscript to the story, word comes to Isaac after Abimelech leaves that his servants struck water. Credit to Isaac!

These six events of Isaac's life correspond to six events in Abraham's life. The ledger below presents Isaac's spiritual debits and credits, comparing them with Abraham, and lists five principles of faith derived from these events.

Isaac's Spiritual Ledger

Event	Abraham's Account		Isaac's Account		Principle
	Debit	Credit	Debit	Credit	
Famine	X			X	Trust God and stay in the land.
Wife Crisis	X X		X		Protect those in your care.
Growing Prosperity		X		X	Handle wealth with wisdom and grace.
Water-Rights Feud		X		X X X	Diffuse hostility when possible.
Covenant Renewal		X		X	Trust the promises of God rather than the promises of men.
Abimelech's Agreement		X		X	

Principles of Faith

There are important principles to draw from each of these events. First, from the famine, trust God in the face of adversity even when your instinct is to flee. When God says, "Stay in the land," do it. Second, from the wife crisis, protect those under your care even when your instinct is for self-protection. Do not put someone you love in moral jeopardy. Third, from Isaac's growing prosperity, handle wealth wisely and graciously, because it comes from the generous hand of God. Fourth, from the water-rights feud, diffuse hostilities when your natural instinct may be to ignite them. Follow Paul's advice, "So far as it depends on you, live peaceably with all" (Rom. 12:18). And fifth, from God's covenant and Abimelech's agreement, trust the promises of God more than the promises of men.

Isaac's Divine Epitaph

Isaac's final epitaph is succinctly stated. "By faith," the writer to the Hebrews tells us, "Isaac invoked future blessings on Jacob and Esau" (Heb. 11:20). This refers to Isaac's patriarchal blessing of his twin sons (Gen. 27).

As a description of Isaac's faith, it carries a mixed message. On the one hand, this is not the patriarch's finest hour. When Isaac decides to bestow his fatherly blessing on Esau rather than Jacob, his decision is based on earthy, unspiritual reasons. He knows Esau disdains his birthright, having sold it to Jacob for a bowl of lentils. Esau and his Canaanite wives and in-laws have brought bitter hardship to the family. And now, with the opportunity to speak a blessing of eternal significance, Isaac chooses Esau because he makes a better venison stew!

Rebekah, with Jacob's complicity, devises the scheme to fool Isaac and defraud Esau. They succeed with goat skins for human hair, borrowed clothes that reek of Esau, and a counterfeit casserole. When the blessings are switched and the plot is discovered, we are somewhat surprised at Esau's bloodthirsty fury. Does he really care that much? Isaac seems blasé, while Rebekah and Jacob are scrambling to make the most of a bad family situation. It is hard to have much sympathy for anyone! Indeed, Isaac is truly an unlikely hero of faith.

On the other hand, the blessing contains an amazing promise full of future hope (Gen. 27:27–29). It is a promise of provision for Jacob and his offspring: "You'll have plenty of grain and wine." It is also a promise of preeminence: "All peoples will serve you. All nations will bow down to you, and your brother will serve you." And it is a promise of protection: "Those that bless you will be blessed. Those that curse you will be cursed."

The lesson of faith for us is this: the life of faith hopes beyond the grave. It is the anticipation that God's blessings are not limited to this life; great things will happen in the world to come. Isaac's blessing of Jacob shows that he, like Abraham, believes in El Olam, the God of eternity, the God who will fulfill his promises well into the future and long after we are gone. That's the point of the Hebrews epitaph. When we trust in the God of Isaac, we possess that same hope.

Isaac's Legacy

Remember three principles from the life of Isaac. First, the life of faith is strengthened by a strong family heritage. Pass it on. Second, the life of faith requires making some tough moral choices.

Do so informed by the promises of God and infused with the grace and wisdom of God. Third, the life of faith recognizes that God's promises extend beyond the grave. Keep your hope alive.

When all is said and done, Isaac's final legacy is his family heritage passed down from his parents. This marks his early years at home, it informs his choices as an adult, and it emerges in his view of the eternal God, El Olam, in his patriarchal blessing. He is undeniably the son of the covenant promise after all.

I was not always pleased with my family heritage. I secretly regretted that I did not have a zinger of a testimony. You know the kind I mean. A well-known celebrity, after living a horrendous life of sin, is marvelously converted to Christ and uses his or her influence to win others to faith. I heard a lot of these at the Portland Youth for Christ rallies held every Saturday night at Benson High School when I was in junior high.

"Why can't I have an exciting conversion story like that?" I would ask myself. "I'd love to tell people how I came out of a life of drugs, alcohol, sex, and organized crime at age eleven to live wholeheartedly for Jesus!"

When I studied at Dallas Theological Seminary, a number of my classmates had exactly that kind of testimony. Some could point to specific evidence of God's supernatural intervention in their lives. I felt regret resurfacing until one friend shared the rest of his story. "Don't ever second-guess your Christian heritage," he said to me. "You're so much further along, and you can't begin to comprehend the pain of the scars I bear." I haven't forgotten. My appreciation for my parental legacy has only grown.

Perhaps you lack that kind of godly family heritage. If so, you are like many of my students at Multnomah University. Unlike thirty or forty years ago, many students come to Multnomah today with lots of baggage: dysfunctional families, little religious training, biblically illiteracy, physical and emotional abuse, struggles with sexual identity, or bitterness from legalistic Christianity. We seek to teach them, train them, and prepare them to minister to a hurting world.

I have concluded that the best thing I can do to repay my parents for their legacy is to pass that heritage on to my daughter. And the greatest thing I can do professionally is to help train my precious students, the future wave of Christian leaders, to be loving ambassadors of Jesus Christ.

If you have not come from a solid family heritage, why not resolve to pass one on to your own children and community? I see no other hope for the church, for our nation, or for our world than for committed followers of Jesus Christ first to become transformed people and then, empowered by the Spirit of God, to impart a rich Christian legacy to the next generation.

CHAPTER 11

JACOB:

THE UNLIKELY WRESTLER

The Least Likely People

Have you ever noticed that the most amazing accomplishments often come through the least likely people?

In 1879 Dr. James Murray was appointed by the London Philological Society to become senior editor of the *Oxford English Dictionary (OED)*. The *OED* was conceived twenty-two years earlier by a group of philologists as a dictionary to contain every single word in the English language, with a documented account of each first written usage. Murray invited scholars, readers, and literary people from across the English-speaking world to read books from every era of the English language, make lists of the words, write a sentence definition, and include a quotation from the earliest source.

Dr. William Minor, who lived only forty miles from Oxford, asked in a letter if he could participate in the project. His credentials were impressive, and Dr. Murray invited him to join. Over the years Dr. Minor submitted some twelve thousand slips of paper with definitions handwritten in a small, elegant script. Though some six million slips were eventually submitted for the *OED* project, Minor's contribution remains significant because most every one of his submissions was used. His chosen words were unique, his definitions precise. For seven years, however, Dr. Murray had never met William Minor. So Murray wrote Minor to arrange a meeting.

"I am unable to come and see you, but you are welcome to visit me anytime," Minor said by return post.

According to a popular fictionalized account, Murray boarded the train to travel the forty miles to the address Minor gave him. He trudged up a long road lined with beautiful poplar trees and arrived at the large house at the end of the drive. Entering through two tall, green doors, he was ushered by a servant up a marble staircase into a spacious room on the second floor. A fire glowed in the fireplace, and oil portraits decorated the walls. In the center of the room stood a large oak desk, and a man of obvious importance sat behind it.

"I'm Dr. James Murray, editor of the *Oxford English Dictionary*," Murray said when he entered the room. "Are you Dr. William Minor? It is a great pleasure to meet you."

There was an awkward silence. The man behind the desk stood and spoke.

"No, I must disappoint you, for I am not William Minor. Rather, I am the superintendent of the Broadmoor Criminal Lunatic Asylum in which you are standing. Dr. William Minor has been our longest resident. He's an American. He is a murderer, and he is hopelessly insane."

This story, told eloquently by Simon Winchester in *The Professor and the Madman,* confirms our observation, doesn't it? Often the most amazing accomplishments come about through the least likely people.

Jacob, the Unlikely Success Story

It is an overstatement to say that Jacob is the William Minor of the Old Testament. Jacob is not, after all, a criminally insane murderer. But he certainly is an unlikely recipient of God's covenantal favor.

Consider his resume. First, Jacob is not the firstborn of patriarch Isaac. Since the firstborn holds the cultural pride of place in the ancient world, Jacob begins with a severe social handicap, and he knows it.

Second, Jacob possesses character traits that should disqualify anyone from shouldering the covenantal mantle of Abraham. Although Abraham is a successful Mediterranean businessman who cuts corners and tells half-truths during his career, we never question his faith in God. Jacob, on the other hand, comes across as a crook from the very beginning, grabbing his brother's heel at birth, bartering for Esau's birthright, abetting his mother in stealing Esau's elder-son blessing, and tricking his way through his relationships with Uncle Laban, his two wives and two concubines, and his twelve sons.

Third, when Jacob meets God face to face at the most decisive moment, it is a wrestling match. There is no "remove your sandals—you're standing on holy ground" when Jacob encounters

God. We don't see awe, fear, respect, or humility in the man. He's trying to grab all he can get from almighty God. While we may not be surprised that Jacob is renamed "Israel"—the one who strives with God—we find ourselves miffed that this man heads the holy nation that God declares to be his chosen people.

Finally, even as a father Jacob has little to commend him. He shows blatant favoritism to the sons of Rachel, and his other boys are out of control. Reuben, Simeon, Levi, and Judah all are mentioned specifically for their outrageous acts. Conspiring to sell Joseph into slavery in Egypt, they lie to their father about him being alive and live that lie for decades.

Three Enlightened Perspectives on Jacob

Let's face it. Jacob is a real rascal. Yet the writer to the Hebrews includes him in the list of unlikely heroes as a man of faith. Jacob meets the Lord on a number of occasions in addition to his wrestling match at Peniel. And he is the covenant-bearer whose name defines a nation.

So, let's examine Jacob's life of faith through three "enlightening" perspectives. First, we will turn a floodlight on Jacob to reveal and examine the flaws in his character through his four major struggles. Second, we will train a searchlight on Jacob to discover evidences of his faith—where they are, how they illuminate his struggles, and what they say to us today. Finally, we will aim a spotlight on Jacob's final act of faith, the patriarchal blessing of his sons. This is the event that Hebrews 11 identifies for special notice.

Three Enlightened Perspectives

Jacob's Four Struggles	Jacob's Growing Faith	Jacob's Final Blessing
The floodlight to reveal his flaws	The searchlight to discover his faith	The spotlight to illuminate his legacy

A Floodlight on Jacob's Four Struggles

His Struggle with Esau

Jacob's struggles with his brother Esau began in the womb (Gen. 25:19–28). Literally. Rebekah is the first to notice it.

"Lord, what's going on?" she may have asked. "I know babies are supposed to kick, but this feels like a herd of male goats on a rampage!"

"Congratulations, Rebekah," the Lord replies. "You're going to have twins. But more is going on here. Two nations are in your womb, and you will give birth to two peoples. And that kicking is prophetic! One will be stronger than the other, but here's the clincher. The older will serve the younger."

Esau is the eldest, but only by minutes. Because his body is red, perhaps covered with fine red hair, they name him Esau, or "Red." Maybe that's the beginning of Esau's surliness—he resented his name! I can understand this. As a boy, I was called "Red" because of my hair color. I hated it too.

Because he emerges grasping his brother's heel, the younger twin is named Jacob, or "Supplanter." No name is more appropriate. Jacob is the one always trying to get more, to get the edge, to gain an advantage. He is number two in the ancestral hierarchy, and he never forgets it. So he tries harder, always trying to beat Esau to the top spot. In this way the struggle in the womb reveals Jacob's character. He's a gamer. He'll try any trick in the book to get what he wants.

The struggle continues throughout the twins' lives, partly because they possess vastly different temperaments. Esau is a hunter, an outdoorsman, a man's man. He loves the chase and loves the kill. Jacob, by contrast, is a sedentary man. Maybe he likes to bake muffins. Esau is at home in the field; Jacob enjoys the tent. Most importantly, Esau is best loved by his father; Jacob is the favorite of his mother. The stage is set for bitter contention.

The next struggle comes with Esau's sale of his birthright (Gen. 25:29–34). Esau apparently lives for the present. If he gets hungry, he goes out and kills something. Jacob, on the other hand, is a planner, a schemer. He waits patiently to seize just the right moment.

That moment comes one day when Esau returns starving from the field. Jacob, working in the tent, has made some kind of lentil stew. Ironically, the literal phrase here is "red stuff," and brother Red is about to get the short end of the stick.

"Oy vey, that smells good," Esau mutters as he enters the aroma-filled tent. "Give me a bowl of that, Jacob. I'm about to die of hunger!"

"Not so fast, Red," Jacob answers lightly. "This is a special order from Mom for dinner tonight. Some Bedouin guests are dropping by, and this will be just about enough." Then he adds, smiling, "You'll only have to wait another three hours."

"How many times have I told you not to call me Red!" Esau growls, with a menacing glint flashing in his eyes.

Jacob ignores the look. "Okay, I'll tell you what. Sell me your birthright and I'll give you a bowl of stew right now. Plus, I'll never call you Red again." Then Jacob lowers his voice. "But I'm serious about the birthright, Esau. I'll only do this if you swear by the Lord God that it's mine. There is no turning back from this, Brother."

Now it's Esau's turn to be flip. "Oh, I'll swear to it if you like. In fact, I'll swear by any god you choose. What do I care about the birthright? Plus," he adds with a sneer, "what good will a birthright do me if I die of starvation?"

And in this simple way, Esau forfeits his precious birthright. The birthright is the promise of a double portion of the father's land and goods, usually to the eldest son. It has broad spiritual implication too, designating the heir as the spiritual leader of the clan. Scripture tells us that Esau "despised his birthright" (Gen. 25:34). Carelessly, he rejects his spiritual responsibilities.

The greatest struggle between the twins involves Isaac's patriarchal blessing (Gen. 27), a story we recounted in the previous chapter. Aging Isaac seeks to bless his favorite son, Esau, even though he doubtless remembers the divine promise that the elder will serve the younger. Rebekah contrives the ruse to deceive her husband and ensure that her youngest son receives the coveted blessing. While this story spells an epic rift between husband and wife, Jacob and Esau are drawn into its vortex. Jacob is directly complicit in the hoax; Esau is outraged at his loss and vows to kill Jacob when Isaac passes on.

Esau never kills his brother, but their relationship is never the same. Jacob fears Esau's vengeance (Gen. 32–33). His troubles with Esau shine a spiritual floodlight on our unlikely hero of faith, who deceives himself into thinking he can manage life for himself. His struggles with Esau are only the beginning.

His Struggle with Laban

Because of Esau's threat to kill Jacob, Rebekah plans to send Jacob out of harm's way (Gen. 27).

I know what to do, she thinks, *I'll send Jacob far away to Haran, where my brother Laban and his family live. He can return after this thing blows over.*

To sell this to Isaac, Rebekah reminds her husband of their common dislike for Esau's two Hittite wives. (We're never told whether Isaac is aware of Esau's death threat.) When Jacob returns twenty years later, we can only infer that Rebekah is dead. What an irony! She who deceives and connives to get the blessing for her favorite son never sees him again.

So Jacob flees to Haran (Gen. 28), Abraham's ancestral city. In an incident strikingly parallel to Eliezer's meeting of Rebekah (Gen. 24), Jacob meets the beautiful Rachel at the well (Gen. 29). The similar details here convince us that the Lord orchestrates this rendezvous. Jacob greets his uncle and family, is welcomed into the home, and falls in love.

Laban is a real piece of work, and he wastes no time schooling Jacob. Noticing the budding romance, Laban sets plans into motion faster than a spider spins a web.

"I'm a fair man, my boy," Laban tells Jacob. "I can't let you work for me without fair wages. Name them!"

Jacob does not even see the trap. "My request is simple," he responds confidently. "I love your daughter Rachel, and I will work for you seven years if I can have her hand in marriage."

Laban hesitates, but Jacob misses the smile. *This is too easy,* Laban thinks. *Too bad Jacob doesn't know the local customs. He could have demanded Rachel's hand today and then paid me with seven years of labor. Perfect! The boy will learn a few more tricks from me before this is over.*

Seven years later, during the seven-day wedding feast, Laban completes his classic bait and switch, grateful that those wedding veils are opaque.

"What in heaven's name have you done?" Jacob storms at Laban when he discovers the woman beneath the veil is plain-looking Leah, not her beautiful younger sister. "I curse you, you miserable trickster. You're nothing more than a . . . than a . . . supplanter!"

"Oh," responds Laban, smooth as silk, "don't you know the tradition that the eldest daughter must marry first? Unless Leah marries, you can never marry Rachel. Believe me, my son, I'm doing you a favor by letting you have Rachel in only seven years. Plus, look on the bright side. You'll have two wives!"

Jacob has little choice but to comply and work another seven years. Laban, of course, has other tricks up his turban. When Jacob finally flees after twenty years (Gen. 31), with his father-in-law hot on his trail, Jacob complains to Rachel, "Your dad changed my wages ten times over, bristled at my success, conspired to undermine me, and even now will thwart our departure if he can. I never did trust the man."

Jacob is right. His father-in-law likely would kill him if God doesn't intervene. "Laban," the Lord tells him in a dream, "say nothing good or bad to Jacob if you value your life. Let them go. This is far bigger than you can possibly know."

Jacob leaves, not knowing how close he comes to losing his beloved Rachel, who secretly has stolen her father's idols. The story underscores how Jacob, the deceiver, is himself ensnared by the deception of others. He realizes from Laban, perhaps for the first time, how hurtful lies and trickery can be. Jacob is far from transformed, but God, ever weaving a web of protection around him, teaches him hard lessons that will bear future fruit.

His Struggle with His Family

Jacob's third struggle is with his own family. Jacob loves Rachel desperately but despises Leah (Gen. 29). As rivalry between the two sisters expands, they bring their handmaidens, Bilhah and Zilpah, into the marriage bed (Gen. 30). While we might be willing to cut Jacob some slack on his bigamy because of Laban's deception, it is impossible to approve this *ménage a cinq*.

The Bible hints that Leah is a woman of faith. Because she is the despised one, God shows her mercy by giving her sons—a strong confirmation that God intervenes for the downtrodden. She names her sons "the Lord sees" (Reuben), "the Lord hears" (Simeon), and "the Lord be praised" (Judah) in gratitude.

Rachel, on the other hand, relates to the Lord with a different spirit. "Lord," she whines, "why are you helping my sister out and not me?"

Try to imagine Jacob's dilemma and the tension in his home. "I can't take another day with Laban," he moans to himself as he walks home from the field. "I'm willing to take the less desirable spotted cattle, but then he accuses me of chicanery when my herd grows.

"I could even put Laban out of my mind for a few hours if I just had a quiet evening in my own tent," he adds aloud with a sigh. "But I'll bet a speckled calf those wives are even now conniving as to where I sleep tonight. I am so tired of their small-minded bedroom politics. What I wouldn't give for a good night's rest—alone!"

Then he stops. "What is it with those mandrake roots anyway?"

And what about Jacob's sons? Reuben humiliates his father by sleeping with Bilhah, one of Jacob's concubines and Reuben's stepmother (Gen. 35:22). Simeon and Levi are so violent they wipe out all the men of the village of Shechem (Gen. 34:25–29). Even beloved Joseph inflames his brothers' jealousy with visions of his grandeur (Gen. 37:5–11). Consequently, the brothers conspire to do away with Joseph though Judah convinces them to sell him into Egyptian slavery, using financial profit rather than familial affection to win his case (Gen. 37:26–27). Later, Judah marries a Canaanite woman, raises two sons so wicked that God slays them, and then sleeps with his daughter-in-law as she plays the role of a prostitute (Gen. 38:1–19).

What a family! Like their father, the sons act deceitfully (Gen. 34:13). You cannot avoid the conclusion that Jacob's covenantal clan is facing utter catastrophe in the toxic climate of Canaan. They will not survive unless something radical happens. Joseph's slavery in Egypt becomes the single thread to fulfill the promise of God.

His Struggle with God

A sobering principle of faith emerges from Jacob's struggles. It is not simply that God refines people of faith through adverse circumstances, though that is true. It is more than that. Jacob's struggles demonstrate that God uses the adversities stemming from our own twisted temperaments and arrogant egos to turn our self-centered eyes to him.

That is why Jacob's fourth struggle is the most momentous: he has a personal wrestling match with the living God (Gen. 32:22–32)! As we will see next, it is this struggle that transforms Jacob heart, mind, and soul.

A Searchlight on Jacob's Growing Faith

Let's turn the biblical searchlight on Jacob's emerging faith and examine the times when God intersects with Jacob and intervenes in his life. The chart below suggests the progressive impact of those events.

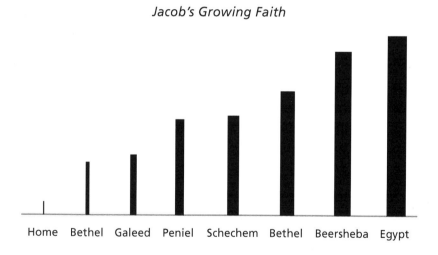

Jacob's Growing Faith

Home Bethel Galeed Peniel Schechem Bethel Beersheba Egypt

Most of the bars in the graph above represent mountain peaks in Jacob's life where he worships God, but Jacob's childhood faith remains a mystery. We may presume he knew about the Lord from his father, Isaac, though there is little evidence his father's faith was his own. During the patriarchal blessing when

Jacob poses as Esau, Jacob says to Isaac, "Dad, the Lord *your* God gave me good fortune" (Gen. 27:20).

Bethel

When fleeing to Haran, Jacob beds down in the desert near Luz and receives a night vision of God standing atop a stairway that reaches to heaven (Gen. 28:10–22). Angels are ascending and descending from Jacob's campsite. God tells him he is the heir to the divine covenant made to Abraham and to Isaac.

The next morning Jacob renames this place Bethel, "the house of God." "God dwells here," he breathes with awe tinged in fear. "This is the gateway to heaven."

Gilead

A second encounter with God occurs twenty years later when Jacob, again fleeing, builds an altar to the Lord, this time at Gilead (Gen. 31). Here Jacob and Laban make a formal covenant to stay out of each other's way, erecting a stone pillar that Jacob names Galeed, or "the heap of witness." Laban swears by the God of Abraham; Jacob, by the Fear of Isaac. Although God utters a warning to Laban, there is no vision for Jacob. Nevertheless, Jacob offers a sacrifice to the Lord. Perhaps he wants God to seal his covenant with Laban with divine protection. More likely he is offering thanksgiving to God for finally releasing him from his wily father-in-law. Whatever the reason, the faint light of faith begins to flicker in Jacob.

Peniel

Jacob's anticipated reunion with Esau precipitates his most significant encounter with God, at Penuel (Gen. 32:22–32). This is vintage Jacob. He does not simply meet God face to face. He wrestles with him!

This event is Jacob's spiritual crossroads, his burning bush. It is not merely an allegorical depiction of Jacob wrestling with God in prayer. No, it is an undeniably historical event underscored by the physical deformity that Jacob has for the rest of his life. What incredible spiritual and prophetic significance! Jacob—the wrestler, the struggler, the deceiver—meets God. It is God and God alone who totally transforms him.

You know the story. Jacob, alone late at night worrying about Esau, meets a man at the edge of camp. With no explanation, they begin to wrestle. In a contest lasting for hours, neither opponent gains the upper hand. As dawn approaches, the unknown contestant, seeking to end the match, simply touches Jacob's hip, apparently dislocating it. Jacob, no longer able to wrestle, can now only cling to the man. He refuses to cry "Uncle!"

"I won't let go until you bless me," Jacob utters through painful gasps.

"What is your name?"

"Jacob."

"Not any more. You are no longer Jacob the Supplanter, Jacob the Trickster, Jacob the Heel-Grabber. From now on you are Israel, 'the One Who Strives with God.' I will give you a blessing more than you could ever imagine and certainly more than you deserve." And Jacob receives a blessing that makes the one he stole from Esau pale by comparison.

This story raises lots of questions. Who is this opponent? Clearly this is a theophany, an appearance of God, most likely a preincarnate visitation of Jesus Christ. Both Jacob's new name, Israel, and the renamed location, Peniel ("the face of God"), confirm that he knows he touches the living God. Hosea later identifies the angel with whom Jacob strives as God himself (Hos. 12:2–4).

But if this is the Lord, why does Jacob seem to prevail? Why doesn't God just dispatch him quickly and decisively? The answer lies in God's desire to meet this man just as he is. Jacob the Supplanter, who struggles and deceives all his life, learns that God is not just a smarter or stronger trickster—a Laban with omnipotence. A sound beating at midnight probably would only harden Jacob's resolve to retaliate next time he has a chance. Through the long, dark hours of the early morning, Jacob learns not only of the futility of struggling with God but of the Lord's supreme patience ending in unmerited blessing. The lesson for us is clear. God meets us on our own turf to make us humble, but he always meets us on his terms to make us holy.

There is never a doubt that God is in charge. In a manner consistent with Ancient Near Eastern custom, the greater names the lesser. Jacob cannot wring God's name out of him. Instead, Jacob is blessed with a new name and a new identity. Jacob's act of renaming the place Peniel demonstrates his faithful gratitude to the God who, he now realizes, walks at his side every day of his life.

A confrontation with God doesn't necessarily mean that a person will change, but a person cannot change unless he has a confrontation with God. And how Jacob is transformed! He begins the night watch as a wrestler trying to gain the edge. He welcomes the dawn clinging to God. He fights as Jacob, the deceiver. He surrenders as Israel, the God-striver. He begins physically whole but spiritually deformed. He returns to his tent physically lame but spiritually transformed.

Do you feel like Jacob? Do you feel like you can do no more than cling to God and ask him to bless you? If so, you are in a prime place to receive God's blessing.

Shechem, Bethel, and Beersheba

The remaining incidents, while significant, are simply commentary on Peniel. Jacob arrives in Canaan and builds an altar at Shechem to worship the Lord (Gen. 33:20), though he must move on because his vengeful, bloodthirsty sons have created irreconcilable animosity in the city (Gen. 34). At God's command, Jacob journeys to Bethel, first purifying his entire camp by throwing out the old gods and unclean garments. Presumably, he even destroys the idols that Rachel stole from Laban. Then Jacob builds an altar at Bethel, where God reaffirms Jacob's new name and renews his divine covenant (Gen. 35). Much later, with the incredible news that Joseph is alive in Egypt, Jacob journeys south to Beersheba and builds his final altar to the Lord (Gen. 46). God permits him to move his entire household to Egypt, where Jacob sees his beloved son return, as it were, from the grave.

This biblical floodlight reveals a second principle of faith. Living by faith requires divine confrontation to produce spiritual transformation. That confrontation will take different forms for each of us. For Jacob the Supplanter, God confronts him in numerous ways, including a wrestling match, to transform him into Israel the God-striver. He is never the same.

The Spotlight on Jacob's Final Blessing

Finally, let's turn a New Testament spotlight on the culminating event of Jacob's life. The writer to the Hebrews takes us down to

Egypt, where Jacob, frail and near death, blesses the two sons of Joseph (Heb. 11:21). (There is no mention in Hebrews of Jacob blessing the other eleven sons, as in Genesis 49.) Jacob gets it right. Crossing his hands, he places his right palm on Ephraim, Joseph's youngest son, and lays his left on Manasseh, the eldest. Unlike Isaac, Jacob intentionally gives the younger the greatest blessing, despite Joseph's protest.

The final principle of faith is the promise of a future. Jacob shows us that living by faith weds unmerited blessing with undeserved hope.

"Wait a minute!" you might be saying. "Jacob's story shouldn't end on such a happy note. You cannot mean that he is reunited with Joseph, enjoys prosperity in Egypt, is surrounded by nearly seventy family members, and bestows a patriarchal blessing on his sons and grandsons. Jacob was a rascal. It doesn't seem fair!"

You are exactly right. It isn't fair. The life of faith is not based on merit. It is based on God's grace alone—*sola gratia*. None of us earn life with God as a reward. It is a gift of God. In his love he transforms us, and from his compassion he blesses us.

Three Principles of Faith

Jacob's Four Struggles	Jacob's Growing Faith	Jacob's Final Blessing
1. God refines people of faith through adverse circumstances.	2. Living by faith requires divine confrontation for spiritual transformation.	3. Living by faith weds unmerited blessing with undeserved hope.
The floodlight to reveal his flaws	The searchlight to discover his faith	The spotlight to illuminate his legacy

Jacob, the Unlikely Wrestler

We have traveled a winding path littered with obstacles as we've walked in the footsteps of Jacob. Dr. Alan Redpath, a Bible expositor of a past generation, once said, "When God seeks to accomplish an impossible task, he takes an impossible man and crushes him!" What an apt summary of Jacob, the unlikely wrestler!

Maybe you identify more with Isaac, who illustrates the contentment of faith. Perhaps you are more drawn to Sarah, who demonstrates the partnership of faith. But if you resonate spiritually with Jacob, struggling to get the upper hand, trying to gain God's blessing, this story is for you. God can transform you. God can use you. God can accomplish the most unexpected things through the most surprising people. In fact, all of us are Jacobs, dependent upon the grace of God. We need God's gracious confrontation to be transformed by him and to enjoy the depth and wonder of his blessing.

CHAPTER 12

JOSEPH:

THE UNLIKELY RULER

The Malaysian Incident

I have many vivid memories of my three years as a merchant seaman sailing the seven seas. But one incident is etched indelibly on my mind for its connection to Jacob's son Joseph.

In December of 1970 I was dispatched by the Marine Firemen, Oilers, and Watertenders Union (MFOW) as a wiper aboard the SS *President Jackson*. This large freighter was heading westward from San Francisco to cities in the Far East and ultimately around the world.

On our global circuit, we pulled into a Malaysian port. The town itself was no more than a simple village, small and undeveloped. Its harbor was so shallow that our ship had to anchor in the middle of the bay, loading and unloading cargo on barges that came out and tied up alongside.

As a wiper in the engine room, I could tell from the activity around me and from the familiar sounds outside the hull that the anchor was set. When we shut down our turbines, it was about three o'clock in the afternoon.

Unexpectedly, the captain spoke over the intercom. "Attention all crew members," he said, his voice squawking through the small speaker. "Unless you have specific deck duties related to the cargo, you all have the rest of the afternoon off. Please assemble on the main deck at once." I was amazed. This was a first since I had come aboard.

The crew ascended the ladders to the main deck and watched the barges tie up. One of them drew our immediate attention. It was an open scow in which two dozen women sat waiting to come aboard. No one could mistake their profession. From their provocative dress, their heavy makeup, and their hardened looks, it was obvious these women were prostitutes sent to service the ship.

In many such ports around the world, the customs agent is king. If a captain wants to move his cargo, whatever the agent requires is law. Bribes and payoffs are the order of the day; conflicts of interest do not exist. On this day, the customs agent demanded that our captain make prostitutes available to the crew as a condition for doing the work. The captain, under pressure to stay on schedule, had very little choice. Soon young Malaysian women walked every passageway of the ship.

My roommate passed me in the hall with a girl in tow. "Our cabin is mine," he whispered to me with a wink. "I don't want to see you the rest of the day."

So here I am, a young man in my early twenties, unmarried and alone. My family lives in Portland. The woman I love is literally half a world away. A Malaysian girl makes explicit overtures to me in the hallway. Further, there is an unspoken code among sailors that what happens overseas stays overseas, so no one snitches. Who would ever know? Would it really matter? And if I do not participate, how will I work with my burly crewmates who will now assume I'm gay?

I make my way down one deck to the small mess hall, waiting out the afternoon with the one or two others who have chosen not to participate. Sitting in that mess hall on a ship anchored in faraway Malaysia, I remember Joseph.

Joseph, the Unlikely, Unlikely Hero

Joseph is a fascinating man. He is unique among those in the Hebrews list of unlikely heroes because nothing seems wrong with him. No moral failure. No character flaws. No devastating habits. No poor decisions. No nothing.

We find little common ground between father Jacob and son Joseph. In fact, we could hardly find two men who stand in starker contrast. Jacob is too flawed; Joseph, too perfect. Jacob is a man whose character we would probably not want to imitate; Joseph is someone with such impeccable virtue that you never could emulate him even if you tried. Jacob the Supplanter is a deceiver. While we can identify with him, would we really want to be his friend? Joseph the Egyptian Governor is a hero. Sure, we might wish to be his friend, but would we ever feel comfortable around him?

Nevertheless, Joseph experiences hurdles in his life that we all face. How he confronts these barriers is immensely instructive as we seek to walk the pathway of faith.

Joseph's Life: Two Competing Perspectives

Let's consider Joseph's life using two racing metaphors with corresponding principles of faith. They are listed below.

The Race of Joseph's Life

Joseph's Spiritual Steeplechase	Joseph's Spiritual Marathon
Overcoming the Obstacles	*Hitting the Wall*
Living by faith means trusting God to guide us through life's obstacles.	Living by faith recognizes God's good purposes in all things.

First, we'll examine Joseph's life as a steeplechase. Joseph is a man who encounters many, many difficulties. He teaches us that living by faith means trusting God to guide us through life's obstacles. Second, we'll consider Joseph's life as a marathon. He is a man who, after running a long race with endurance, hits a spiritual wall—his most treacherous obstacle. In how Joseph responds, we learn that living by faith recognizes God's good purposes in all things. Finally, we'll reflect on Joseph's closing days as he breaks the tape, crosses the finish line, and displays the faith of which Hebrews speaks (Heb. 11:22).

Joseph's Spiritual Steeplechase: Overcoming the Obstacles

The steeplechase is a three-thousand-meter race that rewards speed, endurance, and agility. The runner circles a 400-meter track seven times. Each lap involves clearing four three-foot-high, fixed hurdles spaced evenly around the track. On the other side of the fourth hurdle is a water pit. This twelve-foot-long pool, twenty-seven inches deep near the hurdle, tapers upward to the level of the track.

This unique race is all about overcoming barriers. And Joseph, like a steeplechase runner, teaches us how to trust God to guide us over life's imposing barriers. We'll consider Joseph's external adversity and prosperity and his internal temptations.

The graph below shows the extreme range of external experiences Joseph encounters, from the depths of adversity (in the pit, in Potiphar's house, and in prison) to the heights of prosperity (in Pharaoh's palace and as prime minister of Egypt). The chart also includes the situations which could easily lead Joseph to make poor choices or turn his back on God.

Joseph's Adversity-Prosperity Index

Gen. 37	**Gen. 39**	**Gen. 39–40**	**Gen. 41**	**Gen. 41**
Prophecy & the Pit:	Potiphar's Place:	Prison: *Broken Promises*	Pharaoh's Palace:	Prime Minister:
Betrayal	*Injustice*		*Recognition*	*Power*

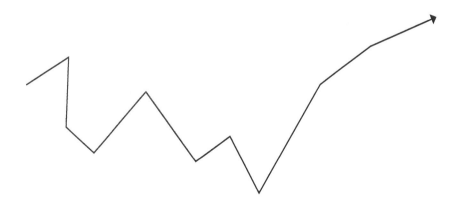

In the midst of external adversity and prosperity, Joseph faces internal obstacles: bitterness toward a heartless family, sexual temptation, despair over broken promises, the deception of Pharaoh's table, and the lure of pride. Let's add these obstacles to the graph below.

Joseph's Spiritual Obstacles

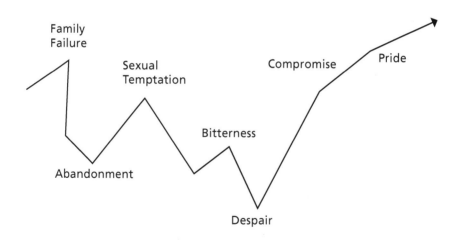

Gen. 37	**Gen. 39**	**Gen. 39–40**	**Gen. 41**	**Gen. 41**
Prophecy & the Pit:	Potiphar's Place:	Prison: *Broken Promises*	Pharaoh's Palace:	Prime Minister:
Betrayal	*Injustice*	*Promises*	*Recognition*	*Power*

Prophecy and the Pit: Family Betrayal and Bitterness (Genesis 37)

Joseph is Jacob's favorite son because he is the firstborn of beloved Rachel—a reason that does not curry favor with his half-brothers. Further, Jacob gives him a special coat with long sleeves (or possibly, many colors) that only underscores Jacob's favoritism. Not surprisingly, his brothers hate the boy for it.

To make matters worse, Joseph dreams about future preeminence, and he lacks the maturity to keep his mouth shut when his already jealous brothers are within earshot.

"Hey, guys," Joseph says with wide-eyed innocence, "I just had a wild dream. I saw all of our sheaves of wheat lying in the field waiting to be picked up and threshed. Suddenly mine stood upright, as if by magic!"

"So what?" Judah asks dismissively.

"Well," explains Joseph excitedly, "all of yours gather around mine and bow down before it. What do think this means?"

"Absolutely nothing," three of them shout out, "except that if you worked harder during the day like the rest of us, you would have fewer foolish dreams at night!"

Simeon says nothing but gives Joseph a shrewd, sinister look that only Levi sees.

"Hey," Joseph continues as if nothing happened, "let me tell you the one about the sun, the moon, and the eleven stars!"

How prophetic these dreams turn out to be! But how hard and lonely is Joseph's path before he sees them fulfilled! When Jacob sends Joseph to check on his brothers and their herds far from the homestead, the brothers conspire in earnest.

"Let's kill him," they say, "and get rid of this crazy dreamer once and for all."

"Wait," cautions Reuben. "Don't kill him in broad daylight. Someone might see. Let's throw him into this well and decide what to do later."

Reuben hopes to rescue Jacob, perhaps as a ploy to mend fences with his father after the concubine incident. But while

Reuben is gone and Joseph sits in the well, Judah smells a shekel to be made.

"Why kill him?" Judah asks, the idea hitting when the Ishmaelite traders appear on the horizon. "There's profit here!"

So the brothers pull Joseph out of the well and barter him for twenty pieces of silver to a caravan that will resell him into Egyptian slavery far, far away.

To say Joseph faced the obstacle of a dysfunctional family is an understatement. His father, Jacob, is a deceiver. His mother, Rachel, is in mortal combat with his stepmother, Leah, for the favor of bearing Jacob more children. Bitterly, they pull their two handmaidens into the fray and use all the kids as pawns in the battle. Think of the confusion. Joseph does not have the problems of a single-parent family; he has those of a quintuple-parent one.

And then there are his brothers—hot-tempered, volatile, jealous men whose actions go far beyond sibling rivalry. I understand sibling rivalry, having two brothers who teased me mercilessly when I was young. But this is nothing compared to Joseph's half-brothers who are out to kill him and who would have succeeded except for the unseen hand of God.

Despite his family's dysfunction, Joseph does not act like a victim. While many play the sympathy card when making extremely poor life choices, blaming family circumstances or other people for the mess they've made of their lives, Joseph continues to make morally wise—and morally difficult—choices without a hint of whining.

Try to imagine Joseph's sense of betrayal and terror. Captured by his own half-brothers, he spends a horrifying couple of days at the bottom of a dark pit, escaping a cruel death only because his brothers want to make a quick buck. The only clue to Joseph's thinking is that he wails from the bottom of the well, a detail the brothers later recall with regret and fear (Gen. 42:21).

And think of his temptation to sink into the dark pit of bitterness. What haunts him more as he bounces on a camel's hump through the dusty desert? Is it the prospect of a short and brutal future as a slave to a ruthless Egyptian master? Is it the hopeless certainty of never seeing his father or family again? Or is it the nagging, painful sense that even God has abandoned him? Whatever Joseph is thinking, and despite his adversity index plummeting, we get no sense that bitterness gnaws at his soul. This is a man who trusts God without conditions.

Potiphar's House: Sexual Temptation and Injustice (Genesis 39)

Sold as a slave to the house of Potiphar, the captain of Pharaoh's guard, Joseph begins a pattern of overcoming adversity that will repeat itself many times. Owned by a master with little regard for the status of a slave, Joseph nevertheless begins to prosper. Joseph's innate leadership, wedded with personal integrity and divine protection, brings prosperity to Potiphar's house. Whatever Potiphar might be, he is pragmatic. Knowing a good thing when he sees it, he promotes the Hebrew slave. The biblical text makes it clear that God is behind all of this. Five times in five verses (Gen. 39:2–6) we are reminded that the Lord is with Joseph, blessing him in all he does. Joseph knows it; Potiphar knows it; and so, it seems, does most everyone else.

Everyone, that is, except Potiphar's wife. It is not long before she tries to seduce the master's handsome slave—repeatedly.

The setup for this temptation is classic: Potiphar is away, the opportunity is perfect, and Potiphar's wife tries to break Joseph's resistance through persistent cajoling day after day.

Anticipating by two thousand years St. Paul's advice to "flee from sexual immorality" (1 Cor. 6:18), Joseph scrams. And what is perhaps even more impressive is his theological thinking.

"How can I sin against the Lord," Joseph asks rhetorically, "and do this despicable deed?"

When she is rejected, Potiphar's wife adds duplicity and betrayal to her list of vices when she becomes the woman scorned. Grabbing the toga of the fleeing Joseph, she gleefully twists this evidence when Potiphar returns home.

"That Hebrew slave of yours came in to make sport of me," she weeps, with crocodile tears.

Potiphar is appropriately furious, throwing Joseph into the most secure of political prisons. Yet there is something hollow about Potiphar's response. Wouldn't a man of his power and position simply behead Joseph, impaling his head on a spike outside the gate as a warning to other insolent slaves? It is likely that Potiphar, knowing his wife's character at least as well as we do, sees through her thin explanation and simply gets Joseph out of the picture. Perhaps he even fears offending the God who is behind Joseph's prosperity—and his own.

But for Joseph, it does not matter much. He loses his freedom and his reputation. He ends up in prison.

It is this story of Joseph that came to me years ago as I sat aboard a freighter anchored in that distant Malaysian port. I could identify with Joseph in many ways. Joseph was in a foreign land far from home and family. He was a young, passionate man all alone. Probably no one back home ever would have known what he did. But unlike me, Joseph faced the additional temptation of encountering a woman, probably beautiful and profoundly powerful, who repeatedly and relentlessly gave him opportunity for sexual pleasure. More than that, she could have repaid him with advantages like his freedom. Besides, Joseph had no earthly reason to count on returning home within three months, as I had hoped to do.

So how does Joseph respond to this persistent, powerful woman? He gives her a response she never expects and is least able to refute. And that was the compelling reason for me: I could not sin against my God. To say that I have never struggled with sexual temptation in my life would not be true. But I can truthfully say that sexual pleasure was not a temptation for me on that day. Through Joseph's story, God reminded me that he was present even though my family was not. He assured me that soon I would return to my family and be reunited with the woman I loved and planned to marry. He made me vividly aware that if I made a sinful choice here, I would either live a lie and bear its guilt silently for the rest of my days, or confess it all and live with its ever-persistent shame.

Ultimately, Joseph reminded me then and reminds us today that when we know the Word of God and are in awe of God, we choose to obey God because we love him, and we refuse to disobey him because we honor him. Joseph chose, despite personal consequences, the route of obedience. I suspect he knew exactly what the consequences of his choice would be. A woman with such power and influence would not take rejection easily. Joseph knew it was simply a matter of time before he would be betrayed and perhaps killed. What an amazing faith he had in God!

Prison: Broken Promises and Despair (Genesis 39–40)

In Potiphar's prison, Joseph could have sulked over the deep injustice of his plight. But there is no hint that he does so. Instead, he bends his will to the narrow confines of his cell and becomes a dungeon success story. Twice, we are told, the Lord Yahweh blesses him (Gen. 39:21, 23), and the warden puts him in charge of the other prisoners. Like Potiphar, the warden never worries when Joseph is in charge.

Eventually, two of Pharaoh's officials—his chief butler and chief baker—end up in jail. (Nothing is said, of course, of Pharaoh's chief candlestick maker.) Both men have dreams, fearful their visions foretell something ominous and worried because they cannot decipher their meaning. In desperation, they consult Joseph.

"God is the only one who knows the meaning of dreams," Joseph reminds them, "but the Lord will reveal the secret of your dreams to me."

After the butler tells his vision of the three grape clusters, Joseph makes his prediction. "In three days you'll be released from this dungeon and restored to your former position," Joseph tells him. "And when you're free," he adds with urgency in his voice, "please put in a good word to the king for me."

The butler absentmindedly agrees.

The baker, encouraged by a promising interpretation, tells Joseph his dream too.

"Are you sure you want to know?" Joseph asks him.

"Of course!"

"Okay. You'll be released in three days too, but you have a different destiny. You'll be led straight to the gallows for your hanging. The birds in your dream are the vultures that will consume your rotting corpse."

That kind of news is enough to ruin a person's day!

Both dreams are fulfilled just as Joseph foretold, but the chief butler quickly forgets his oath to help Joseph in the euphoria of his own good fortune. So, for two long years Joseph languishes in prison, an unknown Hebrew slave and, to the outside world, a silent cipher on the prison rolls.

Joseph has every reason to feel self-pity and anger toward the chief butler and toward God. But the biblical text reports neither anger nor suicidal inclination. Amazingly, Joseph excels in the face of a broken promise. How can he carry on? The same way he responds to sexual temptation and family dysfunction. He hears the voice of God, he knows the will of God, and he harbors a holy fear of God.

Have you ever experienced discouragement and despair because someone you trust failed you? Have you ever sensed that God is the one who failed you? Do the heavens seem as unresponsive as brass when you pray, leaving you to wonder whether God cares or whether he is even present? If so, consider Joseph. His faith is a beacon of hope in the darkness of despair.

Pharaoh's Palace:
Recognition and Compromise (Genesis 41)

Eventually it is Pharaoh's turn for disturbing dreams. First, he dreams of seven fat cows emerging from the Nile River followed by seven gaunt cows that devour them. In a second, parallel dream, seven plump ears of corn are consumed by seven withered ears. Already superstitious, Pharaoh worries about the dreams, and court magi offer no acceptable interpretation. Couldn't any magician worth his salt invent some plausible explanation? But perhaps Pharaoh—like King Nebuchadnezzar some fourteen hundred years later—withholds parts of the dream to ensure his magi are on the up and up. That's when the chief butler remembers Joseph.

"Wait," exclaims the butler, almost dropping Pharaoh's favorite cup with excitement. "There's a convict who can interpret visions. He explained my dream when I was in prison two years ago, and he was spot on. His name is Joseph."

So Joseph is dispatched from Potiphar's prison and summoned to Pharaoh's palace—shaved, washed, and appropriately clothed.

When Joseph finally speaks to Pharaoh, he begins with a disclaimer. "I cannot tell you the meaning of your dream," he explains. I'll bet the chief butler quivers in fear during the deadly hush that follows, as Pharaoh's expression turns dark with impatience. "But my God will reveal its meaning to you," Joseph adds, breaking the silence to everyone's relief. "Your two dreams are God's way of telling you what is about to happen. Yahweh has determined that Egypt will enjoy seven years of incredible agricultural prosperity immediately followed by seven years of such utterly devastating famine that no one will even remember the years of plenty."

Then, unbidden, Joseph boldly adds his own advice. "If Pharaoh is wise, he will appoint a capable man to gather and store the abundance of the seven years of prosperity to ensure Egypt will survive the seven years of famine. Just be certain he is capable, trustworthy, and wise or Egypt will be lost."

Pharaoh is no fool. Looking around at his advisors, he points to Joseph. "What better man can we find than this one who can hear the voice of God?" he asks them, not expecting any answer but his own.

In this way Joseph is exalted to the second most powerful position in Egypt and, one might add, in the world. He becomes the prime minister of Egypt at age thirty (Gen. 41:46).

Can you imagine the heady euphoria of success that Joseph must have felt, especially after being enslaved for maybe six years by this time? His pain and disappointment in adversity is replaced by the seductive pull of prosperity and its companion, spiritual compromise.

Scripture cautions us of this danger. "When you sit down to eat with a ruler," the sages of Proverbs warn, "observe carefully what is before you. . . . Do not desire his delicacies, for they are deceptive food" (Prov. 23:1, 3). The application is clear. Powerful, wealthy rulers often have a self-serving agenda. Beware! Their luxurious trappings can lure you into compromise.

Chuck Colson served as President Richard Nixon's White House counsel from 1969 to 1974. He was assigned the task of convincing both friends and foes of the administration to support Nixon's domestic and foreign policies. Colson's strategy was simple and effective. He would invite senators, governors, heads of state, labor union reps, religious leaders, and anyone with political influence to come to the Oval Office and walk the corridors of power with the President of the United States. For many of these leaders, the palpable feeling of power and the exalted sense of importance was enough to convince them to support the administration's agenda.

Colson, who was not a Christian at the time, observed in *Christianity Today* that religious leaders seemed very amenable to this kind of persuasion. The most susceptible to this strategy, he noticed, were evangelical Christian leaders.

By contrast, Joseph is immune to such enticements. He displays this by his repeated references to the sovereign God: "God will give Pharaoh a favorable answer" (Gen. 41:16); "God has revealed to Pharaoh what he is about to do" (twice, Gen. 41:25, 28); and "the thing is fixed by God, and God will shortly bring it about" (Gen. 41:32).

Joseph knows the Word of God, hears the voice of God, and possesses the fear of God. It shapes his way of seeing the world, even amid the adulation of Pharaoh's court. He simply is not impressed.

Prime Minister of Egypt: Power and Pride (Genesis 41)

Elevated to Egypt's second-in-command, Joseph receives the trappings of power: the signet ring, the royal wardrobe, the gold necklace of office. He even has access to Chariot Force Two, before which people bow when he drives by. Heady stuff for a thirty-year-old.

The potential obstacle here is pride. We know Joseph attributes his ability to interpret dreams to God alone. Plus, he never chalks Egypt's economic survival up to his own wise efforts. The Lord is never far from Joseph's mind during these nine years of intense activity—seven years of plenty and two years into the famine. Joseph names his two sons Manasseh ("God has made me forget all my hardship," Gen. 41:51) and Ephraim ("God has made me fruitful in the land of my affliction," Gen. 41:52). Joseph not only remembers the Lord; he also reflects thankfully on God's gracious provision for him even in faraway Egypt.

Joseph's Faithfulness Scale

Joseph's faithfulness to God does not follow the ups and downs of his experience. Instead, through consistently wise choices, Joseph's spiritual health rises steadily, as the graph below shows. Remember! Joseph hears the voice of God. He knows the Word of God. He possesses a fear of God.

Joseph's Faithfulness Scale

Gen. 37	Gen. 39	Gen. 39–40	Gen. 41	Gen. 41
Prophecy & the Pit:	Potiphar's Place:	Prison: *Broken Promises*	Pharaoh's Palace:	Prime Minister:
Betrayal	*Injustice*		*Recognition*	*Power*

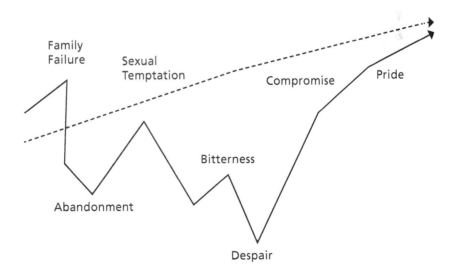

Joseph's Spiritual Marathon: Hitting the Wall

At twenty-six miles and 385 yards, the marathon is a race that sets the standard for endurance running. It requires months of intensive training, including a couple of nineteen- to twenty-two-mile practice runs and a carefully monitored "taper down" period to rebuild the body's reserves before the big event. Even with the best of training, though, the human body in a marathon uses up its stored energy reserves around mile twenty. That is when many runners "hit the wall." Your legs feel like rubber, and your energy simply evaporates. You can consume all the water or high energy gels you want, but all you really want to do is curl up and sleep. It takes determination just to put one foot in front of the other, let alone complete the remaining miles to the finish line. Having run five marathons, I've learned never to take the race lightly, always remaining mentally prepared for hitting the wall.

Joseph faces one of the greatest challenges of his life near the end of his career. Just when he thinks he's conquered every difficulty and leaped every hurdle, Joseph faces a new situation: his ten brothers walk into his life (Gen. 42). In the life of faith, he is about to hit the wall!

Joseph's brothers travel from Canaan to Egypt, the only place where they can buy grain during the great famine. Soon they stand before the one in charge of selling the grain, Joseph, but without recognizing their brother. Joseph is no longer a helpless young man wailing from the bottom of a dark well. He is now the second most powerful man in the realm. He can exact the sweetest and most appropriate revenge.

Joseph "Hitting the Wall"

Gen. 37	Gen. 39	Gen. 39–40	Gen. 41	Gen. 41
Prophecy & the Pit:	Potiphar's Place:	Prison: *Broken Promises*	Pharaoh's Palace:	Prime Minister:
Betrayal	*Injustice*		*Recognition*	*Power*

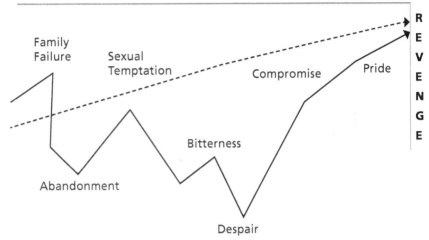

So what does Joseph do? First, he subjects his brothers to a few excruciating tests to make sure they now value honesty and family loyalty. His brothers' compliant actions (Gen. 43–44) and Judah's speech (Gen. 44:14–34) strongly suggest they do. Ultimately Joseph resists the temptation for personal revenge and confers a blessing on his brothers (Gen. 45).

Joseph passes the final test of his faith like a champion. Again, his reasons are theological. He is realistic enough to recognize that his brothers intended evil many years ago; but he is spiritually keen enough to understand that God, perfect in goodness and power, uses even human wickedness to work all things together for good. Rather than revenge, Joseph works to reunite his scattered and contentious family.

A Theology of Revenge

Why does revenge feel so sweet? Why are we drawn to films and stories where the bad guy gets it in the end? Perhaps it is because revenge can sometimes resemble true justice. But make no mistake—it is only a clever counterfeit that we must resist. The Bible gives us a number of principles of responding to revenge, listed in the chart below.

Responding to Revenge

Passage	Principle
Matthew 5:38–42	The "Other Cheek" Principle
Matthew 5:43–48	The "Sunshine" Principle
Romans 12:17–21	The "Coals of Fire" Principle
Genesis 50:18–21	The "Joseph" Principle

First, Jesus teaches, "If anyone slaps you on the right cheek, turn to him the other also" (Matt. 5:39). This "other cheek" principle has nothing to do with self-defense. It speaks of being insulted, not assaulted. Striking someone on the right cheek usually requires a back-handed slap since most people are right-handed. We are not to demand a pound of flesh for an insult. Instead, we are to respond as Jesus does to his tormentors. Turn the other cheek. Don't give place to bitterness. Reject revenge.

Second, Jesus admonishes, "Love your enemies and pray for those who persecute you" (Matt. 5:44). Why? Because that's what our heavenly Father does. Certainly every sinner deserves immediate judgment, but often God shows compassion and patience instead. He allows the sun to shine and the rain to fall on the crops of the wicked as well as the righteous. So, should we hate our enemies, as some Pharisees taught? No. The "sunshine" principle tells to show mercy. We are to be like our heavenly Dad!

Third, the Apostle Paul expresses the "coals of fire" principle when he warns against revenge. "Vengeance is mine," Paul reminds us, "I will repay, says the Lord" (Rom. 12:19). There are some things only God must do; vengeance is one of them. If you get trapped in the vengeance spiral, you will become the very person you seek to repay. Furthermore, revenge shuts down the opportunity for loving restoration. That, I believe, is the significance of "coals of fire." If you return good for evil, people wishing you harm will feel the burning shame of their malice against the backdrop of your kindness. In turn, they may repent. So we must not play God. Instead, we should avoid becoming as evil-minded as the one who offended us and should never close the avenue for loving restoration.

Fourth, the "Joseph" principle teaches us to trust the sovereignty of God. After Jacob dies and is buried in Canaan, Joseph's brothers are understandably terrified, reasoning that with their father out of the way Joseph will exact the revenge they so richly deserve. So they revert to old patterns of lying for self-preservation (Gen. 50:15–21).

"Joseph," they say by messenger, "your father Jacob pled that you forgive us for all our wrong doing."

Joseph weeps as he reads it. How little they know him! How little they know his God!

Gathering them together, Joseph reassures them. "Don't be afraid!" he says. "Am I in God's place? True enough, you meant evil toward me, but God meant it for good. I may be the prime minister of Egypt, but I do not play God."

Neither must we.

Joseph's faith is liberating, isn't it? Biblical faith is like that. It frees us from vengeance, as enticing and sweet as it masquerades to be. And when we forgive someone who has committed a terrible wrong against us—really forgiving them, understanding that the Lord is God—then we are free indeed.

Crossing the Tape

Like the other unlikely heroes of Hebrews 11, Joseph is a man of hope. Before he dies, he arranges for his body to be embalmed, Egyptian style, and entombed in Egypt until the family moves as a people back to Canaan, God's land of promise. Despite all his success, Joseph remembers this life is not all there is (Heb. 11:22).

Joseph teaches us that the life of faith, like a steeplechase, requires trusting God through the obstacles of both adversity and prosperity. It demands obeying God despite the soul-wrenching hurdles of family betrayal, sexual temptation, bitterness, despair, compromise, and pride.

Joseph also demonstrates that in living by faith we, like a marathon runner, may hit a spiritual wall. But faith recognizes God's good purpose in all things, even when we may thirst for vengeance. We can overcome the "wall" and finish the race.

Yes, Joseph is the most unlikely, unlikely hero of faith. But the resources he uses—knowing the Word of God, hearing the voice of God, and harboring a holy fear of God—are ours too.

PART 3

THE PIONEERS

CHAPTER 13

MOSES:
THE UNLIKELY LIBERATOR

The Power of a Simple Choice

Choices, even small ones, can have huge consequences. I'll never forget a small decision I made as a college sophomore—just a miscalculation, really—that would change my life forever.

Earlier I related my plan to hitchhike one summer throughout Europe. I made another decision that spring. Since I intended to apply to law school when I graduated, I decided I would transfer from Westmont College to Willamette University in Oregon the next fall to increase my chances of admission to their law school. At the end of spring term, I packed all my belongings and bid adieu to my college friends in California. This included a farewell to a girl I had dated with hopes for a deeper relationship. Our last goodbye was, I thought at the time, especially warm. In early June I boarded my charter flight from Los Angeles to begin my European adventure.

In mid-July, somewhere in southern Italy, I realized my mistake. I would return to the States two weeks after Willamette began classes. I had planned my European itinerary on Westmont's term schedule, in which classes began in late September. Willamette, however, was on a semester system, and classes began in late August. The prospect of beginning upper-division classes two weeks late at a new university where I knew no students or faculty was daunting. But with no flexibility in my charter flight schedule, I would have to ante up airfare for a different flight home—resources I did not have.

So I decided to return to Westmont in the fall after all. In mid-September I stepped onto Westmont's campus for the first day of classes, greeted by my surprised friends. What I'll never forget is seeing the girl I had dated. The expression on her face said it all: when she said goodbye in June, she meant goodbye!

But within a month after my return, I met a young college coed named Jani, and by October 31 we had our first date. Because of a simple decision based on a seemingly trivial miscalculation, I fell in love with the woman who became my life partner. I bear happy witness that choices—even small, erroneous ones—can have huge, life-changing consequences.

Moses' Family: Unlikely Destinies

Moses' parents are unlikely heroes who make a courageous choice. Their names, Amram and Jochebed, are given neither in the Hebrews passage nor in Exodus where their story is told. We only learn them later, tucked away in Moses' genealogy (Exod. 6:20). In fact, the entire narrative of Moses' first forty years, from his birth to the burning bush, is recounted in a single, compact chapter (Exod. 2).

Amram and Jochebed seem ordinary when we meet them. Members of a slave community, they are new parents to their first son (and second child) and, like most parents, believe him to be the most beautiful baby on earth. Learning that their baby is to be killed, they hide him as long as possible and then release him with the hope that somehow, someway he will survive.

Moses himself is clearly exceptional. God's providential hand protects him from early death, guides his floating bulrush cradle into the royal palace, and sets him on what seems to be a course of political greatness. Eighty years later, Moses faces down the mighty Pharaoh, leads his people on the exodus from Egyptian slavery, and humbly guides a contentious people through forty years of miraculous provision. He is forever known as Israel's great Lawgiver who speaks with God like two old friends in easy conversation.

But Moses missteps, too. His youthful brashness leads him to commit murder. Consequently, he is shunned by the very people he longs to deliver, forced into a lonely, forty-year exile. He marries a Gentile woman who angrily calls him a "bridegroom of blood" (Exod. 4:25), and later suffers grief from his own siblings for his interracial marriage (Num. 12:1). Repeatedly criticized for inept leadership, Moses ultimately forfeits, through his own disobedience to God, his lifelong goal of entering the Promised Land.

Five Life-Changing Choices of Faith

The biblical narrative of Moses' life is vast and rich, spanning the last four books of the Pentateuch. We will consider the five courageous choices made by Moses, his parents, and the Israelites, each mentioned in Hebrews 11 and introduced by the familiar phrase "by faith." These choices are displayed in the chart below.

Five Life-Changing Choices

Unlikely Heroes	Choice	
	Description	*Focus*
His Parents (Heb. 11:23)	1. A New Authority	To obey God over Pharaoh
Moses (Heb. 11:24–26)	2. A New Allegiance	To share mistreatment with God's people
Moses (Heb. 11:27)	3. A New Assignment	To accept the Sinai wilderness over Egyptian slavery
Moses (Heb. 11:28)	4. A New Atonement	To keep the Passover with its sprinkled blood
The People (Heb. 11:29)	5. A New Adventure	To pass through the Red Sea

Let's examine these choices in detail, with an eye to their application to us.

1. Moses' Parents Choose a New Authority

Pharaoh issues an edict of infanticide. All male offspring of this growing slave population, he decrees, are to be killed. To carry this out effectively, he conscripts the Egyptian Midwives Union as his executioners.

"What better way to implement my plan than to use trusted, mothering midwives?" Pharaoh muses, smiling at his own cleverness. "Soldiers would only raise alarm. Midwives can inconspicuously kill the boys during delivery, say it was a hard birth, and no one will know the difference."

The faith of the midwives, named Shiphrah and Puah, is a breathtaking story (Exod. 1:15–22). Pharaoh personally gives them their ghoulish assignment, probably to discourage any disobedience. But surprisingly they conspire to disobey Pharaoh and deceive him. And their plan works.

"Those Hebrew mothers are just too healthy," they report, their eyes round with sincerity. "By the time we arrive, they have already delivered, and we have no access to the newborn. What else can we do?"

Furious, Pharaoh declares an all-out genocide on Hebrew male infants. Yet he accepts the midwives' story with little investigation, and we are privy to the reason why. These women fear the Lord and obey him; and, though they likely expect to die, God favors them with both life and prosperity.

Moses' parents face a similar choice: should they obey God or Pharaoh? Will they disobey a king who would not blink at slaying anyone who defies him? Although nothing is more primal than the fear of death, they are undeterred. They choose, like the Egyptian midwives, to disobey the mighty Pharaoh (Heb. 11:23).

Amram and Jochebed's motivation is pragmatic: they simply want to save their beautiful son. Nothing is stronger than a mother's love for her child, not even death. Of course, the couple may view Moses' unusual beauty as an indication of divine favor, believing that this boy is destined by God for something great. But whatever the reason, they are willing to risk their lives to hide their son, rejecting the king's edict and opting to obey the living God.

The story plays out three months later when Moses' parents can quiet the growing child no longer. Compelled to act, Jochebed weaves the bulrush basket, waterproofs it, settles Moses in this floating cradle, and posts Miriam, Moses' sister, as sentry when the basket is set adrift. Pharaoh's daughter (who names him Moses, a name that sounds like "draws out") pulls the baby from the crocodile-ridden Nile and raises him as her royal son. This only convinces Jochebed that God is at work. That she is paid to nurse him until he is weaned (Exod. 2:7–10) is grace beyond measure!

Let's examine two applications of this story. First, a clear application of Moses' parents' choice to disobey Pharaoh is political: obey the King of kings over any human king. This lesson is found throughout the Old Testament in examples like Daniel, who defies the edict of Darius, the Persian king, by praying to God (Dan. 6); and his three Hebrew companions, who worship God rather than Nebuchadnezzar's golden image (Dan. 3).

Jesus succinctly clarifies this principle, explaining, "Render to Caesar the things that are Caesar's, and to God the things that are God's" (Matt. 22:21). He affirms that the boundaries of human authority come from God alone. Any political leader stepping beyond those boundaries operates outside divine parameters.

Jesus' words form the basis for civil disobedience. We may disobey a governmental decree or a king when obedience would violate our higher allegiance to the law of God. However, we must still retain the honor, respect, and submission toward human government that God requires. As we saw in an earlier chapter, submission is deeper than obedience; it is an underlying attitude of respect. One can obey someone without respecting them, of course, and sometimes it becomes necessary to disobey for conscientious reasons. In those cases, one must disobey only with respectful submission.

A second application is practical. Often we Christ-followers do not show biblical respect for our political leaders. We talk ill about the president of the United States, especially if he is not of our political party. But if Paul can refer to Emperor Nero as "God's servant for your good" (Rom. 13:4), we should speak carefully and respectfully of our nation's leaders whether they share our political persuasions or not.

Let me suggest an antidote to political disrespect. Pray for your president, your senators and congressmen, and your state and local officials. God tells us to. When you do, you may discover, like me, that it is impossible to gossip, criticize, or ridicule someone you pray for sincerely. And while you're at it, pray for your elders and pastors, your bosses and supervisors, your coworkers, and your teachers. And if you still have time, pray for your enemies (Matt. 5:44)!

2. Moses Chooses a New Allegiance

The second choice of faith is made by Moses, who opts for ill-treatment with Israel over treasures in Egypt (Heb. 11:24–26). His is not a choice to overcome fear but one to resist temptation. What led to this choice?

We know little about Moses' early life growing up in Pharaoh's court. Did he shave his head Yul Brynner–style and race chariots, or is he taciturn and withdrawn? Is he being groomed for the Egyptian throne, or does he face anti-Semitic opposition? His ability to write the Pentateuch suggests he is tutored and well educated by the most elite Egyptian scholars in writing, law, and ancient lore. Does he learn how to lead military maneuvers with the skill of a general? What lessons in leadership does he learn from the mighty Pharaoh? What medical arts does he gain from the court magicians? Raised in the lap of luxury, does he accept his opulent living in his youth as a burden or as his due? Does Miriam or Jochebed visit him in the palace, even as his father, Amram, labors as a slave in the brickyard? And as to the plight of his people, does he seethe in powerless frustration or suddenly awaken to their misery out of a cloud of apathy?

One of Moses' great temptations is the potent allure of sin. According to Hebrews, he refuses three kinds of temptations. First, he rejects the temptation of position, refusing to be called the son of Pharaoh's daughter. Likely, he rejects neither her love nor her kindness but rather declines the opportunities of power and influence that this designation could give him and ultimately Israel.

"Joseph accepted a high position from Pharaoh," he could have reasoned, "and look how God used him to preserve the nation!"

But Moses recognizes that God's plans for each person are uniquely tailor-made. I suspect Moses fully discovers just how different this plan is in the crucible of the Sinai desert while he shepherds flocks for Jethro, his father-in-law.

The second temptation Moses refuses is the pleasure of sin, choosing instead ill-treatment with God's people. Make no mistake about it. Sin is enticing. It allures. What's so subtle is that none of us are enticed in the same ways. Each of us has our own areas of vulnerability.

For example, merchant seamen have a well-earned reputation for profanity and drunkenness. After we arrived in port, most crew members headed straight for the nearest bar, always inviting me to come along. When I declined, they may have assumed I had tremendous will power. But actually it did not take a lot of brains to realize that drunkenness in a foreign port was not a bright idea. Watching a young coworker return one night drunk, badly beaten, missing teeth, and robbed of four hundred dollars in cash reinforced for me the stupidity of alcohol abuse. Seeing crewmates writhe in the pain of sexually transmitted disease did the same for prostitution.

Of course, there are sins that do entice me, that pull me away from God. The same is true for you. We must never take a moral vacation but always remember Paul's caution, "If you think you can stand alone, watch out! Failure may be around the corner."

The third temptation that Moses dismisses is the lure of possessions. The archeological discoveries in Egypt over the last two centuries illuminate the vastness and value of this wealth Moses spurned. But spurn them he did. Later, when the people whine to return to Egypt for a cup of onion soup, Moses drops no hint he regrets his decision.

And what motivates Moses to reject the best wealth Egypt has to offer? Hebrews suggests his motives are eschatological and Christological (Heb. 11:26).

Eschatologically, he seeks an eternal reward, like Abraham did. Discontent to reign as Pharaoh of Egypt, he seeks to serve the God of Israel. Dissatisfied with sinful pleasures, he longs for lasting happiness and joy.

Christologically, Moses trades the treasures of Egypt for the "reproach" of Christ, knowing he gets the far better bargain. How can he know this? I imagine some clarity emerges as he pens the *Protoevangelium* (Gen. 3:15), the substitution for Isaac's sacrifice (Gen. 22), the Passover (Exod. 12), the scapegoat (Lev. 16), and his own face-to-face conversations with the Lord on Mount Sinai (Exod. 33). Later, the picture becomes nearly complete for Moses when he stands with Jesus and Elijah on the Transfiguration Mount, speaking of Calvary (Luke 9:30).

Above all, what Moses really chooses over all these temptations is community—identifying with and leading God's people. Moses puts aside position, pleasure, and possessions to identify with God's chosen people.

Do we put aside these things to identify with God's people, the Lord's church? The people of God are indispensable for our protection and vital for our spiritual growth. Our connection to one another is fundamental and organic. We cannot be connected to the Head of the body and remain disconnected from the rest of his body, the church. Moses encourages us to make associating with God's people a habit of our lives.

3. Moses Chooses a New Assignment

The third choice of faith is when Moses leaves Egypt for Midian's desert (Heb. 11:27). This choice entails his flight from Egypt after murdering an Egyptian and his encounter with Yahweh at the burning bush.

At age forty, Moses awakens to the plight of his people when he spots an Egyptian master mercilessly beating a Hebrew slave (Exod. 2:11). "I'll solve this problem here and now," he vows. An impetuous, powerful man, he slays the Egyptian and furtively hides his body in the sand.

Later, while Moses is trying to settle a dispute between Hebrew brothers, they rebuke him. "Oh," says one of the men with a knowing smirk, "are you going to murder us like that poor wretch you left half-buried in the desert?"

Realizing Pharaoh knows his secret, and finding little welcome among his kinsmen, Moses wisely leaves town.

Unwittingly, Moses enters God's forty-year wilderness training program. The Lord gets Moses out of Egypt so he can get Egypt out of Moses! In Midian, Moses begins to shepherd sheep. He learns lessons from the twin mentors of silence and solitude. And for forty years Moses comes to feel at home in the kind of terrain in which he will lead recalcitrant Israelites for another forty years.

In the desert Moses undoubtedly faces the frustration of delay. How did he surmount this? "He endured," we are told, "as seeing him who is invisible" (Heb. 11:27). This refers to God audibly speaking to Moses from the burning bush, a theophany. This vision changes his world. When he returns to Egypt, he appears fearless and purposeful, empowered by the living God.

Do you ever feel like Moses, impatient that life is passing you by? Perhaps you're in a dead-end job leading to nowhere. Perhaps you're in school, even studying the Bible at Multnomah University, but you long to finish so you can put all you've learned into action. Perhaps you are caring for an aging parent or a special-needs child and feel the burden of unending responsibilities.

When I completed my master's degree at seminary, I felt like that. Sensing God's direction toward seminary teaching, I realized I needed to earn a doctorate. But having started late in seminary, in my mind at least, I wrestled with what to do. So I sought advice from one of my professors whom I respected greatly as a scholar, a pastor, and a man of God.

He simply asked, "How old are you?"

When I told him, he took out his pen and made some calculations on paper.

"Well," he said, looking up, "you'll be about thirty years old when you complete your doctorate."

Good grief, I thought, *I'll be over the hill!*

He looked at me for a long time before flashing me a smile. "Dan," he said finally, "you'll still be a very young man."

His words shaped my life. I was looking at it from the standpoint of a twenty-seven-year-old, thinking, *I got to get going. I'm wasting my life.* He had the perspective of decades of actively ministering God's Word.

Do you get frustrated over delay? Moses did—for forty years! Remember, your training here on earth is but for a lifetime. Be willing to follow God's custom-designed training program for as long as it takes.

4. Moses Chooses a New Atonement

The fourth choice of faith is Moses' decision to keep the Passover, with its strange sprinkling of blood ritual (Heb. 11:28). By doing so, Moses chooses the death of an animal over the death of a son (Exod. 11–12).

The new leader of Israel returns from forty years of preparation ready to lead. When he commands Pharaoh to release God's people, Pharaoh's heart hardens. The king and his nation experience nine excruciating plagues, but still, as God foretold, he balks.

"I've got one more plague to show Pharaoh," God tells Moses after he is banned from Pharaoh's presence. "This will break him. He will finally learn that I am God, the only Lord."

"But listen!" God warns. "All Israel must prepare a Passover Seder which they will eat hastily, ready for departure. Be sure they sprinkle the blood of the lamb for the meal on the door-frame of each house, doorposts and lintel. My death angel will visit Egypt that night to take the life of each firstborn son of every household. Only those families protected by the blood will be delivered. The angel will pass over them unharmed."

Moses obeys God to the letter. He never hesitates. But it's easy to imagine others might because the whole ritual seems so unbelievable.

"God wouldn't kill all the firstborn children, would he?" some Israelites ask. "Certainly he wouldn't touch us after all we've been through. After all, we're his people, children of the great covenant."

"And he's protected us from the last five plagues," adds another. "Surely, it's that monster Pharaoh he's after."

"You mean we're to put the lamb's blood on our doorframes?" asks a third. "What possible connection exists between animal blood and my son's life? It's just so, so irrational!"

Such comments are reminiscent of Paul, when he explains that the cross of Jesus is "a stumbling block to Jews and folly to Gentiles" (1 Cor. 1:23). Blood on the doorposts does seem foolish. But it is God's way by which the life of each firstborn in the household could be saved.

Many people think the gospel of Jesus Christ is either too simple or too ridiculous. Every other religion is based on salvation by works. By contrast, Christianity offers a salvation based solely on the work of God. It asks you simply to believe God's promise.

Moses makes a redemptive choice to obey God's plan even though it seems nonsensical. He knows God well enough to take him at his word. As you proclaim the good news, keep the simple, gracious message of redemption clear. Don't dilute it. Don't add to it. Don't muffle it. Proclaim it with boldness and power.

5. The People Choose a New Adventure

The final life-changing choice of faith is the Israelites' decision to cross the Red Sea (Heb. 11:29). The decision is forced by the impending danger of an attacking army, but in the end the people stand in awe of God. Wedged between Pharaoh's army and the Red Sea, the Israelites are motivated by the hope of the Promised Land. In a word, they choose the adventure of a lifetime.

Hebrews tells us the people act "by faith," but it certainly does not start out that way. Departing from Egypt, with living firstborn sons beside them and Egyptian spoils in their saddlebags, the Israelites are rerouted from the faster but dangerous northern Philistine route to the less hostile but longer southern road into Sinai. God guides them with a strange pillar of cloud and fire (the angel of the Lord, another theophany, Exod. 14:19, 24). As a diversion, God leads them directly beside the Red Sea while hardening the hearts of Pharaoh and his army one last time. The Egyptians advance within eyeshot of the trapped Israelites. The pillar of fire positions itself between the two opposing companies, providing a hedge of protection for the long, dark night.

The Israelites are anything but heroes here. They panic, turning to Moses with harsh complaints. Moses bravely calms them but appeals quietly to the Lord. God's purposes here are deeper and more meaningful than simple deliverance. Three times he emphasizes he will gain eternal "glory" over the arrogant Pharaoh (Exod. 14:4, 17, 18).

When morning breaks, the pillar advances over the sea, Moses stretches his rod, and the east wind blows the waves apart. Both companies act by their own faith. Israel, trusting in God, steps into the dry seabed. The Egyptians, trusting in Pharaoh and his six hundred charioteers, enter the sea, panicking when the waves crash behind them and their wheels clog with mud. They are doomed and they know it. Not one survives.

When Israel sees the bodies of the drowned Egyptians, they fear the Lord and believe in him and in his servant Moses. They begin at the west edge of the Red Sea fearful and doubtful, but they obey the Lord's command. They emerge on the other side with a new confidence in the Lord their God.

Theirs is a faith driven by necessity and confirmed by physical evidence, but it is faith just the same. The Red Sea crossing and the Passover Seder remain the two pivotal Exodus events that Scripture repeatedly cites as evidence of the powerful, redeeming hand of God. These events are the Israelites' stake in the ground to remind them of God's power as they continue their adventure with God in the wilderness.

Unlikely Crossroads

Let's review the five critical choices, these five remarkable crossroads. The choice itself, the potential obstacle to a wise choice, the motivation to faithful obedience, and the implicit reward are summarized in the following chart.

Five Life-Changing Choices

Unlikely Heroes	Choice	Potential Obstacle	Motivation	Reward
His Parents (Heb. 11:23)	To obey God over Pharaoh	Fear of their own death	To save their beautiful boy	A new leader
Moses (Heb. 11:24–26)	To share mistreatment with God's people	Appeal of temporal, sinful pleasures	To receive spiritual treasures, not earthly ones	A new community
Moses (Heb. 11:27)	To accept the wilderness over Egypt's luxury	Fear of Pharaoh's anger	To please the God who called him	A theophany
Moses (Heb. 11:28)	To keep the Passover with its sprinkled blood	Fear of the irrational	To save the lives of Israel's firstborn	The Exodus from Egypt
The People (Heb. 11:29)	To pass through the Red Sea	Fear of the impossible	To escape the armies of Pharaoh	The Promised Land

Remember, too, our applications.

- A *new authority* calls us to obey God rather than man, doing so in ways that honor our leaders even if we must follow God's Word.

- A *new allegiance* reminds us to live in community with other believers, a richness far beyond temporal position, pleasure, or possessions.

- A *new assignment* signals to us that our unique calling may require following God's training regimen with its particular timetable.
- A *new atonement* enjoins us to proclaim and live out God's redemptive message of grace in a world that often defaults to legalism.
- A *new adventure* encourages us to embrace the life of faith, not as a dull duty, but as a divine adventure.

Moses, his parents, and his people all make choices that change the course of their lives. His adventure leads him through the wilderness to the top of Mount Sinai where he receives God's Law. Ultimately he joins Jesus on the Mount of Transfiguration. We who follow Christ can follow the example set by Moses, the unlikely liberator, knowing that it will lead to the ultimate adventure, the life of faith in God culminating on Mount Zion.

CHAPTER 14

RAHAB:

THE UNLIKELY ALLY

Three Responses to God

Often it is the people you least expect who respond to God. Nowhere in literature is this more clearly illustrated than in Victor Hugo's classic novel, *Les Misérables*. My daughter Elise has been captivated by this story ever since we first saw the Broadway musical on its Portland tour. Inspired by the story, Elise gave the following perspective in her high school valedictorian address.

> In 1985, a great London musical play was created from Victor Hugo's masterpiece, *Les Misérables*. The director, Trevor Nunn, realized more than anyone the spiritual nature of this story. And on the first day, when he gathered the cast together for rehearsal, he looked at them solemnly and said, "You must remember, above all, this

play is deeply religious." Nunn was right. Three of the main characters of Hugo's novel represent three ways in which people respond to God.

First, there is Thénardier, the innkeeper who represents the atheist—as godless a man as one could ever find. He's a cheat, a liar, and a thief. He will resort to anything, even murder, to gain the upper hand. In one scene of the play, Thénardier, deep in the Paris sewers, is robbing dead corpses of jewelry, finger rings, and gold teeth. Does he have any fear of divine retribution? Absolutely not! "God is dead," he sings in an appalling soliloquy. The only thing that looks down on him, he believes, is the harvest moon. Unfortunately, he represents the way so many think of God.

The second major character is Javert, the police inspector who hounds Hugo's hero throughout the story, totally committed to upholding the law. Himself illegitimate and born in a jail cell, Javert begins to worship the law as he grows to adulthood. Eventually, he becomes the personification of the law, a man without compassion, without mercy, with only justice. He represents the legalist's response to God. In fact, when Valjean extends mercy to him, it is so incomprehensible that he chooses suicide.

Finally, there's Jean Valjean, the hero of the play. His story begins as he is paroled after twenty years of hard labor in prison, emerging as an embittered ex-con, unable to secure work and hounded from village to village. He finally resorts to thievery, stealing from the one compassionate person he meets—a bishop. In the middle of the night, Valjean slips from the house with the silver plate only to be apprehended by the police. As they drag him before the bishop, hoping for the testimony that will put him away again, the cleric says, to everyone's surprise, "No, I gave these to him." And then, handing Valjean his silver candlesticks, he asks, "Would you leave the best behind?"

Flabbergasted, the old ex-con hears the bishop add, "I have bought your soul for God." Jean Valjean, the hardened thief, is redeemed that night. From that point on he chooses the path of redemption, and every choice he makes is governed by compassion and mercy.

That's why I say it's often the people you least expect who respond to the grace of God.

Of all the unlikely men and women of faith we have considered, perhaps the character with the most unexpected response of faith in God is Rahab the harlot. Hebrews 11 makes only two references to Israel's conquest period: the destruction of Jericho's walls (Heb. 11:30) and the faith of Rahab in hiding Joshua's spies (Heb. 11:31). Since only Rahab is named, we will study her life as if she submitted her resume to us to become a woman of faith. We will carefully review her work experience, her greatest achievements, her most challenging decisions, and her expected compensation from the perspective that she is an unlikely candidate for spiritual success. Then we will draw a principle of faith that punctuates each aspect of her story.

Rahab's Unlikely Work Experience

When we speak of unlikely heroes, Rahab surely heads the list. Consider the following two significant strikes against her.

The Wrong Nation

First, Rahab, whose story is told in Joshua 2 and 6, belongs to the wrong political party and ethnic class. She is a loyalist to the king of Jericho and a Canaanite. In a word, she is a citizen of the wrong nation.

Moses leads the Israelites for forty years to Moab, where Joshua becomes their new commander. Joshua's divine mission is to lead the armies of Israel's twelve tribes across the Jordan River into Canaan to conquer it. His divine mandate is to destroy every man, woman, and child in the land.

Why on earth does God order this, many wonder. Let me suggest two possible answers to a difficult question.

First, the Canaanite religion is infectiously depraved. Ancient Canaanite texts confirm, in X-rated language, exactly what and how perverse these practices are. Linking sexual immorality with religious rituals to legitimize temple prostitution becomes a virulent moral virus contaminating anyone, or any nation, it touches. How easy it is to justify the basest sexual lusts when you are simply worshipping your god! Since the Lord brings his people out of Egypt to become a holy nation, the Promised Land in which they will dwell must be cleansed of these abominable practices.

Was God unwise or unloving in doing this? Israel's subsequent history of disobedience in the period of the judges tells the tale. As Israel disobeys God's command, she is infected by idolatry, temple prostitution, and even child sacrifice for centuries. God, in wisdom and in love, knows that infections must be destroyed or they will continue to spread.

Second, God gives the Canaanites four hundred long years to repent. That's the timeline he tells Abraham in predicting the number of years of Israel's bondage in Egypt (Gen. 15:13). Why four hundred years? God explains that the sin of the Amorites, one of the major tribes in Canaan, is not yet complete (Gen. 15:16). Our longsuffering Lord grants them four hundred years to turn from their vile practices. But by the time of the Exodus, there is no repentance, and God's judgment will delay no longer.

Rahab is a daughter of this culture. She's even named after a Canaanite god. She lives prominently as a harlot in the wall of the city of Jericho, the first target on Joshua's military agenda.

The Wrong Occupation

Second, Rahab has the moral stain of being a prostitute. According to Jewish tradition, Rahab is one of the four most beautiful women in history (along with Sarah, Bathsheba, and Esther). Significantly, some rabbinic traditions question whether she is a harlot at all, suggesting instead that she is some kind of official, royal hostess. Proponents cite the king's envoys inquiring about the spies' whereabouts (Josh. 2:2–3) as evidence that Rahab has an official responsibility to alert the king of any strangers visiting Jericho. Other interpreters, wondering why Joshua's spies are visiting a brothel, suggest Rahab simply ran a hotel built into the city wall. But there is no ambiguity in the Greek word that the New Testament uses to describe Rahab. The word *porne* means harlot, and it means just what it says. That's what she is, whether it's her primary occupation or something she does on the side.

But do not miss the important principle. The life of faith is available to anyone regardless of their reputation, their nationality, or their prior lifestyle. Despite the national and occupational strikes against her, Rahab the harlot embraces the God of Israel and becomes a woman of faith. God chooses people not on merit but on grace. If this were not true, Rahab could never qualify. Neither could we.

Do you ever feel disqualified from blessing because of something in your past, or present? Think of Rahab. God's blessing is based on grace. If he can forgive a prostitute in an immoral, godless nation, he can forgive you.

Rahab's Unlikely Achievements

Rahab plays an unlikely but important role in Israel's victory over Jericho (Josh. 2). But her brave action in hiding the spies is only the tip of the iceberg of her faith. To understand the depth of it, we must examine not only her actions but also her bargain with the spies and her motives behind it.

Rahab's Actions

Joshua deploys two spies to scout the enemy; they lodge at Rahab's hotel. Hearing two strangers have arrived, the king dispatches envoys to Rahab.

"Look, we know some Israelite spies are here," they say pointedly. "Hand them over!"

"Yes, they *were* here," Rahab responds lightly. "Didn't know they were Israelites. In fact, I couldn't tell just where they were from. I only figured they weren't from these parts." Then she lowers her voice. "Unfortunately, you missed them. They slipped out the front gate just before nightfall. But I think you could catch them if you start now. They didn't seem in a big rush."

What the envoys don't know is that Rahab has hidden the spies on her roof, under the linens. She acts boldly to protect the enemy spies in her house and lies to the king. She does not merely make some tough ethical choices. She becomes a co-conspirator.

We may wonder why Joshua even sends the spies. Didn't he learn from Moses forty years earlier that spies can get you into trouble? After all, if God assures the victory, why send out scouts? The reason is that Joshua is simply doing his job. Throughout the Canaanite conquest, Joshua uses sound military tactics—many ordered by the Lord—which never are deemed as wasted human effort detached from faith. Divine providence and human responsibility are everywhere compatible in these accounts.

Ironically, Joshua sends only two spies, and anonymous ones at that. His purpose is not to satisfy the twelve tribes but to gain military intelligence. Just as he and Caleb were enough to report the facts to Moses, two are ample for Joshua.

Rahab's Motives

The core of Rahab's story lies in Scripture's candid insight into her faith (Josh. 2:8–14). In this arresting passage where she requests the spies' protection, she reveals her startling spiritual transformation. Consider the four steps of her transformation in the following chart.

Rahab's Spiritual Transformation

Rahab's Heart	Yahweh's Character
1. What she knew (Josh. 2:9)	The purpose of Yahweh
2. What she heard (Josh. 2:10)	The power of Yahweh
3. What she felt (Josh. 2:11a)	The fear of Yahweh
4. What she believed (Josh. 2:11b)	The lordship of Yahweh

First, Rahab hears the rumors, probably better than most from her vantage point in the city wall. She knows that Yahweh (notice how she uses his personal name) intends to give Israel the land, which terrifies every citizen in the region.

Second, Rahab knows the rumors are rooted in recent history. Yahweh miraculously brings his people through the mighty Red Sea and utterly destroys two fearsome adversaries, Sihon (of the Amorites) and Og (of Bashon).

Third, Rahab's heart and spirit evaporate with icy fear when she grasps that the plan of God means the destructions of the Canaanites. Though others know this too, Rahab responds by making a radical, spiritual choice.

Fourth, Rahab embraces the God of Israel as her God. "The LORD *your* God," she says, "*he is God* in the heavens above and on the earth beneath" (Josh. 2:11). With these brief but telling words, Rahab exchanges her allegiance to the gods of the Canaanites for the God of Israel. She is now in covenant with another people.

Rahab's Bargain

Rahab goes out on a limb for these strangers, and after instructing them how to evade capture in the hills, she asks them to protect her and her family.

"Please," she pleads with them as she pushes them out her window and down the scarlet cord dangling above the ground. "Repay my kindness with kindness. Don't let us perish."

"Fair enough," they say, eying carefully the length of the rope. "We'll make that bargain, but with three conditions. First, if you reveal anything about us, the deal's off. Second, keep this scarlet cord hanging from your window. It's the only way we'll remember where you are. Third, and most importantly, keep everyone in the house. There will be no protection for you anywhere else in the city." And with that, they disappear down the wall.

I have called Rahab "the unlikely ally" precisely because of this new allegiance. She now proclaims that she is a daughter of Israel, a woman of faith. She becomes a child of God. An important principle from Rahab's greatest achievements is this: *faith displays concrete evidence in one's life.* Rahab demonstrates her faith by the choices she makes, by the acts she performs, and by her allegiance to the God she embraces.

Rahab's Unlikely Decisions

Rahab makes two ethical choices in this story. She lies to the king about the whereabouts of the spies, and she disobeys the king to preserve their lives. We saw these two dilemmas of lying and disobedience with the Egyptian midwives and with Moses' parents. As with the midwives, Rahab's disobedience to the king is easier to explain. She embraces the God of Israel as her God and switches her loyalties from Jericho and gods of the Canaanites to Joshua and the Israelites and the God of Israel. Her decision to disobey the king thus falls under the category of civil disobedience. Like the midwives, Rahab chooses to obey God rather than man.

The choice to lie to the king is more complicated. Let's consider four ethical approaches in exploring whether Rahab's lying is legitimate. They are listed in the chart below.

Rahab's Lie: Four Approaches to the Dilemma

Approach	Meaning
1. The Single-Value View	Lying is always wrong; God's commands never conflict.

2. The Lesser-Evil View	Lying is always wrong; God's commands sometimes conflict.
3. The Higher-Value View	Lying is only wrong when it does not conflict.
4. The Prior-Obligation View	Lying is always wrong when it violates a prior obligation.

The Single-Value View

Sometimes called the absolutist approach, the single-value view believes lying is always wrong. This is an ancient, long-established position held by theologians like Saint Augustine. Lying is never inevitable, we are told, so it is never necessary or justifiable to lie. Further, there is never a true conflict between the various commands of God. For example, truth-telling will never conflict with life-saving. Since lying is always wrong, Rahab should have told the truth about the spies, leaving the results up to a sovereign God. God will save the spies if he wishes. Since he does not need her lies, Rahab sinned.

This popular view has much going for it. It honors God and his commands as absolute, and it does not require having to choose one value over another. The difficulty of this view in our story, however, is that Rahab's family's deliverance is closely linked to her hiding the spies and concealing their mission to the king (Josh. 2:18; 6:25). Rahab's faith is also connected to welcoming the spies (Heb. 11:31). Some retort that Rahab is rewarded for *hiding* the spies, not *lying* about them, suggesting she could have misled the king without lying. But the story never disassociates the two actions. Perhaps she could have misled them with a creative yet truthful dodge. But what would it be? Should ethical success belong only to the clever?

The Lesser-Evil View

Sometimes called the lesser of two evils, this approach also says that lying is always wrong but that lying is sometimes inevitable because occasionally the moral commands of God conflict with one another. For example, God commands us to value life; he also commands us to tell the truth. Rahab, at a colliding intersection of these two commands, chooses life-saving (the lives of the spies) over truth-telling (not lying to the king).

In this view, the conflict is not a problem with God or his commands. This kind of inevitable conflict occurs only because we live in a fallen world with sin all around us. Since lying is always wrong, Rahab sinned. But God, extending grace to her, will forgive her if she confesses this sin.

What alternative does Rahab have to sinning? According to this view, she has none because she made the best choice she could, the lesser of two evils. Since both options violate God's law, she still sinned even though she made the best choice she could.

The weakness of the lesser-evil view is significant. It fails the Christology test. Jesus, the truly human Son of God, faced every kind of temptation. As perfectly sinless, he made correct moral choices every time. Since Jesus lived in a fallen world among fallen people, he surely would have faced dilemmas like Rahab faced, requiring him to choose one divine command over another. But to do this, Jesus would have had to sin, and we know he never did (Heb 4:15). Since the problem here cannot be in Jesus, the flaw must lie in the view itself.

The Higher-Value View

Another popular view, sometimes called the greater good (or hierarchical) view, holds that lying is only sometimes wrong. It is wrong when it can be avoided, but sometimes lying is unavoidable; and then it is *not* wrong. Indeed, there are times when God's moral commands conflict with each other because of the sinfulness of the human condition. In those cases we must choose the higher value. Unlike the lesser-evil view, however, this approach says God does not blame us for something we cannot escape. So Rahab does lie, but since she chooses the higher value—preserving life over telling the truth—she does not sin.

Some say the higher-value view seems more like moral slight-of-hand than a compelling ethical system. It is really no different than the lesser-evil view, except guilt is removed. But it is unclear how guilt is removed by a God whose moral commands have been disobeyed.

A more serious objection to the view is its subjectivity. How can we say that life-saving is a higher value than truth-telling? God hates both liars and murderers; both actions are prohibited in the Ten Commandments. No matter how we may prioritize these commands, it appears, some choices inevitably will violate God's moral character.

The Prior-Obligation View

The prior-obligation view holds that we must always tell the truth to those to whom we have an obligation. When lying violates that obligation, it is always wrong. When these obligations are clearly defined, there is never a conflict.

This closely resembles the single-value (or absolutist) view. Both views say that lying is always wrong and there is no moral conflict between God's commands. The difference in this view is the insistence that we define each moral absolute biblically and precisely. This is especially true of lying and its close counterpart, deception. Without such precision, conflicts can appear to exist that really do not.

The first three views all define a lie the same way. A lie involves both the *intent* to deceive and an *act* of deception. To deceive someone without intending to do so is not lying; it is simply making a mistake. To intend to deceive without actually deceiving may be perverse, but it is not a lie. Rahab lied by this definition because her action fits both elements: she intended to deceive the king and she actually did.

The prior-obligation view argues that this definition of lying ignores a third important element. A true lie also involves a violation of a prior obligation. Such an obligation may be based either on a divine covenant (like the Mosaic covenant) or on a covenant relationship with another person or community. For example, if you have an obligation based on citizenship, then deceiving a fellow countryman is a violation of your obligation to that person. This is a lie and a violation of God's law. It is wrong.

On the other hand, you have no obligation to someone who makes a claim on you that he has no right to make. You are not obliged, for example, to post a sign on your door that you will be on vacation for two weeks, letting any passing thief know the coast is clear to rob your house. Now here is the tricky part. Is it wrong to turn your house lights and sound system on, preferably controlled by a sophisticated timer, to make a potential thief think you're home when you're really not? The prior-obligation view would say such an act is deception, but it is not an immoral lie. You have no obligation to tell a thief the truth so that he can rip you off.

Notice the important distinction between deception and lying. Deception is morally neutral; lying is always wrong. Joshua practices the deception of ambush against the town of Ai under God's orders (Josh. 8). We practice deception on the basketball court when we fake a pass or shot. These are not immoral acts, because there is no obligation between involved parties prohibiting deception. Deception in a courtroom, however, is another matter. There it is bearing false witness. It is lying, and it is wrong.

Rahab's Difficult Decision

So, does Rahab deceive? Absolutely. She intends to deceive, and she follows through. But does she lie? The prior-obligation view says no, because she does not violate an obligation she has to the king of Jericho. When she realigns herself with the God of Israel and his chosen people, her obligations change. In doing so, she becomes like another warrior in the battle with obligations to protect her new people. In other words, Rahab deceives the king, but she did not lie to him. There was nothing immoral for which she had to repent.

I prefer this view because it holds to an absolute view of lying and does not resort to claiming there are contradictions among God's commands or among his attributes which underlie those commands. Any confusion stems from our failure to define clearly our obligations to one another. This view also helpfully distinguishes deception as morally neutral from lying as morally wrong. This fits many examples we face each day in real life.

The primary objection to the prior-obligation view is a pragmatic one. How can I train my children that lying is wrong, for example, if there are all these loopholes of prior obligation? The answer is to remember that our obligations to one another run very, very deep. We have obligations as human beings to treat every fellow image-bearer with respect and honesty. We have obligations as citizens of our country to treat each citizen with honor. As members of the body of Christ, or a neighborhood, or a company, or an organization, we have obligations to treat one another with due respect, including honesty.

However, the prior-obligation view clarifies the exceptions. It is not a lie to deceive the enemy in battle; it is not wrong to confuse a thief that you're not at home; you are not guilty if you fake out your opponent on the basketball court; and it is entirely permissible to deny you bought a gift for your wife's anniversary when she directly asks you, because you want to keep that beautiful ring you bought her a joyful surprise!

But do not forget the important principle. Rahab the prostitute shows us that living by faith requires clear-headed ethical thinking. Rahab is not the only biblical character that faces such challenging decisions, but she illustrates how allegiance to the one true God truly changes things.

Rahab's Unlikely Compensation

The story ends well for Rahab. She keeps her vow to the letter. She keeps mum about the spies, hangs the red rope out the window throughout the siege, and sequesters her entire family within her home in the city wall. The rewards for her faith are stunning.

First, we see her physical rewards when the walls collapse and the troops storm the unprotected city from 360 degrees around. Her and her family's lives are saved. She now belongs to God's covenant people and will be forever numbered with them. This is the most Rahab dare hope for.

But survival is just a small part of what God has in store, because Rahab receives hereditary rewards. She becomes a link in the genealogy of King David. Matthew's genealogy of Jesus tells us that Rahab (the one time in the New Testament she is not called a harlot) marries Salmon (I like to think she weds one of the spies) and becomes the mother of Boaz, who marries Ruth the Moabite (Matt. 1:5). From Boaz, Scripture traces a direct ancestry to Jesus. What an example of divine grace! Rahab the harlot is also Rahab the ancestor of kings, a mother in Messiah's lineage.

Most importantly, Rahab is a woman of faith and is the recipient of immense spiritual rewards. That is how the New Testament views her in two important passages.

In Hebrews 11:31 she emerges as a *faith-motivated* woman. Her faith is the spiritual impulse to welcome the spies, hide them, and ensure their safe escape. As a result, she not only saves the lives of her and her family but also distinguishes herself from the other citizens of Jericho (who are described as "disobedient"), a recognition of her new allegiance.

In the other scriptural tribute to Rahab (James 2:24–25), she is a *works-justified* woman. "A person is justified by works," James tells us in language that contrasts the Pauline theology of "not by faith alone." To prove this controversial point, he cites our unlikely heroine. "Was not also Rahab the prostitute justified by works," he asks rhetorically, "when she received the messengers and sent them out by another way?" To compound matters, James also cites Abraham's offering of Isaac as proof that the great patriarch of faith is also justified by works (James 2:21). Contemporary theologians get just as exercised over this apparent contradiction as Reformer Martin Luther did five hundred years ago.

There is, of course, no contradiction here. The word *justified* simply means "declared righteous." When applied to you and me, it means that God declares us righteous the moment we place our faith in Jesus Christ. Jesus' righteousness becomes ours. God, seeing Christ's righteousness indwelling us, declares us righteous because of him.

Both Paul and James mean the same thing by justification; the difference is their perspective on the relationship of works to faith. For Paul, the unbeliever's entry into a relationship with God is only by faith (Rom. 3:21–4:25). "One is justified by faith apart from works of the law," he explains (Rom. 3:28). His proof? Abraham is justified by God before he obeys God's command of circumcision (Rom. 4:9; Gen. 15:6). One never can stand before God by his own good works, his own effort. It is always *sola fide*, by faith alone.

James's concern, however, is with the genuineness of faith. He reminds us that faith without works is a useless, dead faith (James 2:20, 26). He agrees with Paul that faith is the requirement for justification (also quoting the Genesis 15:6 reference to Abraham, James 2:23). But he underscores the specific works of both Abraham (of offering Isaac) and Rahab (of preserving the spies) to prove their faith was genuine.

As such, Rahab the harlot illustrates our principle that the life of faith is demonstrated in concrete, active obedience to the living God.

Rahab, the Unlikely Ally

In conclusion, let's review the three principles of faith illuminated by Rahab the harlot. First, as seen in her unlikely work experiences, God extends grace apart from merit and regardless of reputation. Second, as seen in her unlikely accomplishments, the life of faith involves a change of allegiance, buttressed by concrete evidence. Third, as seen in her most challenging ethical decisions, living by faith requires clear-headed thinking. And finally, as seen in her unlikely compensation, the life of faith produces rewards, sometimes earthly ones but always spiritual ones.

Rahab's Spiritual Resume

Rahab's Resume	Principle of Faith
Rahab's work experience	Living by faith is available to anyone regardless of their merit or reputation.
Rahab's greatest achievements	Living by faith produces concrete evidence.
Rahab's most challenging decisions	Living by faith requires clear-headed ethical thinking.
Rahab's compensation	Living by faith issues in heavenly— and sometimes earthly—blessing.

Rahab is an unlikely heroine, no doubt about it. Even fifteen hundred years later, references to her as "Rahab the harlot" retain that shameful nickname. But it reminds us that relationship with God is always by divine mercy, never by human merit. Just as importantly, Rahab displays for us the importance of our new allegiance to the living God Our relationship with the God of Abraham, Isaac, and Jacob; the God and Father of our Lord Jesus Christ; and the God of you and me changes everything, doesn't it? Our loyalties, our relationships, our priorities, and our destinies will never ever be the same.

CHAPTER 15

GIDEON AND BARAK: TWO UNLIKELY WARRIORS

Behaving Badly

A story still circulates through Lockwood family lore concerning an incident involving my father, me, and an ice cream cone. Since I cannot actually remember it, I usually dismiss it on grounds of plausible deniability, but all of my siblings swear it is true because they claim they were there. If it is true, it's not an incident of which I am proud. Likely Dad wouldn't be, either. It is, you might say, a case of a father and son behaving badly.

We attended Central Bible Church in downtown, before it moved in 1957 to its present site near Multnomah. Since we lived in southwest Portland, we would occasionally drive home from church on winding Terwilliger Drive with its magnificent view of the city and Mount Hood. There was always a potential bonus for us kids when Dad did this. This route took us by Peterson's Ice Cream Store, which had the best home-made ice cream cones in Portland.

On this particular Sunday (so I am told), I was seated in the front seat between Mom and Dad. Of course, I began asking for a cone miles before Peterson's came into view.

"I wanna Peterson's ice cream cone!" I shouted.

Dad was in a hurry for some reason, with no intention of stopping. Probably Mom whispered to him, "Dear, just pull up and let Darrell run in to get him one."

"I wanna Peterson's ice cream cone," I chanted again.

So Dad capitulated, pulling onto the asphalt strip in front of Peterson's. Darrell dashed out with some money from Mom and returned with the cone, placing it into my eager hands. Dad merged onto Capital Highway.

I gazed happily down at the ice cream for a moment before my expression changed to a frown. Failing to notice the frustration written on my dad's face, or to sense the tension in the air, I blurted out, "But this is vanilla. I wanted raspberry ripple!"

My father, longsuffering to a fault, rarely let anything tip him over the edge. But when pushed too far, he could act suddenly, decisively, and unequivocally. This Sunday morning was the rare occasion.

Without a word (goes the story), Dad grabbed the cone out of my grip and swept it toward his car window in one deft, elegant stroke. The atmosphere in the car, already tense, grew dark. No one dared breathe. I was old enough to realize I had acted badly, gazing intently at my suddenly empty fist in silence.

But the rest of the family was staring at something else. The driver's side window was shut tight. Without thinking, Dad had firmly thrust the vanilla ice cream cone directly against the glass, on which the crushed cone slowly oozed down.

No one recalls the end of this story. Whether Dad stopped to throw the cone overboard, whether he drove stoically and silently the rest of the way home, or whether he broke the silence with a laugh, I'll never know. It is one of those unknown details I exploit to persuade myself the incident never happened. But if it did happen, on that day two of us behaved badly.

Unlikely Warriors in an Ungodly Generation

Hebrews 11 ends its "by faith" descriptions of unlikely heroes by simply naming six more men of faith in Israel's history: Gideon, Barak, Samson, Jephthah, David, and Samuel (Heb. 11:32). Further explanation is apparently unnecessary because their stories are familiar from the rich detail in the Old Testament. That their order differs from Judges and 1 Samuel may simply be a preference by the author of Hebrews to identify three groups of leaders, with the major character in each group heading the couplet: Gideon and Barak, warriors of the early theocracy; Samson and Jephthah, judges of the later theocracy; and David and Samuel, leaders of the early monarchy. We will consider the first two leaders, Gideon and Barak, in this chapter.

Three of the four leaders (Barak is the exception) are men of faith who behaved badly, and we do them justice only when we understand their historical context. In the final verse of Judges (21:25), we find two themes that aptly summarize the period. One is "There was no king in Israel" (also in 18:1 and 19:1). This not only explains why judges ruled in the land; it also helps us understand the political and military chaos of a nation that suffered through numerous Canaanite subjugations. The second theme is "Everyone did what was right in his own eyes." This accounts for the moral and spiritual depravity of the period.

These two themes are interrelated. Without a king to give strong moral and political leadership, the people will follow their own immoral passions. With a people becoming a law unto themselves, no king can effectively lead.

The question is, how did it come to this? In just a generation from Joshua's victorious conquest, when the nation followed the Lord completely, things are collapsing spiritually. The tribes do not obey Yahweh fully to possess their inherited allotments; and by the time of Samson, the nation is in moral freefall. "There is no king in Israel. Everyone does what is right in his own eyes."

A third theme in Judges gives us a clue to the answer to this question. Seven times we are told, "And the people of Israel did what was evil in the sight of the LORD" (Judg. 2:11; 3:7, 12; 4:1; 6:1; 10:6; 13:1). This phrase informs the structure of the book, introducing six cycles of Israel's downfall. Although twelve judges are named in the book, each cycle focuses on one prominent judge with a familiar pattern: Israel sins, God permits a scourge to oppress them, Israel pleads to God for deliverance, God sends a judge who saves them, and Israel enjoys a period of relative peace. But these six cycles are not simply repeated; they form a downward spiral of rebellion in which the sin deepens, the scourge intensifies, the time of oppression lengthens, the judge declines in moral character, and the period of peace diminishes.

We will consider the first two unlikely warriors in the order they appear in Hebrews 11, emphasizing the aspects of their leadership as charted on the following page.

Two Unlikely Warriors

Warrior	"An Unlikely—	—Man of Faith"
Gideon Judges 6–8 *Cycle 4*	• Initial fear • Final apostasy	• Desired to see God • Obeyed God • Judged Israel well
Barak Judges 4–5 *Cycle 3*	• Not a judge; a warrior • Deprived of "glory" of killing Sisera	• Allied with God's prophet, Deborah • Fought valiantly

Gideon: A Fearful Man, a Faithful Man

Gideon's life is bookended by failure. When God first summons him to lead Israel against the Midianites, he exhibits such timidity and fear that we question what God sees in the man. And at the end of his life, his apostasy with his golden ephod stains his obituary so deeply we wonder why Hebrews even bothers to name him. But named he is, so let's explore why.

Gideon's Fear and Failure (Judges 6)

At the beginning of the fifth cycle in Judges, Israel is savagely oppressed by the Midianites, a loose band of nomadic Bedouins from east Jordan who raid the central plains. After seven years of cruel servitude, Israel pleads to Yahweh for deliverance. The old prophet he sends them does not encourage. One reasonably concludes that God is so fed up with their rebellious idolatry that his judgment is inevitable.

But in his mercy, the Lord sends his angel to Ophrah, a small village in Ephraim where Gideon secretly threshes wheat at a winepress to avoid detection.

"Hail, valiant warrior," proclaims the angel.

Who, me? Gideon thinks, looking around to see if maybe someone else is behind him. No one else is there, and the angel speaks to Gideon as if he matters. Initially Gideon has no clue he is seeing a theophany, so we may infer the Lord appears in a common form—perhaps as the old prophet—and not as a glowing cherub.

Like Moses at the burning bush, Gideon presses the angel with a series of questions designed to make the old man leave.

"Why doesn't Yahweh destroy the Midianites?" he demands, rapid-fire. "And why would he choose me, the baby of one of the least significant families in a small Abiezrite clan of Ephraim? And if you really are God's messenger, why don't you prove it when I bring you an offering?"

The angel patiently answers each objection. "God is going to do something, Gideon," he responds, "through you. The Lord knows you to be a mighty warrior even if you don't. And as to your offering test, bring it on!"

The Lord reveals himself, igniting the sacrifice with his staff and vanishing in a flash. Now Gideon, who holds the common belief that one who looks into the face of God dies, is truly frightened. But God soothes him and explains the details of the plan that he has for Israel, a plan that requires Gideon to live awhile longer.

But not many days later, Gideon demands another sign from God—two more, in fact. First, he asks that his fleece become dew-covered the next morning while the earth remains dry. Then he asks that his fleece stay dry while all the ground around is wet with dew.

Is Gideon exercising great faith here, as many Christian apply this story today? Hardly. Gideon is not humbly seeking God's will, because the Lord has already made his will very clear. Still fearful and doubting, Gideon demands more miracles to prove that God means what he says, when God's simple, unambiguous word alone should suffice.

The other bookend of Gideon's life, the golden ephod incident, is a failure of tragic proportions. After success with the Midianites and instances of wise judging, Gideon asks the people to give him some of the gold from the spoil. They gladly accommodate their champion. With the gold, Gideon fashions an ephod. Though scholars offer many explanations of this ephod, the simplest explanation is best: it is a priestly garment inlaid with golden thread and medallions, glistening with beauty. Gideon, probably copying the Aaronic high priest's ephod, shuns the kingship but covets the priesthood. He makes a garment appropriate to that restricted office so he may stand again in the presence of God. Likely, it also has a pouch containing Urim and Thummim (perhaps two black-and-white stones used to make decisions, Num. 27:21) so he may discern the will of God.

Gideon undoubtedly knew his apostasy was a capital offense, since he knew the Mosaic law, but "there was no king in Israel." Gideon's epitaph says it all. "It became a snare to Gideon," and the people of Israel "whored after it" (Judg. 8:27). "Everyone did what was right in his own eyes."

Gideon's Faithful Obedience (Judges 7–8)

So why is Gideon included as a man of faith with his record of fear and spiritual failure? The same way all of us are: he believes

God, and it is reckoned to him as righteousness. However frail and faltering he appears to us, Gideon exhibits genuine faith and courage in his unswerving obedience to God in destroying the Midianites.

God does not ask Gideon to do the impossible, at least not at first. He wisely gives him the simpler task of destroying the idols and images, the Asherah poles and the altars of the Baal worship on his father's land. Exercising leadership, he takes ten buddies that night and destroys every trace of Canaanite religion in the place, sacrificing on a new altar to the living God instead.

When the villagers, deeply entrenched in fertility-based idolatry, discover that Gideon is the culprit, they demand his life. To our surprise, Gideon's father defends his son, and from that day on Gideon is nicknamed Jerubbaal. He becomes "the one who confronts Baal," and wins!

At God's command, Gideon musters thirty-two thousand men-at-arms from the surrounding tribes of Manasseh, Asher, Zebulun, and Naphtali. His own tribe of Ephraim is not summoned.

That's an impressive showing for our first try, Gideon thinks, while realizing the number pales by comparison to the Midianites who are "like locusts in abundance" (Judg. 7:12). *Maybe we'll get some more when I invite Ephraim.*

But the number is not right for Yahweh.

"Too many," he tells Gideon. "Tell all who do not want to fight for any reason—family priorities, harvest preparation, property care, fear of battle—that they are welcome to go home."

Lord, thinks an incredulous Gideon. *What are you doing?*

But Gideon obeys the Lord, and twenty-two thousand depart, leaving a still-substantial band of ten thousand warriors apparently itching for a fight.

"Still too many," God says. "They must pass my selective service-enlistment test first. Take them down to the river for a drink. Every man who drinks on his belly goes home. Those who lap water kneeling stay." Only three hundred remain.

"I want everyone to know," explains the Lord, "that this battle will be won by me, not by human might. Not even yours, Gideon."

Scholars spill a lot of ink over this story of the three hundred. Most hold to the "alert man" theory. God wants warriors who always keep an eye open and a weapon in hand for the enemy, even when drinking from a brook, they say. The careless are disqualified.

I don't buy it. After all, what will three hundred lonely warriors—whether alert and well-armed or not—do against so many? And that's just the point. God's purpose is to show that the victory comes from him, not the warriors.

I prefer the "old geezer" theory. Who would be the small number out of ten thousand men that would find it difficult even to kneel down beside a brook as their joints creak and their backs ache? Wouldn't it be those aging warriors past their prime? As I enter my sixth decade of life, this interpretation makes more and more sense.

But whatever the reason, Gideon accepts God's choice without complaint and obeys God's unusual tactics to the letter. He divides the three hundred into three groups of one hundred, probably to station them at strategic points around the valley rim. Each is given a torch, a trumpet, and a clay pot. There is no mention of a sword.

Since God's strategy is to throw the Midianites into confusion, this ploy makes eminent sense. Nevertheless, Gideon is afraid. So God gently instructs him to edge to the Midianite camp to overhear a conversation between two guards.

"I had a strange dream last night," says one. "I saw a barley sheaf tumble down the hill and sweep into camp, taking my tent with it. Wonder what that means."

"Oh no!" replies the other, eyes wide in terror. "That clearly means Gideon's army is going to overwhelm and destroy us this very night."

It's hard to imagine a more encouraging message than that, isn't it? So Gideon returns to his men and, by faith, readies them for the battle. The plan works perfectly. When Gideon blows his trumpet, the rest blow theirs, smash the clay vessels hiding the light, and raise their torches to the sky, shouting, "A sword for the LORD and for Gideon!" (Judg. 7:20). The Midianites panic and flee for the Jordan River, killing one another in their haste.

Now Gideon's leadership kicks in, showing the abilities that God knew he had from the beginning. For mop-up operations, Gideon again summons the warriors from the surrounding tribes that had returned home, including the eastern half of Manasseh who can finish the job east of the Jordan. Ultimately, the victory is overwhelming. One hundred fifty thousand Midianites are slain near "the waters," likely where the Jabbock feeds the Jordan. Two Midianite princes, Oreb and Zeeb, are killed by the Ephraimites, who bring the princes' heads to Gideon. Gideon and his three hundred (think of how tired these old guys are now!) continue to pursue the two kings of Midian, Zebah, and Zalmunna, far into Midianite territory, east of Succoth and Penuel. With his three hundred he attacks the remaining Midian camp of fifteen thousand. Once again, they panic, rout, and leave their kings defenseless. Gideon captures them and brings them alive back to his camp near the Jordan, where he kills them.

In this long battle, Gideon shows the kind of wisdom necessary for a judge. When the irritable Ephraimites—his own tribe—complain that he deliberately demeans them by leaving them out of the fighting, Gideon chooses a path of reconciliation to win their allegiance.

But with the two eastern cities of Succoth and Penuel, who rebelliously refuse to aid his exhausted band, he deals with them in harsher, and appropriately different, ways. The elders of Succoth refuse the three hundred men simple nourishment. Selfishly, they want to keep their options open until they know how the battle turns out. Leaving the city a warning, Gideon and his famished men move east. The men of Penuel give the same response.

True to his word, Gideon returns with the two Midianite kings in tow. At Succoth he lashes the seventy elders and officials with briars and thorns in front of the people. At Penuel he destroys their tower and kills all the men. Why the difference? Perhaps in Succoth the elders do not represent the people of an otherwise sympathetic village, and Gideon chooses a discipline that serves as an example to the people of the importance of obeying the instructions of the Lord's judge.

We know less about Penuel, except they are located deeper in Midianite territory and have a tower. Gideon, in destroying the tower, may be removing a military defense facility that could be used willingly or unwittingly against Israel in the future. Doubtless, Gideon senses the entire city is in harmony with their elders' decision, making the city a potential military adversary.

Gideon's Faith

Judges hints that Gideon is a successful judge and a man of faith despite the ephod incident. The land has rest for forty years under Gideon (Judg. 8:28). He dies at a good old age, buried in his father's tomb, and leaving seventy sons—biblical clues of a life well lived. The final verse of this story sums it up. The people, turning again to sin after Gideon's death, did not show steadfast love for Gideon's family "in return for all the good that he had done to Israel" (Judg. 8:35).

In the end, Gideon is a man of faith like so many. He has innate leadership gifts that he himself does not recognize until they are awakened by God. He questions himself and he doubts the word of God, demanding reassuring signs even when his mission is so plain. After his great victory, he doesn't seek the glory for himself or even for his family; rather, he seeks to be constantly in touch with God. Tragically, however, Gideon fails to realize that God's presence cannot be manufactured and that God's voice cannot be summoned at will. When we try using manipulative efforts to do so, they become a snare.

At the same time, Gideon obeys God down to the smallest details. He understands that a small minority plus God is always a majority. Without glory-seeking, he becomes the servant through whom God makes his name known. Then, when God's voice stills, Gideon finishes the work to the very end, bringing victory and peace and administering discipline appropriately. His life teaches us that despite all our flaws and failures, we can, under the mighty hand of God, do good.

Barak, the Unlikely Ally

Barak's main claim to fame—and epical weakness—is that he is eclipsed by a woman. At least, that is the implication of many interpretations of his story. Hebrews includes him as a man of faith in the list with five other male notables (Heb. 11:32). But Barak is never described in Judges as a judge; he is a military commander. Rather, Deborah, a married woman and a prophetess of God, is the one judging Israel (Judg. 4:4). Barak is notable—and sometimes degraded—primarily because he is an ally of Deborah.

Barak, Deborah, and Israel's Fortunes (Judges 4)

When Israel enters her third cycle of sin, she cries out for deliverance from the scourge of the Canaanites under King Jabin. God reveals to Deborah both the man and the plan for defeating Jabin's army commanded by the renowned Sisera, who controls the plains with nine hundred iron chariots. The man is General Barak, and the plan is to muster ten thousand men from the nearby tribes, gather at Mount Tabor, and engage Sisera's army at the Kishon River. God will draw out the confident Sisera on his modern attack vehicles but claim the victory.

Barak's response has the crispness you expect from a military man. "I'll go under one condition, Deborah," he says. "If you go, I'll go. If you don't, I'm staying home!"

"Certainly I'll go," Deborah replies. "But you must know that the road you follow will not lead to your glory. Instead, the Lord will allow Sisera to die at a woman's hand."

Without further objection from Barak, the plan is enacted. He musters the troops from Zebulun and Naphtali for a battle at Kadesh on Mount Tabor. When Deborah gets word to Sisera that Barak is on the move (Judg. 4:7), Sisera deploys all his infantry, including the nine hundred iron charioteers, to engage Barak's forces.

The details of the battle are sparse. Barak gains the upper hand over Sisera's mechanized cavalry apparently by engaging him in the steep terrain of Mount Tabor, catching the army off guard, and forcing the proud general to flee afoot. Barak's ten thousand men kill every one of Sisera's men by the sword. The text is explicit; no one is left alive.

The battle is over except for one detail: the fate of General Sisera. Sisera flees toward Hazor and the safety of King Jabin's palace, passing the tent of the woman named Jael. Earlier we're told that Jael's husband, Heber, a Kenite with distant roots to Moses, has lived harmoniously near Jabin. This grisly tale has the fingerprints of deception all over it. Jael lures the commander to her roadside tent with the soothing promise that he has nothing to fear. When he asks, exhausted, for water, she generously gives him milk to drink and a blanket to cover him. Then, when he's sleeping, free from dread, she impales him through his temple with a sharp tent peg. (Yuck!) Boldly, she points Barak to the corpse when he later passes by, searching for him. What Deborah foretold was accomplished.

Barak's "Loss of Glory"

So, was Barak a man weak in faith and courage? Most question his faith because he is unwilling to go into battle without Deborah present. The evidence cited is Deborah's prediction that Barak will not claim Sisera's defeat for himself; that honor will forever go to a woman.

Others stress Barak's weakness because twice Deborah urges him to action. "Has not the LORD, the God of Israel, commanded you?" she says in summoning him to Kedesh (Judg. 4:6). Later, to begin the battle, Deborah shouts to Barak, "Up! For this is the day the LORD has given Sisera into your hand. Does not the LORD go out before you?" (Judg. 4:14).

I find unpersuasive the argument that Barak is weak in either faith or courage. Deborah's two commands are easily seen as rhetorical questions that emphatically confirm her prophetic gift and reflect the urgency of the situation. They do not, at least of themselves, demand that Barak was a lazy, cowardly, faithless, or reluctant warrior.

More significant is the accusation that Barak is weak in faith or courage because he won't go into battle without Deborah. But Deborah correctly understands that Barak will only fight if the command comes from the Lord. In fact, a better explanation is that Barak seeks to do God's will so much that he will only go into battle when the prophet of God accompanies. His insistence on this has nothing to do with gender; it has everything to do with being in harmony with the word and will of God. Having the prophetess and judge Deborah at his side is a certain, missional way to guarantee he will have victory from God.

If this is a better explanation of Barak's faith-oriented thinking, we must conclude that Deborah's prediction about killing Sisera is not a punishment but a prophecy of the mighty power of God. Like the story of Gideon, the point is that victory belongs to God, not human military might.

Further, neither the narrative (Judg. 4) nor Deborah and Barak's musical duet (Judg. 5) in any way suggests Barak's cowardice or failure. Barak never complains about any loss of glory that might keep a surly, self-centered soldier home. And the Song of Deborah and Barak twice lauds Barak's bravery (along with that of Deborah and Jael) without hesitation (Judg. 5:12, 15).

I wonder whether this criticism more reflects the patriarchalism, or even misogyny, of the interpreters than a weakness in Barak. I believe Barak went into battle with Deborah precisely because he was a brave man of faith who cherished the presence of God in the nation's prominent judge, regardless of gender.

Barak's Valiant Victory

Indeed, Barak's victory over the Canaanites was impressive. After the resounding defeat of the day, culminating in the slaying of Sisera by Jael, the nation, apparently under Barak's military leadership, pressed the fight until King Jabin himself was destroyed (Judg. 4:24). After this, Israel had rest from the Canaanites for forty years (Judg. 5:31). The only biblical reproach in the entire story is that the tribes of Reuben, Gilead, Dan, and Asher stood on the sidelines on the great day of victory (Judg. 5:15–17).

The Tale of Two Warriors

Gideon and Barak are two very different kinds of warriors, and their lives teach us different lessons. Both are military leaders, although Gideon seems unsure of his gifts and must be encouraged repeatedly by the Lord to move into action. Barak, on the other hand, seems born to battle. Both men learn the lesson that their victories belong to God. Gideon secures victory when God throws the enemy into a senseless panic, at the "shock and awe" of three hundred old men breaking jars, blowing trumpets, lifting torches, and shouting. Barak wins his victory over the most advanced weaponry of his day by obeying the word of a prophetess, who directs him to fight iron charioteers in hill country rather than on the plains.

CHAPTER 16

SAMSON AND JEPHTHAH:
THE UNLIKELY JUDGES

Taking Vows

To the best of my recollection, I have made only two vows. And by vows I mean the formal, serious kind made before witnesses with dire consequences if broken.

One was made about fifteen years ago when I was subpoenaed to testify in a medical malpractice case. I appeared in court as a character witness. Entering the courtroom, I immediately put from my mind any idea of lightening up what I thought was a far too somber proceeding. The faces of the twelve jurors and especially the judge's expression proclaimed they were not taking this lightly. When the stoical bailiff asked me to raise my right hand and swear "to tell the truth, the whole truth, and nothing but the truth, so help me God," I answered "I do" as seriously as anyone. My vow was binding for only about five minutes, and I can honestly say I fulfilled it perfectly. They got the whole truth as best as I could tell it.

My first vow has lasted nearly forty years. I voiced it as a young man of twenty-four in an elegant sanctuary in Encino, California. Having persuaded a beautiful and intelligent young woman named Jani to marry me, I successfully hoodwinked her generous parents into thinking I would make a fine husband and son-in-law. On that evening we stood before God, our pastor, family, and friends to exchange our vows of matrimony.

Jani and I wrote our own vows and memorized them so we could look deeply into one another's eyes while speaking from the depth of our souls. Today I can only remember two phrases from those original vows. I told Jani I would "make myself vulnerable to her" and do this "until death separates us." She promised the same. We exchanged rings to guarantee the commitment and shared a kiss—all too brief—to seal it.

We live happily with the implications of this vow every day of our lives. Although so much more than this vow keeps the flame of our love afire, the reality of our commitment to each other before God forged that unbreakable bond that cements our relationship as a couple to this day.

Two Unlikely Judges

Vow-keeping is one theme that unites the narratives of the last two judges of the theocratic period, Samson and Jephthah. Samson is born under obligation to a Nazirite vow that he does not keep; Jephthah makes a rash vow that horrifies us *because* he keeps it!

Samson and Jephthah are contemporaries. Samson stirs up trouble in the west with the Philistines, and Jephthah is likely dispatched eastward against the Ammonites. Samson judges Israel for twenty years; Jephthah's tenure is only six. Perhaps Samson is mentioned before Jephthah in Hebrews 11 because of the power of his story and the length of his judgeship. The chart below displays the characteristics of Samson and Jephthah we will discuss in this chapter.

Two Unlikely Judges

Judge	"An Unlikely—"	"—Man of Faith"
Samson Judges 13–16 *Cycle 6*	• Carnal passions • Violated Nazirite vow	• Divine saboteur • Cried out to the Lord
Jephthah Judges 10:6–12:7 *Cycle 5*	• Outsider reputation • Outrageous vow	• Theologically astute • Tried negotiation • Honored God

Samson, the Unlikely Saboteur

If you think Gideon is a judge who behaves badly, meet Samson. The last actual judge mentioned in the book of Judges (Judg. 13–16), Samson is larger than life; but in moral and spiritual character, he sinks to the bottom of the pond. While acknowledging that God strategically empowers him to fight the Philistines, I would be hard-pressed to include him as a man of faith on any list were it not for his inclusion in Hebrews 11.

Samson's Unlikely Birth

Samson's career begins auspiciously with a theophany, a miraculous conception, and an unusual vow. It is as if fireworks are set off in the first chapter of Samson's story to signal that something unusual, something divine, is about to happen.

Indeed it is. Israel is in the sixth and final cycle of sin. Toiling under Philistine subjugation for forty years, the Israelites neither show repentance nor initiate supplication to Yahweh. Nevertheless, the angel of the Lord appears to Manoah's wife. Barren and childless, Mrs. Manoah is a remarkable woman of faith and wisdom who remains an unnamed cipher throughout the account. The angel has good news.

"Soon, you will conceive and bear a son," the angel tells her, "but you must follow my instructions to the letter. While you're pregnant, eat nothing non-kosher, and never ever consume anything from the vine. Then, when your son is born, make certain a razor never touches his head."

Mrs. Manoah nods silently.

"You need to know why," the angel continues. "He is to be set apart for God's special service as a perpetual Nazirite from the moment he's born."

With that, the angel vanishes.

Manoah's wife immediately repeats the message to her husband, who is absent during the birth announcement. Although his wife refers to the theophany as a man of God whose "appearance was like the appearance of the angel of God, very awesome," Manoah does not know it is the angel of the Lord (Judg. 13:16). Mrs. Manoah, meanwhile, is clearing her kitchen of all half-filled wineskins and grape jelly glasses, disposing of any non-kosher food found within a furlong, and readying the spare bedroom for its new occupant. When the angel returns, he repeats the instructions. Since these are given three times in Judges 13, we realize the child is central to God's purposes.

What an important child he is! Growing to manhood in the village of Zorah, Samson, with his long hair flowing, is blessed by the Lord and feels the Spirit of God stirring within him.

Samson's Unlikely Assignment

Moses' regulations for the Nazirite vow (Num. 6) fit Samson's life in many ways. The prohibitions of using a razor, eating anything unclean, and partaking of the fruit of the vine are all given at the birth announcement. Additionally, a Nazirite could not touch an animal carcass or a dead body.

But Samson's vow is clearly unique. While the usual Nazirite vow was voluntary, temporarily taken as an act of service or devotion to the Lord, Samson's Nazirite vow is divinely ordained from birth. As such, it is obligatory and permanent.

Further, not all the usual Nazirite stipulations are enforced. Samson touches plenty of dead carcasses—human and animal— in his years as a judge. He scoops and eats honey from a lion's carcass in violation of the kosher laws. Probably he drinks wine during his wedding feast. Since the Holy Spirit does not depart from Samson for any reason except the cutting of his hair, we conclude that the only prohibition of the Mosaic Nazirite vow that pertains to Samson is the razor. A close reading of the angel's instructions shows it is Mrs. Manoah, not Samson, who is prohibited from touching the fruit of the vine (Judg. 13:4, 7, 14).

Samson is distinct among the judges in other ways too. First, of course, he is extraordinarily strong. Hollywood always portrays Samson as a huge brute of a man. I like to think of him as a small man, maybe about my size. If he were, his superhuman feats become all the more surprising to the Philistines and his divine power all the more obvious to Israel.

Second, Samson is not a military commander. Nowhere during his twenty-year judgeship do we find him mustering an army against the Philistines. Apparently, that is neither among his skill set nor part of God's strategy, perhaps because the nation has reached a point where they are unable to marshal such a force. Instead, Samson initiates individual, often clandestine, raids against the Philistines that nip at their heels and stymie their plans.

Third, he has a weakness for women. From his initial falling in love with a Philistine girl, his later weakness for prostitutes, and his final demise at Delilah's barber shop, Samson harbors a passion for the ladies that both infuriates the Philistines and leads him into moral disaster.

In short, Samson is a saboteur and a womanizer. He is the James Bond of the Old Testament!

Samson begins his divine 007 assignment by falling in love. While this understandably upsets his parents who want him to marry a nice Jewish girl, we are told that this is "from the LORD" (Judg. 14:4). God appoints the hot-blooded and hot-headed Samson to go down and make trouble with the Philistines.

And make trouble he does. When the Philistines cannot puzzle out Samson's riddle about the honey and the lion and are unwilling to ante up the price of thirty expensive suits, they turn nasty, threatening to burn his new bride in her home unless she pressures Samson for the secret. Samson, furious at their extortion, kills thirty Philistines at Ashkelon to pay his wardrobe tab.

Hostilities escalate from there. When his wife's father gives her to another man, Samson destroys the Philistines' wheat harvest with one hundred fifty pairs of foxes running amok among the fields and barns with torches tied to their tails. When the Philistines avenge their losses by burning his wife and her family, Samson slays one thousand of them with a donkey's jawbone at Ramath-lehi (renamed "the hill of the jawbone").

Samson's Sad Demise

Samson's career as a judge unfolds in two stages: the story of his defeating the Philistines (Judg. 14–15) and the story of his ultimate demise (Judg. 16). Both stages are punctuated by the closing statement, "He judged Israel twenty years" (Judg. 15:20; 16:31).

The declining moral tone of Samson's downfall is set early as he trysts with a Gazite prostitute (Judg. 16:1–3). Even so, he uses his supernatural strength to escape from the Philistines lying in wait, fleeing with the city gate, massive framework and all.

But the story of the notorious Delilah grabs center stage. The only woman mentioned by name in the story, she is Samson's match; she uses a familiar extortion with Samson to uncover the secret of his strength. Unlike their tactics with Samson's wife, however, the Philistines make no threats against Delilah's life. They simply entice her with 5,500 silver coins (a king's ransom of 1,100 from each of the five rulers, or a total of about 140 pounds of silver). After three unsuccessful tries, Delilah pries Samson's secret from him, and he submits to her razor.

Samson, unaware the Spirit of God has left him (Judg. 16:20), is easily captured, blinded, bound in bronze fetters, and brought to Gaza to grind grain. We are not told how long he endures this humiliation, only that his hair begins to grow again. Eventually, the Philistines plan a great feast to praise their god Dagon for their victory over the fearsome Samson. He is taken to the temple to entertain the three thousand guests. While they play, Samson prays that God will strengthen him one last time to avenge his eyesight. Though the Spirit of God is not explicitly mentioned, Samson pulls down the temple with restored supernatural strength. "So the number whom he killed at his death," we are told, "exceeded those he killed in his life" (Judg. 16:30).

Samson's Unlikely Faith

Dr. John Mitchell often said, "God can draw a straight line with any crooked stick." What a portrait of Samson!

Indeed, God uses the carnal Samson to accomplish his sovereign purpose to "begin to save Israel from the hand of the Philistines" (Judg. 13:5). But Spirit-empowerment never excuses Samson from acting in an immoral, ungodly way. It never excuses us, either.

Samson is Spirit-empowered, without question. Three times, we are told, the Spirit of the Lord "rushed upon him" to perform works of supernatural strength (Judg. 14:6, 19; 15:14). We may presume his other supernatural deeds are a result of the Spirit's work too, until the Spirit leaves him (Judg. 16:20). This does not mean, however, that the Spirit of God approves everything Samson does, including visiting the prostitute. The Holy Spirit's "coming upon" or "filling" someone in the Old Testament refer to God's sovereign empowerment to accomplish his specific, often theocratic, purposes. He can use believers (Moses), unbelievers (Balaam), or carnal believers (Samson) to accomplish his will. Spirit-empowerment says nothing *in itself* of a person's spiritual character.

By contrast, Spirit-indwelling in the New Testament is permanent, given only to believers, and given to all believers for their spiritual maturity (John 14:15–16; Rom. 8:9–11). Spirit-empowerment does not function this way. In Samson's case, the

Holy Spirit enables him to be an effective saboteur to fulfill God's purposes; his womanizing is his own undoing.

So why is Samson included in the Hebrews list of the faithful? I can offer two reasons. First, God appoints him to divine service from his mother's womb, much like Jeremiah the prophet and John the Baptist. One might argue that God's prenatal choice of Samson to service is consistent with the Father's pretemporal choosing of those who will be "in Christ" (Eph. 1:4–5). Second, Samson cries out to the Lord at the end of his life for one more chance to avenge himself on the Philistines. While this is not the spiritually uplifting prayer of a Moses or Daniel, it reveals that Samson has access to God's presence, even as a blind, humiliated prisoner.

Not much to go on, is it? But perhaps that's the point. Our relationship with God is entirely by faith. Hebrews 11:6 says the one drawing near to God must believe that he exists and that he rewards those who diligently seek him. Samson's final prayer shows he believes both.

Jephthah, the Unlikely Vow-Keeper

The paradoxical nature of Jephthah's judgeship is starkly captured in Scripture's one-verse introduction: "Jephthah the Gileadite was a mighty warrior, but he was the son of a prostitute" (Judg. 11:1). Add to this his reputation as an outlaw and his reckless vow, and we may well wonder why this man is listed among the Hebrews 11 faithful.

Jephthah, probably from the tribe of Manasseh, is the unacknowledged son of his father, Gilead, whose name also designates the entire Transjordan region and a prominent village near the Jabbok River. Gilead's name suggests he was a man of position and influence, and Jephthah likely believes he is destined for honor too.

Unfortunately his half-brothers think otherwise. They banish him from the family home, denying him any inheritance. Jephthah flees far into the desert northeast of Ramoth-gilead and into the region of Tob. He surrounds himself with "worthless fellows" (Judg. 11:3), forming an outlaw band that survives, apparently, by raids on unsuspecting caravans.

Meanwhile, Israel's sin worsens as she enters the fifth cycle of sin (Judg. 10:6–16). Scripture lists seven gods or groups of gods that the Israelites worship: the Baals, the Ashtaroth, Syrian gods, Sidonian gods, Moabite gods, Ammonite gods, and Philistine gods (Judg. 10:6). This suggests that Israel, at a sevenfold level of idolatry, is now completely immersed in wickedness. In his anger, Yahweh delivers the nation over to two oppressors, the Philistines and the Ammonites. He is moved to mercy only when Israel backs up her words of repentance by putting away these gods.

This is when the Gileadite elders, desperate for deliverance, summon Jephthah to rescue them from Ammonite oppression. Examine with me two important strands of Jephthah's story.

Jephthah, the Wise Negotiator

A valiant and experienced warrior, Jephthah does not immediately scurry off to battle. He pauses to ensure two things: first, that the wily Gileadites will do what they promise; and second, that the Ammonite king has a chance to negotiate for peace.

We understand Jephthah's hesitancy to fight for Gilead. Can he trust the people who heartlessly exiled him? Now, when they need his help, he insists on assurance that they will keep their word. The Gileadites make a solemn vow before the Lord at Mizpah, promising leadership to Jephthah in exchange for victory over the Ammonites.

More surprising is Jephthah's pursuit of peace with the Ammonite king. Such negotiations were probably common, a bit of formal sparring before the real fighting began. But Jephthah impresses us with his grasp of the historical, political, and theological issues that divide Israel and the Ammonites.

The Ammonite king plays along. "This is a simple property dispute," he says through his messengers. "Years ago, when Israel migrated from Egypt, she took my land between the Arno and Jabbok Rivers illegally by force. Give it back and avoid a fight."

"Not so fast," Jephthah responds. "Israel never took your land. In fact, we took pains to avoid conflict with the Edomites, the Moabites, and the Ammonites, our brothers by Abraham's covenant."

"No," snaps the king imperiously, "you took Ammonite land by battle. Brush up on your history!"

"You're the one who needs the history lesson," answers Jephthah. "Sihon, king of the Amorites in Heshbon, took Moabite land illegally and opposed us. We fought and defeated him because he prevented our peaceful passage through the region."

"Oh, so you admit taking Moabite land belonging to the Ammonites?" replies the king sarcastically.

"We conquered the *Amorites*," retorts Jephthah with growing impatience, "not the *Ammonites*. Besides, Moab has lived peaceable with us for three hundred years without once disputing ownership!

"However," asks Jephthah, playing his theological trump card, "if the land really belongs to you, why haven't your gods retaken it in the last three centuries? Let the one true God decide the issue right now!"

Jephthah's faith is impressive. Not just a warrior, Jephthah is a theologian. He understands his own nation's history and

Yahweh's important role in it. Would that we understand the Lord's working in our stories so we may contend effectively and theologically for what is right and true!

Jephthah, the Rash Warrior

With the Spirit of God empowering him, Jephthah heads south from Mizpah to Ammonite country east of Jordan and east of the tribe of Gad. The details of the battle are sketchy. We know neither how many troops Jephthah commands nor from what tribes they come, although Ephraim is doubtless uninvolved (Judg. 12:1). We are not told of the size of the Ammonite army, what kind of military hardware they have, or what strategies Jephthah plans to use. We only know Jephthah makes a vow to the Lord prior to the battle and that the Lord gives him a decisive victory (Judg. 11:30–33).

To appreciate Jephthah's faith in God, we must understand his vow. To do this, let's consider four vital questions.

First, why does Jephthah make this vow? The simple, probable answer is that Jephthah is scared. He grasps the resolve of the Ammonites, the disparity between the armies, and the uncertainties of conflict. He pleads with Yahweh for divine help, promising to do anything—even sacrificing the first thing he meets when he enters his house—if the Lord will only give him victory.

This vow is connected to the earlier vow that Jephthah and the elders of Gilead make before Yahweh (Judg. 11:9–11). And when he begins peace negotiations with the king of the Ammonites, Jephthah argues within the covenant framework of God's "vow" to Abraham to bless even Abraham's fringe descendants, the Edomites, Moabites, and Ammonites. Jephthah knows that God never violates his word, and he realizes God's people must keep their word too. While this neither explains nor justifies his making a rash vow, it gives us insight as to why Jephthah is so resolute in keeping it.

Second, what is Jephthah's vow? In return for victory in battle, Jephthah promises to sacrifice to the Lord whatever comes out of his house. Then he adds, "and I will offer it up for a burnt offering" (Judg. 11:31). It is that last phrase that divides biblical scholars and chills readers. The majority of scholars take the phrase "burnt offering" at face value. Jephthah promises to slay whatever creature meets him at the door, they contend, and to offer it up with fire to the Lord. The proof, they say, is Jephthah's anguished response when his daughter meets him at his threshold with the music of victory. Hearing of his irrevocable vow, she insists he keep it (Judg. 11:36), only requesting a two-month postponement so she may weep with her friends over the fact she will never marry and raise a family (her "virginity"). When she returns, we are told, Jephthah does exactly as he vows (Judg. 11:39).

A minority of scholars, reflecting a relatively recent tradition, believe such human sacrifice would never be permitted by God or practiced by a man of faith. Besides, they argue, why would his daughter be so concerned about her virginity when her life is at stake? Rather, her father is committing her to a life of celibacy; Jephthah's personal sacrifice is to have no heirs.

I wish this second view were true. Unfortunately, the biblical phrase "burnt offering" is too specific to suggest such a nuanced meaning as "life of celibacy." Additionally, human sacrifice exists in the theocratic period of the judges, and even men of faith commit rash acts and make rash vows they later regret. Therefore, I must conclude that Jephthah did, in fact, take his daughter's life and sacrifice her to the Lord.

Third, why does Jephthah keep such a terrible vow? Jephthah understands, as do all Israelites, that Yahweh takes vows made in his name very seriously. "You shall not swear by my name falsely," Moses is told, "and so profane the name of your God: I am the LORD" (Lev. 19:12). Elsewhere we read, "If a man vows a vow to the LORD, or swears an oath to bind himself by a pledge, he shall not break his word. He shall do according to all that proceeds out of his mouth" (Num. 30:2). And further, "If you make a vow to the LORD your God, you shall not delay fulfilling it, for the LORD your God will surely require it of you, and you will be guilty of sin" (Deut. 23:21).

Perhaps the story of Joshua's covenant with the Gibeonites (Josh. 9) enters Jephthah's mind. Who could forget that Joshua keeps his oath to the Gibeonites even though they enter it fraudulently? More likely, Jephthah remembers his own vow made before God with the Gileadites. "If I do not fulfill this burnt-offering vow made in my soldiers' hearing," Jephthah may reason, "what is to prevent the treacherous Gileadites from reneging on their word?"

The answer is clear: Jephthah makes a vow to Yahweh; and however rash it is, he has to keep it.

Fourth, should Jephthah have kept this rash vow? The ethical issue remains as to whether this vow, or any vow, should be kept without exception and regardless of the consequences. Jephthah's story seems to argue that this is the case, since no divine voice excuses him from the vow. Furthermore, both Jephthah and his daughter are firmly convinced that his vow to the Lord should be kept. Some even suggest that Jephthah proceeds with the sacrifice, hoping God will stop him as he did with Abraham and Isaac. For these reasons, the argument for fulfilling the vow seems strong.

However, I take the opposite view. Jephthah's vow to slay his daughter as a burnt offering should not have been followed; neither should we fulfill such foolish vows. My reason is twofold. First, Scripture is clear that no one may deprive another innocent person of life or limb. In fact, slaying an innocent person violates God's clear mandate: "Fathers shall not be put to death because of their children, nor shall children be put to death because of their fathers. Each one shall be put to death for his own sin" (Deut. 24:16). Why, then, would God require Jephthah to take his innocent daughter's life, just because he rashly vows it?

Second, the Mosaic passage on vows (Lev. 27) suggests that some things vowed to the Lord may be redeemed with the payment of an appropriate price. For example, if a person vows a piece of property to the Lord, he can redeem it by paying the ransom price plus a fee (Lev. 27:16–25). While there are exceptions to this—for example, one cannot redeem with money a person sentenced to death (Lev. 27:29)—a strong case is to be made that Jephthah could fulfill his vow by redeeming his daughter with an appropriate payment. Perhaps the reason he does not goes back to the theme of the book of Judges: "There was no king in Israel. Everyone did what was right in his own eyes."

Let's be clear. God takes vows seriously, and we must avoid making rash ones. If we make a vow before God, we must fulfill it or bear the guilt of disobeying God. But two wrongs do not make a right. Harming or killing an innocent person is never an option, even if part of an oath.

Jephthah's Unlikely Faith

Despite our understandable aversion to the story of Jephthah's vow, Scripture views Jephthah as a man of faith. We see it in his thorough understanding of Israel's history and glimpse it in his confidence in Yahweh as the covenant-keeping God of Israel. Jephthah exhibits faith in negotiating with and fighting the Ammonites, and his confidence that God can defeat the Ammonites remains firm. Both he and his daughter clearly understand God's character of faithfulness and truthfulness as they seek to honor the oath. That he was rash in making the oath is beyond question, but this does not mute his sincere and unshakable faith in Yahweh.

Conclusion

With our consideration of the four warriors and judges of Israel mentioned in Hebrews 11 complete, let's recap some important applications as displayed on the following chart.

Four Unlikely Warriors

Warrior	"An Unlikely—	—Man of Faith"	Application
Gideon Judges 6–8 *Cycle 4*	• Initial fear • Final apostasy	• Desired to see God • Obeyed God • Judged Israel well	• Put aside fear and obey. • Seek spiritual intimacy God's way.
Barak Judges 4–5 *Cycle 3*	• Not a judge; a warrior • Deprived of "glory" due to fear?	• Allied with God's prophet • Fought valiantly	• Seek a godly ally. • Disregard self-glory.

Samson Judges 13–16 *Cycle 6*	• Carnal passions • Spiritual blindness • Violates Nazirite vow	• Divine saboteur • Cried out to the Lord	• Simply believing God is vital. • Do not confuse giftedness with godliness.
Jephthah Judges 10:6–12:7 *Cycle 5*	• Outsider reputation • Outrageous vow	• Theologically astute • Seeks negotiation • Honors God	• Grasp God's faithfulness. • Understand God's lordship over history. • Avoid rash vows.

With Gideon we learn to put aside our natural fears as we respond to the call of God. We are to resist making "ephods"—any counterfeit shadows of spirituality—to regain our sense of intimacy with God.

With Barak we discover the value of allying ourselves with other servants of God, regardless of gender, in order better to obey God's will. We seek to follow God's path faithfully, regardless of who gets the credit.

With Samson we understand that our relationship with God is extended *sola gratia*—by grace alone. We must take care never to confuse giftedness with godliness.

And with Jephthah we treasure a deepening understanding of our God as a true and faithful covenant-keeping God who is deeply involved in our own story. At the same time, we are to avoid presuming on God's mercy by making outrageous vows we may live to regret.

CHAPTER 17

SAMUEL AND DAVID:
THE UNLIKELY LEADERS

Hearing God's Voice

In some churches I would not qualify to be a minister of the gospel. The reason is simple: I have never heard God's voice. I mean "voice" in a literal way. Such as hearing a voice that could be captured on a digital recorder and replayed so that anyone—believer or skeptic—could hear it. Or listening to the voice Jesus used for over thirty-five years with his family, his disciples, the multitudes, and his enemies. Or encountering the voice God used with scores of men and women in the Old Testament.

When a friend says he has heard God's voice, I sometimes push him for a concrete explanation. "Is God's voice tenor, baritone, or bass?" I ask with a smile.

"Well, it wasn't actually an audible voice," he'll concede, "but I felt God's presence with a clear message. In that sense, God spoke to me as surely as if his voice was broadcast over a loudspeaker."

I do not deny that this can happen. In fact, I have prayed from time to time that God would speak to me in such a way. So far he has not. This does not mean, however, that I have not sensed God's leading.

I will never forget sitting alone in an apartment in Salem, Oregon, one October evening in 1971. I was one month into my first semester of law school at Willamette University's College of Law. That September, I had moved from my parent's home in Portland to a small studio apartment that smelled like fried fish in a greasy diner. It was located on State Street, not far from Oregon's state capitol and the university. I purchased a truckload of law books for my courses in contract law, criminal law, property law, torts, and civil procedure, facing a towering amount of reading each evening for classes the next day. Like every student, I was required to be ready to discuss the details of a case and its legal principles on the spot in any class.

In mid October I was struck with an earthshaking realization: one went to law school to become a lawyer. "Why would I want to do this?" I asked myself. Recognizing that our adversarial legal system requires attorneys to defend clients, not necessarily to argue for the truth, I became disillusioned, discouraged, and depleted (though today I wouldn't struggle with our legal system as I did then). I sat in my studio apartment, separated by 909 miles from the woman I loved, feeling adrift and alone and wondering what this crossroads meant.

At that moment my empty soul was recharged with new purpose. I was filled with the overwhelming desire to invest my life in a ministry of the Word of God. I did not want to become a lawyer. I did not want to read tomes of case law and do Bible study on the side. I wanted to devote all my energies, all my abilities, all my gifts and talents to teaching and preaching the Holy Scriptures.

This was not an unexpected insight, however. God had been preparing me for this for a year and a half. But I am as certain today as I was on that October evening—especially having completed over thirty-two years of service at Multnomah University—that God was directing me to my life's calling, even though I never heard his audible voice.

In this chapter we consider two unlikely leaders. We will meet the kingmaker Samuel, a man who heard God's actual voice and learned how to listen. We will also meet David, the first dynastic king who knew how to follow God's leading, even though he never heard God's voice himself.

Samuel and David—the final two names in the list of six unlikely judges and warriors—are the early architects of Israel's monarchy. Although Hebrews names David first, we will begin with Samuel to retain a more coherent biblical chronology. The biblical stories of Samuel and David are so numerous and extensive that we cannot do justice to the breadth of these men's lives here. For that reason we will focus on two characteristics of leadership: Samuel embodies what it means to listen to God's voice, and David is a man after God's own heart.

Samuel, the Unlikely Listener

Samuel is an expected entry into faith's hall of fame. Of the tribe of Ephraim, he functions as the hinge in Israel's unfolding history. He is the last of the judges and travels a circuit throughout Israel to the end of his days. He gives spiritual leadership to the nation but does not command Israel in battle. He is a prophet who delivers God's message to Israel's people and kings. He is a kingmaker who establishes the monarchy by anointing Israel's first king, Saul. Finally, Samuel anoints David as king in Saul's place, establishing an eternal dynasty fulfilled in Jesus Christ.

But this judge, kingmaker, and prophet is not perfect. He fails as a father when his two sons, Joel and Abijah, grow up to be greedy and unjust. Israel demands a king partly because they refuse to be governed by Samuel's corrupt sons.

Nevertheless, Samuel is a man who hears the voice of God and continues to listen to God even from beyond the grave (1 Sam. 28). This theme of listening to God in the story of Samuel's boyhood years is shown below.

Listening to God

Samuel's Unlikely Birth	Samuel's Unlikely Mentor	Samuel's Unlikely Summons
Born of Hannah, a godly, barren woman who prays to Yahweh	Raised by Eli, the priest in Shiloh who raises contemptible sons	Receives from God a fourfold summons when visions are rare
God listens	Eli and his sons do not listen	Samuel listens
1 Samuel 1:1–2:11	1 Samuel 2:12–36	1 Samuel 3:1–21

Samuel's Unlikely Birth

Much like Samson, Samuel is born of a barren woman who vows not to use of a razor on her son's head (1 Sam. 1). In Samuel's case, however, his parents, Elkanah and Hannah, are named, and special emphasis is placed on their piety. Hannah, though deeply loved by her husband, is bitterly discouraged by her barrenness and by the jibes of Peninnah, Elkenah's other wife. On an annual visit to Shiloh—the site of the tabernacle and the residence of Eli the priest—Hannah sinks into the darkest despair. Praying fervently for a son, she vows to dedicate the child to the Lord all his life, apparently as a Nazirite, if only Yahweh would grant her request.

Eli watches her silent praying and assumes the worst—that she is drunk in God's house. When he finally sorts out the truth, he prays for God's compassion. Soon, Hannah supernaturally conceives and gives birth to a boy she names Samuel, which means "heard by God." The theme of listening that punctuates Samuel's boyhood story begins with the Lord's listening to Hannah's passionate prayer.

Samuel's Unlikely Mentor

Hannah and her husband are as good as their word. As soon as Samuel is weaned, Hannah takes him to Shiloh to dedicate him to the Lord's service. Her prayer of thanksgiving (1 Sam. 2:1–11) is a classic paean that likely inspires Mary's *Magnificat* (Luke 1:46–55).

Though Hannah visits him annually with a new suit of clothes, Samuel is raised by Eli the priest. Eli is himself a swing man of sorts. Besides his priestly role at Shiloh, he also judges Israel for forty years until his death at ninety-eight years of age. Scripture speaks more to Eli's failure as a father than to his success as a judge (1 Sam. 2:12–36). His two sons, Hophni and Phinehas, are morally and spiritually despicable. They treat the offerings of the Lord with contempt by securing (through extortion if necessary) the best portion of each offering for themselves, including the fat reserved for God alone. They brazenly commit fornication at the doorway of the tabernacle in sight of all.

I doubt that any parent in their right mind would want their child raised by Eli.

"Hannah, do you really mean to entrust our little son to Eli?" Elkanah asks, with evident concern in his voice. "You know how he spoils his sons."

"To be honest," Hannah responds, "I share your concern. But I vowed before Yahweh our God, and I cannot disgrace his name or ours by backing out of it."

"I'm aware of your vow," her husband counters. "But I'm thinking of Samuel. What's to prevent our boy from following the bad examples of Hophni and Phinehas? Their blatant rebellion against God, plus Eli's blind eye to it, could lead Samuel down the same destructive path. I've got a bad feeling about this!"

Hannah pauses. "I do too, Elkanah. But we have no choice but to trust that the God who brings life out of the death of my barren womb can protect and bless our child, even beyond our greatest fears.

"You know how much I love you, Hannah," Elkanah says finally. "Do what you think is right. I will not interfere."

Despite his parents' concerns, Samuel thrives at Shiloh. In a deliberate contrast to the evil deeds of Eli's sons, the narrative three times emphasizes his spiritual growth. Samuel ministers to the Lord (1 Sam. 2:11); he grows in the Lord's presence (1 Sam. 2:21); and he continues to grow in stature and in favor with God and man (1 Sam. 2:26, using language later applied to Jesus in Luke 2:52).

The theme of listening continues. Eli hears how much the people deplore the practices of his sons. He tries to reason with the boys, but they rebuff their father, continuing on their wicked path. The section ends with Eli listening to the voice of a prophet, who predicts an awful judgment on his house.

Samuel's Unlikely Summons

The centerpiece of Samuel's early years is his hearing God's voice in the night, which is highlighted by the statement that visions from God are rare in those days (1 Sam. 3:1–21). The time between the prophecy to Eli of the destruction of his house (1 Sam. 2) and God's nocturnal call to Samuel may have been years. Perhaps this gap confirms that Eli and his sons are finished as God's instruments of prophetic word or priestly service, even though they will live on for some years to come.

God's voice to Samuel in the middle of the night is an audible one. Samuel hears it and wakes, thinking Eli needs him. Obediently, he runs to the sleeping Eli and awakens him, ready to serve.

"Go back to bed," Eli says sleepily. "I didn't call you."

I must have been dreaming, Samuel thinks, rubbing his eyes.

God calls his name a second time, and then a third. Each time Samuel runs to Eli. Samuel does not recognize God's voice, we are told, because God's word is not yet given to him. What surprises us is that it takes Eli so long to realize that God is summoning the young protégé. Perhaps Eli doubts that God's voice will speak again in Israel. Or maybe he clings to the belief that he will continue as the primary recipient of God's revelation.

At any rate, Eli finally clicks. "It is the Lord," he tells Samuel. "The next time he calls, answer him like this: 'Speak, Lord; your servant hears.'"

On the fourth occasion, God calls Samuel and stands before him. Samuel not only hears a voice speaking in the darkness; he witnesses a theophany (confirmed later by the reference to a vision in 1 Samuel 3:15). God's message to the young Samuel affirms the Lord's earlier judgment pronounced against Eli's house. It is not only certain; it is imminent. God reminds Eli through Samuel that this will occur not just because of his sons' wickedness but also because of Eli's failure to restrain them. The final refrain is chilling. No offering can atone for this evil, says the Lord. Not now, not ever.

The next morning, Eli compels Samuel to reveal the vision's message. When Samuel does this fully and faithfully, Eli accepts the word of judgment without complaint.

Samuel has heard God's audible voice. More important, he listens.

The Theme of Listening

The theme of listening comes full circle. The God who listens with compassion to Hannah's prayer also notes the blasphemy of Eli's sons. Eli listens to the people's complaints but is incapable of restraining his wicked sons, who themselves do not listen to their dad. Eli hears God's final message forecasting terrible destruction on Eli's house; but God next speaks to the boy Samuel. Samuel hears and listens, faithfully reporting what God has spoken. This launches Samuel's career as a judge, prophet, and kingmaker guided by the voice of God.

David, the Unlikely King

No one would question David's inclusion in Hebrews 11. Perhaps the only surprise is that he is not singled out for more attention. As the second king of Israel, David is without dispute the nation's greatest monarch, the one through whom God establishes an eternal dynasty that culminates in Jesus Christ, the Son of David and Son of God.

David's accomplishments are impressive. As a teenager watching his father's sheep, he shows courage, confidence, and charm while deferring to his father and seven older brothers, who apparently don't think he amounts to much.

Being anointed king of Israel by Samuel in a secret ceremony in tiny Bethlehem does not go to his head. He serves Saul faithfully for years and seizes Saul's scepter only after the king's death on the battlefield.

David wears his kingly crown with majesty. He is an able military general who finally defeats the Philistines and is a canny political leader who rules with wisdom and grace. He can forge unlikely personal friendships with Jonathan, inspire unquestioned loyalty in his military "mighty men," and unite a nation battered with schism.

Most important, he is a man of immense love for God. He is unafraid to dance with joy before the Lord even though his wife hates him for humiliating himself. He possesses a strong sense of justice and longs to honor God by building a magnificent temple. When God denies this request, David accepts both this and the promise of an everlasting dynasty with equanimity.

But David is not without serious defects. He marries eight wives—often with motives that seem to violate Moses' warning against acquiring many wives (Deut. 17:17)—and takes concubines for political purposes. We wonder why God is silent on these practices that fall so short of his ideal of monogamy. David is an indulgent father who rears some incorrigible kids. In dealing with his rebellious son Absalom, David succumbs to a blind nepotism that threatens to tear the kingdom apart.

Worse are his failings with Bathsheba and Uriah. When he should be leading his troops, he's ogling the beautiful Bathsheba bathing in the nude next door. Whether or not she is complicit in this tableau does not justify David's immoral behavior. In an episode that has the marks of power abuse written all over it, David summons her, sleeps with her, and impregnates her. When she informs him that she bears his child, David resorts to a series of despicable maneuvers, from a heartless cover-up attempt to a thinly disguised military feint that guarantees Uriah is slain.

God's displeasure of David runs deep. Nathan the prophet condemns David in no uncertain terms, and David's love child ails and dies. Despite David's genuine repentance (Ps. 51) and God's forgiveness (Ps. 32), David's legacy remains blemished. "David did what was right in the eyes of the LORD and did not turn aside from anything that he commanded him all the days of his life," Scripture tells us, "except in the matter of Uriah the Hittite" (1 Kings 15:5).

Nevertheless, David is a man after God's own heart. With this background, we shall explore David's divine calling to Israel's throne to reveal his spiritual core. Accordingly, we will examine the cameo of David's calling in the context of Saul's disobedience and Samuel's assignment, as summarized in the following chart.

A Cameo of David's Calling

Saul's Disobedience	Samuel's Assignment	David's Kingship	
God's Priority	God's Standard	God's Perspective	God's Choice

The Lord seeks a man after his own heart.	Obedience is better than sacrifice.	Man looks on the outward appearance, but God looks on the heart.	"I have found in David the son of Jesse a man after my heart."
1 Samuel 13:14	1 Samuel 15:22	1 Samuel 16:7	Acts 13:22

Saul's Disobedience

Although Samuel anoints Saul as king reluctantly, he grows fond of this tall monarch who seems equally hesitant to wear the crown. After his anointing, Saul is quickly pressed into military leadership, leading Israel's armies in victory against the Ammonites in a move that begins to renew the kingdom. Samuel, apparently believing his work is done, delivers his farewell address to Israel (1 Sam. 12).

But things do not go well. Again, Saul musters his warriors, who are frightened and trembling, to meet the Philistines near Gilead as he awaits Samuel's arrival at Gilgal to offer a pre-battle sacrifice to the Lord. When Samuel does not show after seven days, Saul impatiently offers the sacrifice himself. At that very moment Samuel arrives and, despite Saul's excuses, informs him that Saul has lost his dynasty because of his disobedience. "The Lord has sought out a man after his own heart," he declares (1 Sam. 13:14). In the ensuing battle, it is Saul's son Jonathan and Jonathan's armor-bearer who rout the Philistine army.

Events unravel for Saul. Samuel instructs Saul to attack the Amalekites, warning him that every living being of the Amalekites must be destroyed. "Leave nothing alive; take no spoil" is the direct order. Saul defeats the Amalekites but saves king Agag and many of the valuable livestock from destruction. Once again, Samuel confronts the disobedient Saul, who offers lame evasions before finally blaming his soldiers for taking the best animals to sacrifice to the Lord.

"Enough!" shouts Samuel. "Remember, Saul, obedience always trumps ritual. Your first disobedience cost you the dynasty. This one will cost you the throne!" (1 Sam. 15:22–23). Samuel is deaf to Saul's tearful pleading. When Saul tears the garment of the departing prophet, Samuel retorts, "So will the kingdom be torn from you." With that Samuel slays King Agag (hacks him to pieces, we are told) and departs (1 Sam. 15:33).

The story of Saul is one of the saddest in Scripture. With two acts of disobedience, he begins his descent into jealousy, fear, and paranoia from which he never emerges.

Two questions arise. First, is Saul a man of faith? Though the evidences are sparse for a definitive conclusion, I am inclined to think that he is, based on the single statement, "God gave him another heart" (1 Sam. 10:9). Second, why does the Lord reject Saul for two seemingly trivial acts of disobedience, while David's folly of adultery, murder, and cover-up does not disqualify him either from the throne or the dynasty? The answer is clear. It is not the magnitude of sin that matters to God, since even the smallest sin is an affront to his holiness; it is the God-centered orientation of one's heart. David seeks God with his whole heart; Saul's heart was hardened to him. This timeless principle applies to us today.

Samuel's Assignment

Samuel discovers that his ministry to Israel is far from over. God instructs him to travel to the village of Bethlehem, to the house of Jesse, and anoint one of the sons (whom God will show him) as Israel's next king. The old prophet fears that if Saul learns of this, he will kill him—the first indication in Scripture of a dark side of Saul's nature. But Samuel obeys, using a ruse of an offering to the Lord to cover up his real purpose. He makes certain Jesse and his sons are invited to the consecration.

When Samuel meets the family, he is especially impressed with Eliab, the eldest. *He has to be the future king,* Samuel thinks to himself. *This is easier than I thought.*

"Not so fast," the Lord tells him (1 Sam. 16:7). "You're using the usual human standards of appraisal—looking at a man's height, stature, and physical appearance. That's not my standard. I look where you cannot; I look at the heart." Then the Lord continues, "I have rejected Eliab. Keep looking!"

So Abinadab, Shammah, and four other sons of Jesse parade before Samuel. All are impressive human specimens.

"I've rejected them all, Samuel," the Lord says.

"Is this all of your boys?" Samuel asks Jesse, at a loss of what to do.

"Well, there is another, my youngest," Jesse answers slowly. "But he's out in the field tending sheep. I just assumed you wouldn't want—"

"Send for him now! We won't eat until he arrives," Samuel says, cutting him off.

When David enters fresh from the sheepfold, he is handsome too. Scripture describes him as "ruddy," which I prefer to interpret as a redhead, like me!

"That's him," the Lord tells Samuel. "Anoint him Israel's king, and do it now."

David's Kingship

We are not told of David's response to being anointed by Samuel, only that the Spirit of God rushed upon him, a sign of empowering. What we do know is that an unspecified number of years elapse before he finally takes the throne. The lengthy episodes (1 Sam. 16–31) of his serving Saul as court musician and armor-bearer, defeating Goliath, befriending Jonathan, marrying Saul's daughter Michal, fleeing from Saul, living as a fugitive, sparing Saul's life, and fighting Israel's enemies with his own loyal men all occur prior to Saul's death.

Throughout all of this, David's heart seeks the Lord. This characteristic becomes a standard for evaluating other kings of Israel. The assessment of Solomon (1 Kings 11:4) and Abijam (1 Kings 15:3), for example, is that they are kings whose hearts were not fully devoted to the Lord, as David's was.

David's final epitaph is spoken by the apostle Paul in his message in Antioch: "[The Lord] testified and said, 'I have found David son of Jesse a man after my own heart'" (Acts 13:22).

Listening to God's Voice

We have considered Samuel and David with a specific emphasis. Both are men who hear God's call, listen, and obey. Their experiences differ, of course. As God's prophet, Samuel hears the Lord's audible voice throughout his life, from God's fourfold summons to him as a boy at Shiloh to God's direction to anoint David as king. David listens to God too, but we are never told that God speaks to him directly. God communicates to David through prophets like Samuel and Nathan and wise counselors like Ahithophel and Hushai. While the means of communication vary, the divine source of these messages is indisputable. These two men of faith consistently respond in obedience to God's voice.

Have you ever heard the audible voice of God? If you have, congratulations! If not, you may wonder how God speaks to us today in ways undetected by the human ear. And make no mistake: he does still speak. Let's consider five ways God communicates with us today: through Scripture, through creation, through human counsel, through our minds and souls, and through adversity.

First, God speaks to us through the Scriptures. Scripture is the word that the psalmist hides in his heart (Ps. 119) and the whole counsel of God that the apostle proclaims (Acts 20:27). Together, the Old and New Testaments are God's full and sufficient message that infallibly explains God's wonderful character, Christ's completed work on Calvary, the blessed hope of Christ's return, and the principles of life and godliness in which we walk. Meditate on God's holy Word (Ps. 1). Study it diligently (1 Pet. 1:10–11). Feast on it daily.

Second, God speaks to us through his creation. The heavens declare God's intelligence and character (Ps. 19); even the invisible attributes of God are proclaimed by creation (Rom. 1:20). Creation is not an infallible witness, of course, because the fall, the curse, and death have distorted the witness of creation. Spiritual blindness also confounds unbelievers from clearly seeing God in creation. Nevertheless, creation is one of God's textbooks for our instruction. Become curious about the creation. Observe the evidences of beautiful design and harmony imbedded in the cosmos that testify to the power of our God. Rejoice in creation's beauty.

Third, God speaks through wise human counselors. One of the greatest gifts that God gives to us, besides his Word and his Holy Spirit, is fellow believers in the body of Christ. We are designed to be connected to one another, and in the company of many counselors there is wisdom (Prov. 11:14). Wise men and women surround us to encourage, rebuke, correct, and instruct. They are human incarnations of Christlike values that we must imitate (Phil. 3:17). Identify those men or women who can surround you with love and encouragement. Draw on their wisdom for guidance. Rely on their comfort during barren times. Become accountable to them for personal godliness.

Fourth, God speaks to the mind and soul. God promises that as believers we have a new capacity to understand spiritual things because of the indwelling Spirit of God (1 Cor. 2:12). We are to renew our minds and carefully discern the will of God (Rom. 12:2). Use your mind to apply biblical principles to your decisions and to weigh the merits of your options, the significance of your circumstances, and the validity of others' advice. Do not ignore heartfelt feelings of caution, but through prayer, meditation, and counsel investigate whether red flags come from the Spirit or your own reluctance. Be willing to listen carefully to your heart.

Fifth, God speaks through adversity. In his book *The Problem of Pain*, C. S. Lewis puts in perspective God's purposes in pain. "God whispers to us in our pleasures, speaks in our conscience, but shouts in our pain," Lewis writes. "It is His megaphone to rouse a deaf world."* Believing that there are no accidents with God (Rom. 8:28), we recognize that adversity is a way he directs us. God may use adversity to close a path we have pursued, while opening another, unforeseen opportunity. Adversity may

---

* C. S. Lewis, *The Problem of Pain* (San Francisco: HarperSanFrancisco, 1996), 91.

remind us of God's character and promises. It may mold us for the higher purpose of deeper intimacy with him. Trust God's purposes. Rest in God's promises. Accept God's discipline. Wait on God's direction.

The chart below summarizes the five ways of listening to God that we have explored.

The Art of Listening to God

What to Listen To	How to Listen	Scripture
God's Word	Learn how to study the Bible. Study it regularly.	Psalm 1
Creation	Marvel at its design. Look for God's attributes.	Psalm 19 Romans 1
Wise Counsel	Seek wise counsel. Be accountable.	Proverbs 11:14
Mind and Soul	Use your reason. Weigh your circumstances. Listen to your heart.	Romans 12:2
Adversity	Trust in God's purposes. Rest in God's promises. Accept God's discipline. Wait on God's direction.	Romans 8:28

The most important thing to remember is this. God's direction is not so much about where he wants us to go or what he wants us to do. It's mostly about what he wants us to become: men and women after God's own heart.

CHAPTER 18

THE UNNAMED FAITHFUL:

THE UNLIKELY VICTORS

A Question of Identity

As a boy growing up without television, I cherished a boyhood hero: the Lone Ranger. Every weekday evening after dinner, I would run to the radio and tune in station KWJJ to hear the latest episode. The program always opened with the stirring strains of Rossini's "William Tell Overture." I still get goose bumps when I hear that music. Then the narrator would come on. "A fiery horse with the speed of light, a cloud of dust, and a hearty 'Hi-Yo, Silver!' The Lone Ranger!"

I even had 78 rpm records of eight of the early episodes, and I would play them over and over. My favorite was the first episode, which told the story of how Dan Reid became the Lone Ranger.

Dan Reid and his brother were Texas Rangers. They and four other Rangers were on the trail of the notorious Cavendish Gang, a ruthless band of outlaws, cattle rustlers, murderers, and thieves led by Butch Cavendish. They had received a tip from a reliable scout that the Cavendish Gang had their hideout in a nearby canyon. So the six mounted up and rode to the canyon to capture them.

What they did not know was that they had been betrayed. The Cavendish Gang was there all right, waiting in ambush. The Rangers entered the narrow opening to the box canyon single file on horseback. When all six Rangers were in the canyon, the Cavendish Gang, hidden in the rocks around the canyon rim, opened up, cutting them down with withering rifle fire. Soon the bodies of all the Rangers were scattered on the canyon floor. Convinced they were dead, Butch Cavendish and his gang rode away.

At nightfall, a lone figure entered the canyon. He was an Indian. He carefully examined five of the bodies of the Rangers and pronounced all of them dead. But when he examined the sixth body, the body of Dan Reid, he discovered he was still alive. Carrying him to a nearby cave, the Indian dressed the Ranger's wounds and began to nurse him back to health with his knowledge of tribal medicine. Then, returning to the canyon floor, he buried the dead bodies of the five other Rangers. He dug, however, six graves, forever concealing the truth that one of the Rangers was still alive.

Two days later, Dan Reid's fever broke and he awoke to see an Indian bending over him.

"I am Tonto," the Indian told him. "Years ago we were blood brothers. I called you Kemo Sabe. This means faithful friend."

"What about the others?" Reid murmured. "What about the other Rangers?"

"Other Rangers all dead," Tonto replied. And then, in words that will never be erased from my boyhood memory, Tonto added, "You only Ranger left. You lone Ranger."

That night Dan Reid made a vow that he would pursue the Cavendish Gang and bring them to justice. He realized he would need to hide his identity to be successful and to protect his family. So he chose a black mask to conceal his face. For the rest of his life, Dan Reid rode the plains as the Masked Avenger, the Lone Ranger.

The final verses of Hebrews 11 refer to nameless people. Many are likely Old Testament prophets, since "the prophets" is the last category specifically noted (11:32), and some of the descriptions fit what we know of them. Even so, their earthly identities are concealed from us, known only to God. Anonymous as they are, these nameless people are victors, true heroes of the faith.

The descriptions of these heroes can be divided into two groupings: the faithful who experience miraculous deliverance in this life (Heb. 11:33–35a), and the faithful who endure adversity, suffering, torture, and martyrdom without earthly vindication (Heb. 11:35b–38). For brevity's sake, I will display the descriptions of these unlikely victors in two charts below. I have included some suggestions as to the possible identities of the nameless men and women described in these verses.

Unlikely Victors, Earthly Deliverance

In the first grouping, Hebrews emphasizes miraculous, earthly deliverance: conquest, justice, fulfilled promises, escape from fire and sword, and achievement of military victory out of weakness. Some of these descriptions clearly identify certain figures, such as Daniel and his three companions in Babylon. Others seem to be apt descriptions of Gideon, Barak, Samson, Jephthah, David, and Samuel. All, of course, represent faithful men and women who bear common witness to the strong arm of God. The list impresses us with the abundance and diversity of God's miraculous dealings with his servants.

Unlikely Victors, Earthly Deliverance

Verse	Description	Possible Identities
11:33	They conquered kingdoms.	Joshua, David
	They enforced justice.	Joshua, the Judges, Samuel, David, Solomon
	They obtained promises.	Joshua, David, the Prophets
	They stopped the mouths of lions.	Daniel
11:34	They quenched the power of fire.	Daniel's three Hebrew companions
	They escaped the edge of the sword.	David, Elijah, Elisha
	They were made strong out of weakness.	Gideon, Barak, Jephthah, Samson, David, Esther, the Maccabeans
	They became mighty in war.	
	They put foreign armies to flight.	
11:35a	Women received back their dead through resurrection.	The widow of Zarephath and Elijah; the Shunammite hostess and Elisha

Heavenly Victors, Earthly Sufferers

In the second grouping, the mood darkens. The earthly outcome of the lives of these faithful ones is not triumphal. They face adversity, suffering, and death, often in horrific ways. They confirm Jesus' view of Israel's history as a story of her leaders murdering her prophets (Matt. 23). These sufferers are not as easily identifiable in Scripture. Some Old Testament figures, like Isaiah and Jeremiah, have explanations based in tradition; other figures may have lived in the intertestamental period. This list impresses us with the immovable faith of men and women as they walk through the valley of the shadow of death.

Heavenly Victors, Earthly Suffering

Verse	Description	Possible Identities
11:35b	Some were tortured.	Seven brothers of 2 Maccabees
11:36	Others suffered mocking and flogging.	
	Others endured chains and imprisonment.	Jeremiah
11:37a	They were stoned.	
	They were sawn in two.	Isaiah
	They were killed by the sword.	
11:37b–38	They went about in skins of sheep and goats, destitute, afflicted, mistreated, wandering about in deserts and mountains, and in dens and caves of the earth.	Elijah

Some of these descriptions fit people in the New Testament too. The apostle Paul, for example, is stoned, flogged, imprisoned, and eventually killed by the sword. The ultimate example of suffering, of course, is the scourging and mocking of Jesus, the preeminently faithful One, which culminates in the unspeakable torture of the cross.

Lessons from Unlikely Victors

The closing verses of Hebrews 11 deliver two important insights. First, the world is not worthy of such people (Heb. 11:38), and second, none of them received what is promised. This last insight repeats the conclusion mentioned earlier in the chapter: "They all died in faith, not having received the things promised" (Heb. 11:13).

At first glance this conclusion, coupled with the final list of faithful men and women who suffered and died in terrible ways, makes us wonder. Is the life of faith worth it? Why are the promises unfulfilled? Can we live up to these standards of faith? To address these important questions, we will consider the five concluding observations below.

The Hope of a Heavenly Home

First, God promises a heavenly homeland to people of faith. Hebrews reminds us that everyone in this chapter—from Abel to David—seeks a homeland guaranteed by God. Since Abraham is asked to move his entire household to the land of Canaan, it is easy to assume this homeland is a physical locale. Nothing could be further from the truth! If it were, Hebrews tells us, Abraham would run back to Ur when things get bad, or Moses would return to Egypt (Heb. 11:15). But since they never do, it is clear

that they have a heavenly homeland in view, a city with foundations, whose builder and architect is God (Heb. 11:10). That is
why the faithful die with an unfulfilled promise but pass away
with hope, not bitterness. They know God will fulfill his promise
to them in the future, beyond the grave.

A Longing for Heaven

Second, every person of faith yearns for this heavenly home.
People of genuine faith possess an insatiable longing for heaven
(Heb. 11:16). No earthly kingdom satisfies. No marble palace,
temple, or monument substitutes for that divine destiny that is
far, far better. They consider themselves aliens and exiles in this
present world (Heb. 11:13), rejecting its values and dismissing its
pleasures. C. S. Lewis expresses such longing in *Mere Christianity*, when he writes, "If I find in myself a desire which no experience in this world can satisfy, the most probable explanation
is that I was made for another world."* The unlikely heroes of
Hebrews 11 desire such a world.

Divine Deliverance of the Faithful

Third, God may intervene to bring glorious victory to his
people. In a variety of ways, God brings incredible blessings
out of impossible circumstances. Virtually every story we have
considered in this book recounts the amazing intervention of
an omnipotent and compassionate God to accomplish his good
purposes on the earth. Sometimes he brings down city walls,
raises the dead, or defeats immense hostile armies. Usually he
uses weak, frail, fearful, flawed, and ordinary people like us to do
it. And he can do it today.

---

* C. S. Lewis, *Mere Christianity* (San Francisco: HarperSanFrancisco, 2001), 136.

Righteous Suffering of the Faithful

Fourth, God may allow his faithful ones to suffer adversity and martyrdom. God does not guarantee our success, victory, or prosperity in this life. Abel is slain, Samson dies blinded under the rubble of a Philistine temple, Isaiah is sawn asunder, Jeremiah is stoned, and countless prophets are killed by Jezebel's sword. Jesus goes even further and predicts that in this present world we will have tribulation. He explains that if the world hated him, his followers cannot expect easier treatment (John 15:18). Nevertheless, he offers us deeply-rooted comfort. "Take heart," he reminds us, "I have overcome the world" (John 16:33).

Because of this principle of suffering, any prosperity theology of health and wealth crumbles in the shadow of the tombs of the unnamed victors who suffer terrible deaths without receiving the promise. Are these faithful ones betrayed by God because they die this way? No! The world is not worthy of them; they now live among the cloud of witnesses who inhabit a heavenly homeland.

Postponement of the Promise

Fifth, God postpones the fulfillment of his promise to us until Christ returns. The promise of a heavenly homeland is delayed until all men and women of faith can enjoy it together. "Apart from us," we are told, "they should not be made perfect" (Heb. 11:40). In what sense are the unlikely heroes now imperfect in their heavenly home? They do not yet possess their immortal and glorified bodies. That summative event will occur when Christ returns for the rest of us who long for his coming. Then and only then will we be reunited with the Savior and join the entire assembly of the people of God. That is not, of course, the end. It is only the beginning.

The Spectators of Faith

The conclusion to Hebrews 11 is actually found in the first two verses of Hebrews 12. "Therefore, since we are surrounded by so great a cloud of witnesses," we read, "let us lay aside every weight, and sin which clings so closely, and let us run with endurance the race that is set before us, looking to Jesus, the founder and perfecter of our faith, who for the joy that was set before him endured the cross, despising the shame, and is seated at the right hand of the throne of God" (Heb. 12:1–2).

All of the men and women of faith we have discussed, all of these unlikely heroes—whether named or unnamed, leaders or followers, warriors or travelers, famous or ordinary—are divine examples to encourage us to finish well.

The author's imagery is powerful. Each of us, like a runner in the greatest marathon of our lives, stands at the starting line with 26.2 miles to go. All around us, the stadium is filled with people who have successfully run that race. Just before the gun fires to signal the start, they rise to their feet with a vigorous ovation and exuberant cheering, encouraging us to finish well, no matter what. For just a moment, we glance up. There stands Abel, Abraham, Sarah, Moses, and Rahab with expressions of inner peace and outward joy, pulling for us, encouraging us.

The starter's pistol cracks, and we set off at our individual paces, recalling that none of the heavenly spectators in the area ran the race perfectly. Some were beset with weights of distraction they had to set aside. Others were bespotted with clinging sins that required cleansing. But they all ran, and they all finished.

But that's not all. As we begin to get in stride for the long race ahead, we glance across at the finish line on the other side of the oval track. One lone figure catches our eye. Though standing tall, he is disfigured, with scars on his hands and brow. We recognize him as the only one who has run this race flawlessly, in record time. He is the epitome of endurance and racing perfection, and he awaits each runner who crosses the line.

If you think about it, Jesus is the unlikeliest hero of all. He is unlikely not because there is anything flawed, broken, ordinary, or undistinguished about him. He is none of that. As the King of kings and Lord of lords qualified to sit on the divine throne, Jesus is the most heroic of all. No, what is so unlikely is that he ever ran the race at all. He certainly did not have to. He had nothing to prove; there was no reward he did not already possess; there were no records he had not already shattered. Jesus chose to run the race we run so that we might claim a victor's crown. He endured the agony of the cross and disregarded its shame to secure our victory.

So how should we run our race? We run it like Jesus did: without distractions, without bending the rules, without short-cuts, with joy, with endurance, with the cheers of the innumerable unlikely heroes of the faith ringing in our ears, with our eye on the finish line, and with our heart on the prize of God's upward call.

And why should we run this race? We run it simply to be greeted in the eternal city by its architect and builder. We finish to hear him say, "Well done, good and faithful runner. Join me, joyfully, in the finisher's circle!"

THE FOUNDATION

OF FAITH

Back to the Basics

The summer after my freshman year in college, my family embarked on a fishing expedition into the Bob Marshall Wilderness area of north-central Montana. Our plan was to pack in to Big Salmon Lake (a trip of roughly twelve miles, we thought) and catch the gigantic rainbow and eastern brook trout we knew were there.

After a long drive from Portland to Montana in our old Ford pickup, we arrived at the trail head, Holland Lake, late in the evening. The next day, by the time we were prepared to depart, it was after ten in the morning. "No problem," we said to one another. "We can easily make the twelve miles to Big Salmon before dark." With justifiable optimism, we set out.

The day stretched out longer than we imagined. By 8:30 p.m. Dad and I, a half an hour ahead of the others, reluctantly concluded that we had misjudged the distance. Uncertain how much farther the lake really was, we made an executive decision: unpack the horses, set up a temporary camp, and hike into the lake first thing next morning. Thirty minutes later, when the others arrived with looks of surprise, dinner was cooking. No one complained, although Mom, seeing the sleeping bags laid out on the flat tent canvas, did ask why the tent was not standing. "This is just temporary," Dad explained confidently. "Besides," he said, pointing upward, "look at the clear sky. There will be no rain tonight." Then he added the words that would haunt us for the rest of the trip: "Remember, I was born and raised in Montana!"

After dinner, surrounded by darkness, we crawled into our sleeping bags, exhausted from the day's trek. Dad, ever the woodsmanship teacher, reminded us to protect our belongings from the elements. I drifted off to sleep with his final exhortation: "Be sure to put your matches and watches inside your boots and cover them with your hat to keep out the rain." I vaguely wondered why he would warn about rain after what he said earlier, particularly with the moon shining so brightly.

The next thing I knew, I was stabbed awake with the flash of lightning and its almost simultaneous crash of thunder. Sitting upright, I felt that heavy downpour of a mountain cloudburst so typical of hot summer nights in the Rocky Mountains. This was no light drizzle. It was a torrential baptism that quickly puddled the campsite and the flattened tent. In fact, so quick and intense was this rain that water began flowing into the open mouths of our sleeping bags before we realized what was happening.

Soaked, all of us wondered the same thing: *What time is it?* and *How long until morning?* In the darkness I could feel Dad pivot in his soggy bag and reach for his watch and flashlight.

Ker-plunk! was all I heard as Dad's hand plunged into his hat, now full to the brim with water. His watch, matches, and flashlight lay at the bottom. When he retrieved his watch, thankfully waterproof, he whispered the bad news. "It's only 12:30 in the morning."

It is interesting what comes to your mind in challenging situations, or rather what does *not* come to mind. On that pitch-black August night in Montana's wilderness, I was not thinking about which political party might regain the White House. I did not wonder whether interest rates were rising or falling. I was unconcerned about the stock market. Questions about my fall class schedule vanished. Instead, dramatic circumstances redirected my priorities. In the blink of an eye, I was focused on the basics: how to dry off, how to warm up, and how to last the five long hours of darkness until daybreak.

In our spiritual pilgrimage, sometimes it is wise to return to the basics. In this chapter, we shall do just that, reflecting on the fundamental meaning and implications of living a life of faith before God. As we investigate the meaning of true, biblical faith, we will follow three trails: the confusion of faith, the meaning of faith, and the necessity of faith.

The Confusion of Faith

To understand what faith is, we must first examine what it is not since there is much cloudy thinking about faith. While it should not surprise us that many nonbelievers misunderstand the nature of genuine, biblical faith, I am amazed that many believers are equally confused. Therefore, we will consider three widely held distortions, or myths, of faith.

The Myth of Mystical Faith

The first myth is that faith is primarily mystical. The mystical view of faith affirms the idea that faith is believing something whether or not it seems reasonable. I call it the "blind leap" approach. It is faith *without* reason. In this view, to be a person of faith requires closing one's mind. Faith and reason are seen as contradictory, incompatible with each other. While many widely accept this as a correct meaning of faith, there are two opposing responses to it.

Rejecting the mystical. One response to mystical faith is to reject faith altogether. I am a member of the Portland Society of Magicians (PSM), an interesting group of people! Its membership includes believers like me who enjoy learning and using illusions in our teaching and evangelistic ministries. But the PSM also includes many who are secularists, some quite hostile to Christianity. I'll never forget overhearing a conversation between one of the members and a guest. The member (whom I'll call Carl) is rightly considered an elder statesman among magicians in the Northwest. The guest, whom I did not know, was obviously a Christian. The two of them were discussing Christianity, and Carl guided the conversation with his definition. "Faith," he said, "is by definition that which you cannot prove." To Carl, an intelligent rationalist, faith is irrational; and he would have nothing to do with it. "That kind of faith," he argued, "means sacrificing your mind." He went on to explain that he was an agnostic when it came to God.

Agnosticism, of course, is a safe position because it says, "I don't know!" When it comes to the question of God, it proclaims, "I don't know whether there is a God." Pleading ignorance is safe because it shifts the burden of proof to the one who seeks to prove something (that God exists, for example).

By contrast, the atheist who says, "There is no God," faces the greater difficulty. He must prove his denial. This is impossible to do since it requires a virtually omniscient grasp of all knowledge to show that there is no God. The atheist must demonstrate he knows all there is to know in the universe, has searched the cosmos from beginning to end, and can confirm without reservation that no God is to be found. Few atheists are so arrogant as to try this. Those who try come across as silly. They remind us of Yuri Gagarin, the first Soviet cosmonaut. According to Nikita Khrushchev, when Gagarin returned to earth, he reported that he saw no God in space. Theists, of course, loved to retort, "Just step outside the capsule and you'll see him!"

The late J. Edwin Orr, author and apologist, spoke on agnosticism a number of years ago in a lecture at Multnomah. There are two kinds of agnostics, said Orr. One is the *ordinary* agnostic, who says, "I do not know whether there is a God." The ordinary agnostic honestly expresses his intellectual uncertainty, and the Christian apologist can introduce him to the biblical truth about the one, true God. The second kind of agnostic is more popular. This is the *ornery* agnostic, who says, "I don't know if there is a God, but you don't know and no one knows, so don't try to tell me."

Carl, my friend from the Portland Society of Magicians, falls into the ornery category. "How can I believe in the Christian God?" he asks. To him, the God of the Old Testament is a God "whose hands drip in blood" because he commanded the annihilation of the Canaanites—men, women, and children. Carl's agnosticism stems from a very specific and incorrect understanding of faith: "Faith is by definition what you cannot prove." To Carl, being a person of faith means committing intellectual suicide.

Embracing the mystical. Unlike Carl, others embrace a mystical faith but are less concerned about the object of their faith. We often see this with the so-called New Age religions, popular for their postmodern rejection of reason.

A most vivid example of embracing an "irrational," mystical faith occurred in the early 1980s, when a group of people wearing clothes the colors of the rainbow made their pilgrimage to Central Oregon to follow an Indian mystic called the Rajneesh. Inundating the little town of Antelope, Oregon, he and his followers renamed it Rajneesh Purim. I will never forget the initial, enthusiastic response by many sectors of Oregon's society. The business community, for one, was ecstatic over the coming of the Rajneesh because his grand construction projects spelled economic hope for many workers and suppliers still mired in an economic slump. Even our local newspaper, *The Oregonian,* was uncharacteristically supportive of this overtly religious enterprise.

The followers of the Rajneesh accepted a mystical definition of faith and embraced it as their own. The Rajneeshees, as they were called, were not society's castoffs, homeless, or down-and-outers. Most who gathered in Rajneesh Purim were well educated, highly professional, and in many cases wealthy. They relinquished their wealth and resigned their jobs to enter this commune with a man who claimed to be a god.

Theirs was a mystical faith because of its irrational object. The Rajneesh was called the Bhagwan, the "enlightened one." In other words, he claimed to be a god. The ridiculousness of this claim became evident several years later when the Bhagwan's house of cards began to tumble. As the U.S. Immigration Service initiated steps for his deportation, his spokesperson, a high-ranking woman in the organization named Ma Anand Sheela, gave an explanation that should have said it all. "I'm sorry," she protested, "he's too old and sick to move."

Now, think about this. Here is a man who claims to be god with willing, compliant followers. But he cannot board an airplane because he is too old and sick. This echoes the prophet Elijah's sarcastic remarks made against the false and impotent idols of Baal during his dramatic confrontation with the priests on Mount Carmel (1 Kings 18:27), doesn't it? The situation would be laughable if not for the tragic spiritual implications for thousands of sincere but misled followers.

But this story's greatest irony emerges in a reporter's interview with one member of the Rajneesh community, the daughter of the late California Congressman Leo J. Ryan. (Ryan himself was murdered in 1978 while investigating the cultic Jonestown settlement in the South American country of Guyana, shortly before members committed mass suicide.) Ryan's daughter was a follower of the Rajneesh. A reporter asked Ryan's daughter the inevitable question: "If the Bhagwan asked you to commit suicide, as cult leader Jim Jones asked his followers, would you do it?" Without hesitation, she replied, "Absolutely."

People who embrace mystical faith are all around us. Likely, in the years to come, more and more will become "people of faith" but will care little about whether the object or content of their faith is credible or reasonable. They will accept not a biblical faith but a mystical view to fill the vacuum in their lives.

The Myth of Emotional Faith

There is a second myth of faith: faith depends on how it makes you feel. This is the emotional view of faith. I call it "feel good" faith.

A number of years ago, a guest editorialist wrote an op-ed piece in *The Oregonian* that recounted a personal experience. The writer boarded a plane, she explained, and just before takeoff an elderly woman—described as being a bit frumpy—sat down in the seat next to her. The woman appeared nervous, the reporter said, as they buckled their seat belts. After they were airborne, the older woman uneasily turned to the reporter and asked, "Do you believe in Jesus as your personal savior?"

The reporter responded, "I don't talk about religion because I think it is a very personal matter." The column concluded on a rather smug note: the older woman had no good comeback, and she left the reporter alone the rest of the flight.

The author's point, of course, is quite clear. Religion is a good thing, and in our pluralistic society any religion you choose is fine. You have the right to believe what you want. But religion is personal. Do not dare to impose your beliefs on me.

Perhaps you have heard someone say something like that. In responding to such a view, remember two important things.

First, religion *is* personal. It had better be. If a worldview or religious system is only theoretical, with no provision for hope and guidance for life, then it is irrelevant and easily dismissed. Such an approach is a philosophy, not a religion. Make no mistake about it: Christianity is a religion, pure and true. Remember what James says: "Religion that is pure and undefiled before God, the Father, is this: to visit orphans and widows in their affliction, and to keep oneself unstained from the world" (James 1:27).

Second, pure religion is true. It is much more than personal relevancy. The tragedy of the reporter's self-righteous answer is that she ignores the question of veracity. While it might be interesting to discover what a friend *feels* about the resurrection of Jesus Christ, for example, one's feelings have little to do with it. For if in fact the tomb was empty because Jesus conquered death, and if he appeared alive to the disciples to demonstrate his victory, and if he is living in heaven at the Father's right hand to return for those he has called, then the truth of these claims stands as a matter of eternal importance.

Even more to the point, the same resurrected Jesus who conquered death and promises to return to earth also claimed, "I am the way, the truth and the life. No one comes to the Father except through me" (John 14:6). This "exclusivist" claim may not be politically correct, but that does not change its central, historical reality. Accept it as true or reject it at your peril. It has little to do with whether you *feel* it is true; it has everything to do with whether it really happened, and whether Jesus Christ means what he said.

The Myth of Intellectual Faith

There is a third, perhaps subtler, confusion. It is the myth of intellectual faith. In this misunderstanding, faith is the affirmation of a collection of propositional truths. I call this the "grocery list" view of faith. Like all of these views, it contains elements of truth, but restricting our understanding of faith only to a doctrinal statement is a distortion. Again, James reminds us of the inadequacy of trusting doctrine, regardless how orthodox, alone. "You believe that God is one," James says, "you do well. Even the demons believe—and shudder" (James 2:19). And if the demons are as doctrinally orthodox as anyone, James implies, be warned. Merely affirming theological truth is no guarantee of a personal relationship with God.

The myth of intellectual faith finds several expressions. Unfortunately it is evident in many Bible-believing churches. Such churches, including solid evangelical ones, often require the signing of a doctrinal statement or creed as a requirement for membership. Yet pastor after pastor can tell stories of members in good standing who eventually come to faith in Christ after years of self-deception. It's not that people willingly mislead church leadership when they join, but an unbalanced emphasis on doctrinal conformity without a corresponding accountability to personal holiness can perpetuate empty intellectualism.

The myth of intellectual faith is also evident in well-known scholars who replace childlike faith with intellectual theories. In 2000, the late ABC news anchor Peter Jennings moderated a television special called "A Search for Jesus." Disappointingly, the program showcased a number of world-renowned New Testament scholars who argued that the Jesus of history is not the Christ of the Gospels. The Gospel records, they argued, contain very little we can trust about the Jesus of history. Rather, the ample material about the Christ of the Gospels was manufactured by the early church and is therefore historically unreliable. The task of responsible scholarship, they claimed, is to use critical assumptions and rational arguments to peel away the layers of invented stories about Jesus (the miracles, his claims to deity, and the resurrection, for example) to discover the true historical Jesus.

What is interesting about these scholars is that many consider themselves to be men of faith. While rejecting the Gospels' account of Jesus' life and teaching, they affirm the so-called Christ event, finding solace and hope in what Christ symbolizes. Theirs is a most interesting mixture of the intellectual and the mystical. They possess an intellectual belief in a critical view of the history of Jesus, yet they embrace a symbolic view of the Christ story. The apostles and the early church knew nothing of such a schizophrenic faith!

Finally, mere intellectual faith can camouflage outright unbelief. One summer, my wife Jani, daughter Elise, and I were driving home from Southern California. We stopped in the quaint town of Ashland, Oregon, for a brief lunch in beautiful Lithia Park. Seated at a picnic table not far away was a tall man with long, blond hair dressed in a white sheet. Since we had seen several similarly dressed men hitchhiking that day, I was curious.

I approached him and asked, "Would you like some of our lunch?"

"Thank you," he responded. "I won't accept anything for myself, but I will accept your offer as an offering to Krishna."

Now I knew. I was mildly surprised because I thought Hare Krishnas wore saffron gowns and were bald, but this man apparently belonged to a different denomination! Not having much time, I asked, "Tell me, why have you rejected Christianity?"

His response was instructive. "Oh, I haven't," he said.

"Well, what do you believe about Jesus?"

"I believe Jesus Christ was the Son of God who died for the sins of the world," he answered earnestly.

I was flabbergasted. He could have signed the doctrinal statement of many evangelical churches.

"What do you mean that 'Jesus is the Son of God'?" I asked.

"We're all sons of God," he said. "We all have that divine spark within us; Jesus just had it a little more. But, if we follow the right path, we can gain that too."

And so the conversation went as he discussed sin, morality, and redemption—using biblical words with entirely unbiblical meanings. The final danger of intellectual faith is that it is possible to say the right words and mean the wrong thing. It is even possible to know the meaning and possess no relationship with God at all.

The Meaning of Faith

Out of this confusing rubble, we now seek to build a proper understanding of genuine, biblical faith. Before suggesting a definition, we shall first look at faith in two different yet complementary ways. First, we will examine three biblical phrases that together outline a full-orbed understanding of biblical faith. Second, we will explore three time frames of faith imbedded in Hebrews 11:1 that understand faith from our temporal perspective of the present, the future, and the past.

Three Biblical Phrases for Faith

For centuries, Christian thinkers have recognized genuine faith as more than a mystical leap, an emotional feeling, or simple intellectual affirmations. Theologians, for example, frequently speak of three aspects of faith, *notitia*, *assensus*, and *fiducia*, or the intellectual, emotional, and volitional aspects of faith. More popularly, C. S. Lewis, in an essay in his *God in the Dock*, identifies genuine faith as a combination of intellectual belief (Faith A) and trusting faith (Faith B). Building on these observations, we will examine three pivotal biblical phrases that capture Scripture's bigger landscape of faith, an approach used by Charles C. Ryrie in his *Basic Theology*.

The first phrase is "believe *that*." This is a favorite of the apostle John in his first epistle. He writes, "Everyone who believes *that* Jesus is the Christ has been born of God" (1 John 5:1). This verse emphasizes content. Biblical faith demands that you embrace central propositions of truth in order to become a child of God. For example, John emphasizes the importance of such propositions as Jesus' messiahship ("Jesus is the Christ," 1 John 5:1) and his full humanity ("Jesus Christ has come in the flesh," 1 John 4:2). Belief grounded in content is central to biblical faith, although by itself it is insufficient.

The second phrase is "believe *in*." John uses this frequently in the fourth gospel, where it acquires almost a technical meaning of "saving faith." We find it in the familiar verse, "For God so loved the world, that He gave his only Son, that whoever believes *in* him should not perish but have eternal life" (John 3:16). This phrase is not just about doctrinal content, although knowing truth about Jesus is a prerequisite. This phrase speaks of having confidence in Jesus. Whereas "believe *that*" emphasizes truth, "believe *in*" highlights trust. Are they connected? Absolutely. Are they distinct? Certainly. Can you have one without the other? Unfortunately, yes, and that is precisely where distortion enters. Trust without truth produces a mystical faith unconnected to any credible object. But truth without trust fosters an intellectual faith, a cold orthodoxy without relationship. The biblical picture demands both. A person errs in choosing one or the other.

The third phrase is "believe *on*," a favorite expression of the apostle Paul. In Romans 10:11 Paul says, "Whoever believes on Him will not be put to shame" (NKJV). This phrase emphasizes commitment, the perfect complement to belief in content and confidence in Christ. Whereas the other components pertain to truth and trust, this one pertains to troth. *Troth* is an archaic word formerly used in traditional marriage vows. It means commitment, and for an alliterationist like myself, the three words *truth*, *trust*, and *troth* form a perfect threesome.

These three aspects of faith stand in a vital cause-and-effect relationship. First, one must believe in fundamental truths about Jesus Christ, although that alone will not save. Second, one must channel this knowledge into trust in the Savior, triggering a relationship. Third, that relationship is to grow and mature into a commitment that governs choices and decisions.

But that is not the end, because living faith develops and deepens. Committed action creates a hunger for more truth, which leads to greater trust, which incites a more fervent commitment, and the cycle spirals upward. This deepening faith, where all three intersect, is biblical faith.

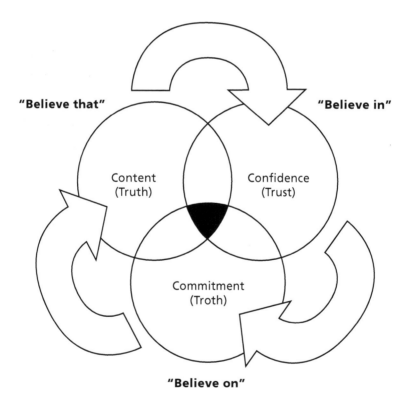

This interlocking relationship between truth, trust, and troth was beautifully illustrated a number of years ago at the inauguration of the Portland Center for the Performing Arts. The city of Portland, after renovating its venerable Paramount Theater into the Arlene Schnitzer Concert Hall, built a multistory complex of three performing arts theaters just across the street to complement it. In 1987, as the venues prepared to open for their fall schedules, plans were made for an inaugural celebration. As part of the evening's entertainment, Philippe Petit, a French high-wire artist, was hired for $35,000 to perform his breathtaking act, bathed in spotlights, between the two buildings six stories above the pavement.

In great secrecy Petit traveled to Portland to prepare for the event. He lacked one thing, however: a young and agile female volunteer to cross the wire with him. Not long before the deadline, an event organizer spotted a young woman named Ann Seward at an evening dinner party. She appeared to be the right size and sufficiently athletic, so he approached her and asked if she would be willing to volunteer.

Although she was interested, Seward responded as any sensible person would: she wanted much more information. She discovered Petit to be an internationally known performer with a twenty-five-year legacy of success. Widely respected, he had performed flawlessly on international venues far more challenging than Portland's Broadway and Main. As yet, though, Seward had exercised no faith. She was at the initial content-gathering stage but open to take the next step. "I'd like to meet this man," she said to an *Oregonian* reporter, "and see if I trust him."

Indeed, the next step was building trust. The French artist invited Seward to inspect his studio. There he set up his high wire as it would appear the night of the celebration, but only eight feet high. Petit climbed onto the wire and challenged Seward to dislodge him. Try what she would, he was immovable. And so, with growing confidence, she began to rehearse with him on the taut wire eight feet above the floor.

Eventually, Seward agreed to participate and prepared for the big night. That evening, at the climax of the festivities, the spotlights illuminated the French performer and his wire. He moved effortlessly back and forth between the tall buildings, each time performing increasingly complicated and daring maneuvers. Finally, it was time for Ann Seward. Up to this point, she had developed a kind of faith. She believed intellectually that Petit could carry her across the wire safely. She came to believe through repeated experience that she would be safe in his routine. But only if she made the commitment to be carried across herself would she exercise what we know to be biblical faith.

She did make that commitment. To the awe and applause of the crowd far below, she traveled safely on Philippe Petit's back across the high wire. Her performance was the talk of the city.

That is biblical faith. It is a commitment to act with total trust that God will keep his word and perform faithfully. But it is no blind leap. It is based on a confident relationship with God built up by layer upon layer of enriched experience and grounded in the objective truth of the character and purpose of God.

Three Time Frames of Faith

Our primary text suggests another important way of looking at faith. Hebrews 11:1 supplies a threefold time frame to faith. The first is the present. The author begins, "Faith is." Faith characterizes our life right now, in the present moment. It is a present confidence in God.

The question is, how can we trust God when all of life sometimes seems to be collapsing around us? Part of the answer lies in the second part of the verse: "Faith is the substance of things hoped for." This time frame includes the future. Faith must have a future dimension; if it did not, it would not be faith. Faith is the assurance that the promises now unfulfilled will someday be realized in all their richness.

The complementary idea to future faith is hope. The Bible frequently speaks about hope, and it is important to understand that biblical hope stands in sharp relief from wishful thinking. Imagine that one of my students approaches me after class. I ask him, "How are you doing in the class?"

"Well," he says, "I hope I get an A."

"I hope you do too. How are your assignments coming?"

"Well," he hesitates, "I flunked the first exam, as you know, but I intend to study more than one hour for the next one."

"Good thinking. How about the paper?"

"Well, I know it's due next Monday, and I haven't started it yet, but I plan to get on it this weekend."

"How are you doing on your reading?"

"Well, I'm a little behind, but I'm sure I'll catch up. I find Millard Erickson's *Christian Theology* a little boring. Still, I hope I get an A."

What kind of hope is that? While this student's hope is sincere, it is no more than wishful thinking.

Biblical hope is vastly different. Suppose I ask another student in the hall, "How are you doing in the class?"

"Well, I hope I get an A," she says, smiling.

"I hope you do too. How are you doing on those assignments?"

"I got an A on the exam, and I'm already reviewing my notes for the next one."

"How's the paper coming?"

"I'm not quite done yet, but I've done all my research, and I'm halfway through first draft. I'm really excited about the topic. It's unfortunate you gave us a ten-page limit. I'm already on page twenty."

"Keep it to ten," I tell her. "How about your reading?"

"Yeah, I'm up on all of it. I'm really learning a lot. In fact, I really like Erickson's approach."

Now, has this student earned an A? Not yet. Could she drop the ball? Sure. But at least her hope has some roots in reality. That is like biblical faith. It is still future—still uncertain from our human perspective—but it is anchored in something concrete, not hovering in the vapor of wishful thinking.

The third time frame is the past. Hebrews calls this "the evidence of things not seen." Why do I believe God when he says something is going to happen for me in the future? Because God has demonstrated in the past that he keeps his promises. Our God is perfectly trustworthy.

That is why God constantly reminds Israel of her history. The prophets and the psalmists repeatedly refer to God's powerful deliverance of Israel from Egypt, the parting of the Red Sea, and the collapse of the walls of Jericho. This reminds them that their God is the one true God who is absolutely faithful to his Word. He can be trusted to fulfill his promises.

Biblical faith, then, has these three temporal dimensions. First, we stand in the present moment, eager to live step-by-step as we walk with God. Second, we look toward the future. This requires hope because we do not yet see what is in store for us. Third, we look back, remembering the past and knowing we can trust God for the future because he has repeatedly demonstrated his faithfulness in history. The following chart visualizes the nature of faith within these three time frames.

The Time Frame of Faith

"—the evidence of things not seen"	"Faith is—"	"—the assurance of things hoped for"
Past evidence	Present confidence	Future hope

This understanding of faith makes God's intervention in human history, and our understanding of it, so important. These divine, historical events are like stakes driven deep into the soil of human experience. They become unshakable memories that constantly remind us, "This is something that can only be explained by God's faithfulness." Have you planted such a stake that testifies to God's faithfulness? Perhaps for you the stake was planted when you trusted Christ. Maybe your conversion produced such a radical transformation that there is only one way to explain what happened: the supernatural radically invaded your life.

Such a memory, such a stake, proves immensely valuable when we go through periods of doubt. When we begin to wonder whether God is near, or even real, we can remember that stake. "I don't know what's happening now," we may say to ourselves, "but one thing I know. God met me and changed me, and I'll never be the same. I can believe that when God promises to protect me, he will do it, even though I don't see how."

I do not remember the exact moment of my conversion, because I was saved at a very early age. But I still need a stake when the winds of life buffet me and I have doubts and questions. At those moments (and they come to all of us), I return to God's

Word and reclaim the stake of Jesus' resurrection. I have studied the resurrection story many times from many angles, and I stand convinced that the tomb is empty today because Jesus is alive. To me there is only one explanation for the details of the text, the secular evidences of history, and, most important, the radical psychological change in the disciples that led them to martyrs' deaths. That is that the risen Jesus of history presented himself to his disciples alive. No other explanation will do. The resurrection remains one of the most irrefutable events in human history. With that historical stake driven deep in the ground, everything Christ claims for himself, and for us, falls into place.

Perhaps you have asked yourself, "Do I really have a secure confidence that God is who he claims to be?" Perhaps you have an emotional faith, a mystical faith, or an intellectual faith, but you have never entered into a personal relationship with Jesus Christ. My friend, do not turn another page without experiencing the most wonderful thing that a human being can experience—a personal relationship with the living God.

A Definition of Biblical Faith

Understanding the three biblical phrases of faith and the three time frames of faith suggested by Hebrews 11:1, we can now consider the following definition.

A Definition of Faith

Faith is the *present* confidence that God will fulfill his promises in the *future* because he has proven faithful in the *past*.

Let's sum up. First, faith is the confidence in the present. This means I believe God's promises right now. Second, faith is hope for the future. I will trust his promises today because I know he will fulfill all of them in the future. Third, faith is grounded in the historical evidence of God's faithfulness. His performance record is one hundred percent. Biblical faith is incredible because it is rooted in an incredible God.

The Necessity of Faith

Finally, we must ask, is faith really necessary? To answer this, we turn to our text in Hebrews 11:6. It's crucial to notice what the writer does *not* say. He does not tell us, for example, "And without faith, it is very hard to please God, but you can do it." The text does not read, "Without faith, it is difficult for fundamentalists to please God." It does not even suggest, "Without faith, some people can please God if they truly live a good life, tithe to the church, and have compassion for the poor." Never! That's the worldview of every other religion. By contrast the text says, "Without faith it is *impossible* to please him, for whoever would draw near to God must believe that he exists and that he rewards those who seek him."

Three verbs in this verse are instructive: *please, draw near to,* and *seek.* By themselves, these are not God-honoring activities. People seek God all the time. The Muslim seeks God. The Rajneeshee longs to please God. The Hare Krishna walks a path he thinks will bring him to God. Unfortunately, as the Bible reminds us, this simple act of seeking does not result in spiritual reconciliation, because the impulse to seek a higher, transcendent being is simply part of being human. It is a vital vestige of our being divine image-bearers. But because of sin's contamination, such seeking only pleases God when it is done in faith. Only when we seek him and draw near to him *in faith* does God justify us. Just as it is impossible to please God without faith, so seeking God and drawing near to God are futile without faith.

Jesus perfectly illustrates the necessity of faith in his encounter with the rich young ruler (Matt. 19:16–30). In this story, the Lord is walking along with his disciples when a young man approaches him.

"What must I do to inherit the kingdom of God?" he asks Jesus.

Jesus answers with a question, "Have you obeyed all the commandments?"

"Oh, yes," the young man answers, "I've obeyed all of them."

Now, I don't believe he did. Scripture clearly teaches that no one can obey God's law perfectly. But Jesus does not challenge the young man on this; rather, he looks at him with love.

He says, "There is one thing you *lack*. Sell everything you have, give it to the poor, and follow me."

The narrator tells us that the young man turns from Jesus and walks away, filled with sorrow because he is very rich.

What an arresting story! I often ask myself, "Under what circumstances would I tell a young person with great wealth, who asks me how to have eternal life, to sell everything he has and give it to the poor?" But Jesus did.

After the young man leaves, Jesus turns to his disciples. "It's easier for a camel to get through the eye of a needle," he says, "than it is for a rich man to enter the kingdom of God."

What crosses your mind when you hear that proverb? I'll tell you what the disciples think. They are absolutely shocked. They ask, "Then, Lord, who in the world can ever be saved?"

And that's when Jesus gives his familiar response. "With man it is impossible," Jesus tells them, "but with God all things are possible."

With unmistakable clarity, Jesus declares that entrance to the kingdom of God is based on faith, not on works or wealth. That is why Jesus emphasized, "There is one thing you lack." The young man did not lack material wealth. He did not lack human righteousness. But he woefully lacked the humble and childlike faith in God that admits, "I am utterly helpless to come to God on my own." All his pride and self-sufficiency is distilled in that simple act of turning away from Jesus.

Do you see the point? One enters God's presence not by what one *does* but by *whom one knows*. It is impossible with us. Human effort, personal merit, material wealth, social status, ethnic identity, and philanthropic generosity are insufficient for gaining eternal life. It is only possible with God. And the avenue through which God grants entrance to a perfect heaven for sinners like us is by grace through faith.

With faith it *is* possible to please God. If you have never accepted that free gift, there is nothing easier. And there is nothing that will change your life more, with eternal implications, than that acceptance of that free gift. Do it today!

A DAY ON MOUNT JEFFERSON

It was noon on a Saturday in August 1993, and I knew we were in deep, deep trouble. Our adventure had begun rather well. The day before, my two climbing partners, Jerry S. and Jerry G. (the "J-2 Guides"), and I trekked about five miles from the trailhead at Whitewater Creek Road, where we parked my van. By day's end we climbed to an altitude of 6,400 feet, a thousand feet above verdant Jefferson Park on the northern slope of rugged Mount Jefferson in Central Oregon. Our goal was to climb what many consider to be the most difficult peak in the state. Establishing a cozy campsite on a level space right at the edge of the glacier, we bivouacked high enough to escape the clouds of mosquitoes that are the bane of campers in the park below.

After arising at a sensible 4:00 a.m., we ate breakfast, organized our packs, and secured the camp. Well-rested and well-fed, we were on our way by 5:00 a.m. The weather looked friendly as we made our way slowly but purposefully up Jefferson Park Glacier. After navigating several crevasses, we skirted around the *bergschrund* (the crevasse that is formed where the glacier first pulls away from the mountain) and spent an hour circumnavigating a rocky pinnacle.

Moving eastward and upward, we climbed the upper tier of the glacier. This stretch was a membrane of sheer ice, sloped at a nail-biting fifty degrees. We traversed this obstacle gingerly, securely roped together and carefully belaying one another as we zigzagged up the icy slope. As the least experienced climber, I stood in the middle position, kicking my twelve-point, steel crampons into the ice and making sure each foothold was secure before taking the next step. Each of us carried a lightweight but razor-sharp ice axe in each hand. Sinking the tip of one axe securely into the ice (and sometimes swinging it repeatedly at the stubborn surface) before releasing the other axe, we repeated this procedure footstep-by-footstep, pickhold-by-pickhold up the steep incline. Even with these precautions, I would instinctively draw close to the glacier, kneeling against the ice in a misguided effort to hug the slippery surface for security. Immediately Jerry G. above me would call out sharply, "Stand up! You don't have crampons on your knees!" That was his firm and necessary way of telling me to trust my equipment and keep all twelve crampon points on the ice. My life depended on it.

We traversed the upper glacier without mishap. After a brief rest we confronted our next challenge: a near vertical "chimney," or rocky shaft, approximately 150 feet high. Then, with ropes and pitons, we ascended another fifty-foot, ice-and-rock cliff that led us to the summit ridge. At the top of this ascent is a structure called the "eye of the needle." This rocky formation of boulders is stacked in such a way as to form a small opening, just wide enough for a single climber to wriggle through. We squeezed between the rocks and onto the summit ridge. From there we could see both the vastness of Jefferson Park Glacier immediately below us and the summit rising from the ridge directly ahead. Without unexpected delays, we would be able to summit in roughly two hours. We stood congratulating ourselves with grins on our faces. It was noon.

What had been a spectacular climbing day suddenly became potential disaster. As often happens in the Oregon Cascades, the favorable weather turned abruptly into a whiteout. Clouds bearing both sleet and snow formed quickly and descended on us. Within minutes we were enveloped by fog and, shortly thereafter, by freezing rain.

I was shivering with cold by the time we got out and pulled on our all-weather, Gortex parkas. In these circumstances, it did not take us long to make a decision. We had to get down off the mountain, and we had to do it fast.

Fortunately for me, my guides were accustomed to such alpine challenges. They exploded into action. Uncoiling both of our 150-foot climbing ropes, they knotted them together into a single 300-foot loop and prepared for a series of breathtaking rappels down the sheer ascents we had painstakingly inched up all morning. While I adjusted my climbing harness for the descent, fixing a figure-eight rappelling ring onto my harness loop, the two Jerrys strapped a length of webbing around one of the boulders with a single carabiner dangling from it. We needed a secure rappelling point to permit the rope to be pulled free through the carabiner when we reached the bottom. The strap and hardware would have to be left behind, a small price to pay for a rapid escape from the icy weather.

Careful teachers that they were, the J-2 Guides reminded me how to lock onto the rope, how to play out the trailing end of the rope as I descended, and how to push out from the lip of the cliff. Keeping my knees flexed, I was to use my legs both to propel myself outward for another downward drop and to protect my body as it swung back toward the rocky face. The guides explained the importance of timing my push-outs with the gradual release of the rope in my gloved but tightly clenched fingers. "Of course, you've done this before," Jerry S. said as I stood atop the cliff with my back to Jefferson Park Glacier a thousand feet below. "You might find it easier if you don't look down." With that, Jerry S. stepped backward into the void.

I nodded silently to Jerry G. as if understanding everything completely. I thought it unwise to admit at that moment that I had never rappelled anything before.

Nevertheless, I pushed off, and for some mysterious reason the timing of my releasing the trailing rope, my downward movement, and my legs absorbing the shock of swinging back into the cliff was perfect. It was one of the most exhilarating sensations I've ever had. For a moment I even forgot the miserable weather, my soggy clothes, and our immediate alpine peril.

In seconds I was standing at the bottom of the fifty-foot face, waiting for Jerry G. to joins us. When he did, we pulled the rope free and set up for the next and longer, 150-foot rappel that would take us to the top of the ice sheet. We repeated the rappelling process three more times, dropping in 150-feet increments in a fraction of the time it had taken us to climb just hours earlier. With each descent, the visibility improved, the angle of inclination lessened, and our spirits lifted. Within an hour and a half of standing on the summit ridge, we paused for a break just below the *bergschrund*.

Steepness was not our challenge now; endurance was. Still needing to keep warm, we plodded down the moderately inclined glacier in the general direction of our camp, still roped together, with crampons strapped on our boots and ice axes in our hands for security. The snow had obliterated our early morning tracks as well as the visibility of dangers. Jerry S., who took lead position for this leg, met one such hazard, stepping into a small crevasse whose opening was covered with soft snow. Fortunately Jerry was holding his ice axe horizontally. As he slipped downward, both the axe head and the pointed metal tip of the axe handle wedged into the tapering sides of the small opening, holding him securely until he could scramble out. Jerry continued to lead, as neither I nor Jerry G. volunteered to take his place.

We neared our campsite located on one of five fingers of bare rock that reached upward into the glacier. But in the fog it was invisible. I was of no use in recalling the location of our camp; in my early morning enthusiasm I had not looked behind me periodically to note our point of origin. I was confident, though, that my experienced and careful guides would have no trouble with the simple task of finding our tent.

So I was a bit anxious when I overheard the two Jerrys arguing about it. We were not facing a disaster, of course. Our altimeter would guide us to the 6,400 feet elevation of our camp. If we descended the wrong rocky ridge, we could traverse the remaining ridges at that elevation until we found the right one. But no one was in the frame of mind to expend that kind of energy this late in the day.

Jerry S. prevailed and selected the second ridge. And when I saw our small, blue tent fifteen minutes later, was I glad he did! We did not procrastinate. Within twenty minutes we had changed our clothes, rolled up the tent, repacked our bags, and headed toward the car. When we finally pulled away from the trailhead parking lot in my van, it was with a deep sigh of relief.

Lessons of Mount Jefferson

Mount Jefferson taught me many things that day. Oh, I grew in my skills as a mountaineer, certainly. But more importantly, God used this mountain and the experience of attempting to climb it to remind me of important principles about the life of faith. Let me mention three central lessons.

First, I trusted in reliable, experienced, and seasoned guides. The J-2 Guides were not infallible, of course, but their vast knowledge and time-honed experience meant the difference between survival and disaster. No human guide can control all circumstances, whether ascending mountains in the Oregon Cascades or confronting mountains of doubt in the spiritual life. But God places human guides along our spiritual paths to give the necessary instruction, caution, and encouragement we need for spiritual success. To attempt either an alpine adventure or a spiritual summit without a reliable guide is more than folly. It is an arrogant disregard for one of the key provisions God makes available to each of us who desires to walk the pathway of faith with him: the wisdom and encouragement of other believers.

Second, I owed my life to well-designed equipment and the knowledge to use it. Insulated, snug-fitting boots with spiked crampons easily attached or detached with thickly gloved hands in forty-miles-per-hour winds spelled security on steep ice. Warm layers of polypropylene, wool, Gortex, and other "space-age" fabrics guarded me like sentinels against hypothermia. And I entrusted my life to technical gear such as an alpine climbing rope, a secure harness, alloy carabiners, and other climbing hardware. I appreciated as never before how brave (or perhaps foolhardy!) were the accomplishments of previous generations of climbers and explorers who succeeded at incredible exploits without today's technology.

I realized anew that God provides many important spiritual resources for us as we seek to walk with him. His primary resource for our spiritual growth is his infallible Word; all other resources are explained and appropriated through the thoughtful understanding and application of the Scriptures. Like a good mountaineer, our challenge is to familiarize ourselves with the entire counsel of God, to understand how to apply it correctly, and to trust its sufficiency for our spiritual health and survival even in the midst of overwhelming obstacles.

Third, I noted new connections between mountaineering and the life of faith. In both enterprises, you set goals, you plan with care, and you exercise wisdom. Yet climbing requires taking one step at a time. Much of it seems to be just monotonous trudging, demanding resolve and endurance. But the monotony is interrupted by wonder. The beauty of creation and the breathtaking grandeur of a massive mountain provide frequent intrusions on your senses that quickly dispel even the most exhaustion-laden tedium. It is this beauty that leads me to applaud George Leigh Mallory's famous mountain climbing rationale: "Because it's there!" In my spiritual walk I am struck with the wonder of God's grace in guiding me into paths of joy, fulfillment, and wonder.

Crisis can erase boredom too. For that reason, adventures of mountaineering and faith require constant diligence and alertness. While the rewards are great, so are the stakes. This same grace, I've learned, also accompanies me in the midst of spiritual crises. Crisis in God's economy is not a time when he abandons me; it is, rather, a venue for the divine Potter to shape me more and more into the kind of vessel that reflects the image of Jesus Christ.

The Adventure Begins

In this book we, like intrepid explorers, surveyed the wide panorama of faith-principles from a familiar biblical promontory: Hebrews 11. We traced a veritable who's who of human mentors who have traveled faith's path before us. Like mountaineers, they were not infallible. They failed. They were finite. They never saw the whole picture. But they were men and women of faith. As such, they obeyed God and bore his divine endorsement.

We looked closely at Abraham, who taught us how to walk, worship, and prevail throughout the journey of faith, and Sarah, who illustrated the implications of the partnership of faith. Delving deeply into the Old Testament materials behind the Hebrews sketches, we turned the biblical spotlight on Abel, Enoch, Noah, Isaac, Jacob, Joseph, Moses, Rahab, and numerous other unlikely heroes of faith who left legacies for our learning.

We have examined the meaning of faith as it is formed in crucible of human experience and adversity, distinct from the secular myths of unbiblical notions of faith. We've met over a dozen men and women who have accepted the same adventure we face and for whom God has proven himself faithful.

Now it's your turn to embrace the principles of spiritual living that prepare us for the most exciting adventure there is: approval by the living God.

Let the adventure begin!